Financial Reporting and Analysis

Financial Reporting and Analysis

John Dunn

A John Wiley and Sons, Ltd, Publication

This edition first published 2010
© 2010 John Wiley & Sons Ltd

Registered office
John Wiley & Sons Ltd, The Atrium, Southern Gate, Chichester, West Sussex PO19 8SQ, United Kingdom

For details of our global editorial offices, for customer services, and for information about how to apply for permission to reuse the copyright material in this book, please see our website at www.wiley.com

The right of John Dunn to be identified as the author of this work has been asserted in accordance with the Copyright, Designs and Patents Act 1988.

Wiley also publishes its books in a variety of electronic formats. Some content that appears in print may not be available in electronic books.

Designations used by companies to distinguish their products are often claimed as trademarks. All brand names and product names used in this book are trade names, service marks, trademarks, or registered trademarks of their respective owners. The publisher is not associated with any product or vendor mentioned in this book. This publication is designed to provide accurate and authoritative information with regard to the subject matter covered. It is sold on the understanding that the publisher is not engaged in rendering professional services. If professional advice or other expert assistance is required, the services of a competent professional should be sought.

Library of Congress Cataloging-in-Publication Data

Dunn, John, 1959-
Financial reporting and analysis/John Dunn.
     p. cm.
Includes bibliographical references and index.
ISBN 978-0-470-69503-6 (pbk.)
 1. Financial statements. 2.   Corporations–Accounting. I.   Title.
HF5681.B2D78 2010
657′.3–dc22   2009037090

A catalogue record for this book is available from the British Library.

Set in 11/13 pt Goudy by Thomson Digital, India
Printed in Great Britain by TJ International, Padstow, Cornwall

For Wendy

Contents

About the Author

John Dunn is a lecturer at the University of Strathclyde in Glasgow, where he teaches financial accounting and auditing. He is a qualified accountant with extensive experience of examining for professional bodies.

Preface

There are two hurdles to overcome when studying accountancy. The first year involves coming to terms with lots of mechanical material that is often quite difficult to relate to. Learning double-entry bookkeeping, arranging the resulting balances into a trial balance (and breathing a sigh of relief when it balances), and using the trial balance to prepare a set of financial statements (with another sigh of relief when those figures seem to balance too) are all challenges. Having mastered the basics, it is sometimes just a little unnerving to discover that there is quite a jump from first to second year. The difference is that intermediate-level classes start to introduce human nature into the process.

People generally make accountancy far more complicated than it really has to be because they can be greedy, deceitful, or just afraid of the consequences of telling the truth. Or they are honest and upright citizens who simply wish to present a realistic picture in the accounts. It is difficult to tell which of these attitudes the people preparing the accounts had when they were preparing the statements, and so the credibility of the figures has to be underpinned by rules. So far, so good, but setting rules in the real world can involve lots of compromises. Sometimes the rules seem quite illogical, and that is often because regulating intelligent people who are motivated to misbehave often means thinking several steps ahead. Sometimes the rules require lots of thought and judgement, and sometimes they just impose a course of action because experience has shown that any discretion in a particular area will just be abused.

Two words of encouragement . . .

First of all, it is really the human factor that makes accountancy interesting. Accountants are generally well paid and respected. If their craft was just the mechanical processing of double-entry bookkeeping transactions, then there would be very little need for recognition and reward.

Secondly, the jump from second year to third is far less pronounced. The topics that are taught at subsequent levels may be more complicated, but the difficult part is simply appreciating how the process of setting and applying the rules works.

About this book

This text is written with a view to being 'student friendly'. To that end, there is a danger that it might lack some of the features that look good at first sight and then turn out to be more difficult to live with once the book has been bought and paid for.

Firstly, the content has been cut down to save time and effort in reading. Conversations with students indicate not only that large and impressive-looking tomes are difficult to carry but also that the realities of combining part-time work with full-time study can make a shorter read more welcome.

There are some references to further reading in most chapters, but the emphasis is on suggesting places to look for further information. Every intermediate accounting class is at least a little different from every other, and so indicating ways of finding things out is a little less restrictive than a detailed bibliography.

The questions at the ends of chapters are intended to be accessible and provide the opportunity to practise. The hope is that there are sufficient questions to practise on without offering an overwhelming amount.

The book is supported by a website www.wileyeurope.com/college/dunn. It is hoped that the materials that can be found there will be useful to teaching staff and students alike. It is certainly an area that will develop in response to feedback.

PUBLISHED ACCOUNTS

1

Contents

Learning Objectives

After studying this chapter you should be able to:

- appreciate that accounting must be regulated if it is to provide credible information;
- understand the basic presentation requirements for financial statement, as laid down by the accountancy profession;
- prepare basic accounting statements in an organised and efficient manner.

Introduction

This chapter is intended to bridge the gap between your introductory studies in accounting and the intermediate level that is the subject matter of this text. You might find that you know a lot of this material already, although that does not mean that it would be advisable to skip anything. At the very least, you will have had the summer vacation in which to forget a lot of the basics. Furthermore, this chapter presents the basics in terms of the aspects that you really need to know in order to proceed to the next level. Thus, there might be something new that will make a huge difference to your progress hidden away in the body of the 'revision' material.

One of the most important things that you need to understand in studying financial reporting is that the whole discipline is entirely man made. There are very few concrete realities that arise in the preparation of financial statements. Admittedly, there are cash flows into and out of the business's bank accounts and there are resources that its managers can direct and control, but the manner in which these are accounted for is open to a great deal of discussion and debate. We might have reached a stage where a lot of the arguments have been resolved, but there is no reason why the financial statements that you have seen in your studies to date have to be as they are. This is an important point, if only because understanding the interests and the ideas that have shaped accountancy is one of the most interesting aspects of the subject.

Two Jokes About Accountants

The contested nature of accounting practices can be seen most clearly in the fact that there are two quite distinct strands of accounting humour:

Jokes that make accountants sound boring
Q: How do you drive an accountant crazy?
A: Unfold a map and refold it along the wrong creases.
Q: How do you identify extrovert accountants?
A: They look at your shoes when they are talking to you instead of their own.

Jokes that make accountants sound corrupt
Q: How many accountants does it take to change a light bulb?
A: What number did you have in mind?

An employer asked all of the applicants for accounting jobs 'what does two plus two equal?'. The successful applicant was the one who replied 'what do you want it to equal?'.

There are two stereotypes of accountants:

On the one hand, there is the quiet introvert in a cheap polyester suit (which was chosen for its resistance to wear and tear rather than style). This individual spends vast amounts of time poring over ledgers and bookkeeping records and is generally uncomfortable in the company of other human beings.

The other image is of a brash, smartly dressed 'captain of industry', who is capable of talking lenders and investors into financing deals and taking risks so that everybody else loses while he or she prospers. The accountant does not necessarily tell lies in the process of doing so, but often presents the truth in a misleading way.

Neither of these images is at all fair (even though most accountants love accountancy jokes), although it must be admitted that there are aspects of accountancy that might have helped to create these impressions.

But Seriously . . .

The accountant as a dull, grey obsessive probably dates back many years and can be blamed partly by the impressions created in popular fiction. For example, Dickens had characters who were bookkeepers. The impression has persisted, and that might be partly due to the process of becoming an accountant. There are various rules and procedures that have to be taken at face value and learned. Sadly, the most effective way to come to terms with this material is to practise until the techniques become second nature.

Rather than viewing the idea of practising as a chore, you should view it as an investment. One of the important concepts in education is that of transferable skills. A transferable skill is one that can be used in contexts other than the narrow confines of the course itself. Practising on a range of accountancy questions will help you to develop the ability to work with figures. You will also learn to break complex problems down into a series of manageable activities that can be dealt with one at a time.

> **Think!**
>
> Stop and reread the previous paragraph. It leads on to the next stereotype because it takes a fact that a reader might find unpopular (that you need to invest time and effort in order to acquire certain skills) and presents it in a more appealing way (by focusing on the benefits, rather than the time and effort).

The accountant as a purveyor of half-truths arises because of the manner in which a number of so-called accounting scandals have been reported in the press. Typically, these scandals do not involve someone actually telling an outright lie and fabricating a set of numbers. Rather, one or more parties argue that the accountants have misled them by presenting facts in a misleading way. For example, a company has had a bad year and the directors might want to try to improve the figures.

One way to improve accounting numbers is to indulge in 'creative accounting'. That normally involves reading the rules and looking for gaps that enable the directors to say 'where does it say that I can't do that?'. For example, a payment that is normally accounted for as a cost might be treated as an asset. Doing so would enhance the profit figure and make the balance sheet look stronger. The pressures that cause this behaviour and the accountancy profession's response will be discussed frequently in subsequent chapters of this book. Rather than give examples at this stage, it is sufficient to point out that there are whole books devoted to the topic of creative accounting. Arguably, the first was a book entitled *Accounting for Growth: Stripping the Camouflage from Company Accounts* by Terry Smith, a prominent investment analyst (Smith, 1992). In spite of the ongoing work of the accountancy profession and its rule-making programme, which is designed to make creative accounting increasingly difficult, there has been a steady stream of similar books on this theme. Try inserting the phrase 'creative accounting' in an on-line bookseller's search facility. One of the latest offerings runs to 584 pages (see Jones, 2009).

A related approach to enhancing figures is sometimes referred to as 'aggressive accounting'. This involves introducing a deliberate bias into any estimates or assumptions associated with preparing figures. For example, optimistic estimates of asset lives for depreciation purposes will reduce the cost and increase reported profit. In many ways, aggressive accounting is more difficult to prevent through regulations than creative accounting, but it is also more difficult to make a substantial difference to the final figures in this way. There are limits to the possible life expectancy of a piece of equipment. Creative accounting is almost certainly more of a problem because readers can understand that the directors might push an estimate to the limits of credibility, but they struggle with the notion that accountants cannot state categorically how a transaction or a balance should be accounted for.

Enron – An Extreme Case of Bad Accounting

Accounting scandals crop up from time to time. Invariably, they attract a great deal of attention because they usually involve somebody suffering a great deal of harm. This section will look at a few of the broader implications of the Enron case, without getting bogged down in the detail.

Before we start, it should be stressed that cases such as Enron are not daily events. Indeed, catastrophes of this magnitude do not necessarily happen every year or even once in every several years. They do, however, have a massive impact when they do occur because the various stakeholders who rely on financial statements look for reassurance that something will be done to prevent this from happening again.

Enron was a major US company that collapsed in 2001. The issues that concern us most are not the fact that the company failed. Rather, the problem is that the company was made to look like an attractive investment through some rather underhand accounting techniques. These techniques came to light largely because of a clerical accident.

The technicalities of what happened are really not all that relevant at this stage. It is enough to know that Enron wanted to borrow heavily without showing the resulting balances as liabilities in its financial statements. The company also wanted to remove some power stations from its balance sheet because they did not make a huge amount of profit relative to the amount invested in them. It did not want to sell them off completely, though. The solution was to create a complicated series of business ventures called 'special-purpose entities', which borrowed heavily from outside lenders and shareholders and used the resulting cash to buy Enron's power stations.

> **Think!**
>
> Why would a company want to exclude borrowings and assets from its financial statements?

Ideally, a company would always wish to seem highly profitable and low risk. The key to seeming profitable is to have large profits relative to the resources used to generate those profits. Thus, excluding assets from the balance sheet would make the business appear efficient. One of the ways to appear less risky is to reduce borrowing. Heavy borrowings increase the risk that the company will struggle to pay interest and make repayments when they fall due. Removing liabilities from the balance sheet will make a business seem less risky.

Setting up business ventures in the way that Enron did would not normally have affected the figures because the financial statements of business ventures under the control of a company are normally combined with its own (we will return to this concept in Chapter 12 when we discuss the preparation of consolidated financial statements). Thus, the total assets and liabilities should have been the same. Enron got round this by looking very closely at the rules in force at the time and setting up the ventures in such a way that they did not quite meet the criteria for inclusion in the accounts. Doing so meant that the company seemed to be more profitable and less risky.

There is a problem with making things disappear in this way. Just as a magician might make an object seem to vanish, the reality is that nothing has changed. The object is still there even if it has been hidden inside a secret compartment. Enron could change the impression created by its financial statements, but it was still effectively liable for the borrowings and was still effectively the owner of the assets. It did not become more profitable or less risky because it was able to distort the figures in its financial statements to make it look like a better investment.

The crucial point about this story is that presenting the financial statements in this manner was misleading, but it was not technically in breach of the accounting rules. At least, that was the case until the discovery of an error in the setting up of one of the special-purpose entities. Large companies are required to have their financial statements checked and reported on by an external auditor. Enron's auditor discovered that one of the special-purpose entities had been set up in such a way that it should not have been excluded from the Enron Group and its figures had to be added in. The effect of this was to recognise a loss of $1.2 billion in the financial statements. Not surprisingly, the shareholders could not understand how such an enormous adjustment could even be possible, and the whole creative accounting scheme quickly unfolded. Enron collapsed shortly afterwards, making itself the biggest bankruptcy ever at that time.

In the years since Enron, the US government has passed legislation in the form of the Sarbanes–Oxley Act which, among other things, has tightened up on the regulation of the accountancy profession. Arguments will rage on as to who was ultimately responsible, but there are some very simple lessons that we can take from this:

• Preparing financial statements is not a simple, mechanical activity. There are often choices to be made. Sometimes those choices are made by managers who wish to make the financial statements more representative of reality, and sometimes the choices are biased.

- Those managers who do bias financial statements are sometimes motivated by personal greed, but sometimes they feel a sense of identification with the company and they are keen to strengthen its position rather than benefit themselves.

- The wording of the rules governing accounting is extremely important. Any ambiguity or gaps will be open to exploitation. Many of the accountants involved in preparing and auditing financial statements are extremely honest and are keen to reflect reality in their financial statements, but the rules have to deal with those who simply wish to comply with the letter of the law even if the resulting figures are misleading.

Principals and Agents

Agency theory is a branch of economics that is devoted to the behavioural implications of entrusting decisions to a third party. That is what happens in the case of virtually all large companies. The shareholders are the principals and they invest by buying shares. The directors are their agents. The directors must have the freedom to make decisions on the running of the company, and the shareholders cannot have a great deal of input into this process. In a perfect world, the directors will always act in the best interests of the shareholders, but it is easy to doubt whether they always will.

Think!

Identify some of the ways that directors might abuse the shareholders' trust.

The simplest and most obvious form of abuse would be outright theft from the company. For example, the directors could simply authorise excessive expenses claims for one another. Such behaviour would clearly be criminal, but it would be very difficult to detect, and so the chances of getting caught would be slim.

The directors could misbehave in more subtle ways that might cause more harm than stealing from the company. For example, they might not exert themselves to make the best possible profit. Or they might refuse to take realistic and responsible business risks even though they are justified by the potential returns. Looking at the directors' behaviour from a purely economic perspective, it would be logical for them to put in the least possible effort or to avoid even acceptable risks because the shareholders will enjoy the benefit at the directors' cost.

Concerns that the directors might misbehave will deter shareholders from investing, and that will stifle the creation of large and efficient businesses.

The agency problem can be tackled to some extent by trying to design reward packages that motivate the directors to act in the shareholders' interests. This approach can be seen in practice because many companies pay their directors bonuses that are linked to profits, or they give them a stake in the company.

The agency problem can also be tackled by monitoring the behaviour of directors, and that is where accounting statements come in. If the shareholders have access to credible and informative financial statements, then they can review the directors' performance. If the directors are not performing adequately, then they risk replacement.

The Enron example illustrates one shortcoming of the monitoring approach. The directors have control over the bookkeeping and accounting systems and they have to be responsible for the preparation of the financial statements that are used to monitor them. Even if the directors' statements are subject to an external audit, as was the case for Enron, the auditors must be able to measure the financial statements against some benchmarks, otherwise they will be unable to form a meaningful view on the quality of the information that is being checked and reported on.

The accounting rules that are described in this text are an important part of managing the relationship between principals and agents. History suggests that some directors are prepared to make their companies appear more profitable or more secure in order to retain their shareholders' confidence. Accounting rules are frequently designed to deal with specific areas where problems have arisen. For example, you should be aware of the concept of depreciation from your previous studies. We will discuss this in more detail in Chapter 8 of this text. For the moment, it is worth noting that there have been problems in accounting for depreciation over the years. Should buildings be depreciated? Should an asset be depreciated if it is revalued, and should that depreciation be based on the revalued amount or the original cost? Answers to these questions can be found in International Accounting Standard 16 *Property, Plant, and Equipment.*

Standard-setters have had an extremely responsible and difficult task. They have to design rules that deal with problem areas without alienating the companies whose accounts are going to be affected. They also have to retain the trust of the readers of financial statements, so the rules that are published must be logical and should lead to better accounts.

Directing resources to improving accounting involves thinking about areas where abuses are likely to occur. It often helps to think about the directions in which preparers might like to distort financial statements.

What do Readers Like to See?

You should know a reasonable amount about the interpretation of financial statements from your prior studies. There are two key ratios that are extremely relevant to understanding a company from the business side of things.

Profitability is measured in terms of the return on capital employed ratio:

$$\text{Return on capital employed} = \frac{\text{Profit before tax and interest}}{\text{Shareholders' equity} + \text{long-term liabilities}}$$

There are other formulae for calculating return on capital employed, but this is the only one that we need for our purposes. The numerator is the pre-tax 'return' earned for the shareholders and lenders who provided the company with its long-term finance. The shareholders are entitled to the profit, which is expressed before tax to show the gross amount earned. The lenders are entitled to interest. We divide this figure by the total amount invested by the shareholders and lenders to arrive at a measure of management's ability to generate a return from a given investment.

In an ideal world, the shareholders would prefer that the business earned the highest possible return on capital employed. If management can make the profit figure higher or the valuation of capital employed lower, then the return on capital employed statistic will be improved.

Return is only part of the picture. Anyone interested in investments will also be very interested in risk. Gearing is one of the most important ratios for measuring risk:

$$\text{Gearing} = \frac{\text{Long-term liabilities}}{\text{Shareholders' equity} + \text{long-term liabilities}}$$

Gearing is just the proportion of long-term finance that comes from borrowing. A higher ratio implies an increased risk. Heavy borrowing means a higher annual interest, which means that there is a possibility that any downturn will leave little or no profit left over for the shareholders. Heavy borrowing also means that the company's assets will have to be spread thinner if the company fails, so the lenders will have less chance of being paid in full from the proceeds of winding up the business.

It would be far too simplistic to sum up the whole of the interpretation in terms of these two ratios. It is, however, surprising just how many creative schemes have the effect of boosting return on capital employed, reducing gearing, or both. In other words, it is often worth thinking about these two ratios when looking at the background to a particular accounting rule.

Presentation of Financial Statements

We will explore the whole process of setting accounting standards in the next chapter. This section will lay some foundations for that by looking at the formatting requirements for the main financial statements. This will give you an opportunity to revisit the basic accounting statements, but will do so from the perspective of the formal presentation requirements laid down by the accountancy profession.

The main rules relating to the format of a set of accounting statements can be found in International Accounting Standard 1 *Presentation of Accounting Statements* (IAS 1). A revised version was published in 2007, and so some companies may have financial statements in issue that were published before the revisions came into effect.

The two statements that we shall focus on for the remainder of this chapter are:

- the statement of financial position (also known as the balance sheet);
- the statement of comprehensive income (which can be broken down into two statements, the first of which is the income statement and the second of which shows other components of 'comprehensive income', such as gains on revaluation).

IAS 1 requires that both of these statements be shown in very specific ways. For example, the statement of financial position should be in the following format:

ABC plc
Statement of financial position as at 31 December 20X8

	£m
ASSETS	
Non-current assets	
Property, plant, and equipment	30
Goodwill	15
Other intangible assets	11
Financial assets	5
	61
Current assets	
Inventories	8
Trade receivables	9
Other current assets	2
Cash and cash equivalents	4
	23
Total assets	84

EQUITY AND LIABILITIES
Equity
Share capital	20
Retained earnings	21
Other components of equity	1
Total equity	42

Non-current liabilities
Long-term borrowings	16
Long-term provisions	4
Total non-current liabilities	20

Current liabilities
Trade and other payables	8
Short-term borrowings	5
Current portion of long-term borrowings	2
Current tax payable	3
Short-term provisions	4
Total current liabilities	22

Total liabilities	42
Total equity and liabilities	84

Thus, the statement of financial position shows the company's assets, broken down between non-current and current assets and further subdivided within each category. The second part of the statement shows how those assets were financed in terms of equity and liabilities, with liabilities broken down between non-current and current.

The format shown above should be regarded as mandatory. Even if you have used an alternative approach in your previous studies, IAS 1 lists a number of specific items that must appear on the face of the statement of financial position and provides a very similar example to the above as an illustration of good practice. From now on, you should get used to treating this as a compulsory format. If you practise on as many questions as possible, then you will find that using the prescribed format becomes second nature.

IAS 1 also lays down requirements for the layout of the statement of comprehensive income:

ABC plc
Statement of comprehensive income for the year ended
31 December 20X8

	£m
Revenue	56
Cost of sales	(24)
Gross profit	32
Other income	2
Distribution costs	(4)
Administrative expenses	(7)
Other expenses	(1)
Finance costs	(3)
Profit before tax	19
Income tax expense	(5)
PROFIT FOR THE YEAR	14
Other comprehensive income:	
Gains on property revaluation	1
TOTAL COMPREHENSIVE INCOME FOR THE YEAR	15

This statement indicates how the shareholders' wealth has increased through both trading and non-trading activities. This company earned a profit after tax of £14 million. In addition, wealth increased by a further £1 million because of a gain on the revaluation of non-current assets.

There are two variations on the above presentation:

- The first variation is to split the statement into two. It would be perfectly acceptable to have an 'income statement' that was used to calculate profit. That would be exactly as the statement shown above, except that it would stop at the profit for the year. In that case, the company would have to provide a second statement showing the total comprehensive income. Such a statement would start with the profit for the year and would adjust for the other components of comprehensive income. This text will use the simpler approach, which is to provide a single statement of comprehensive income, rather than two separate statements.
- The second variation is to show the expenses by type of expense rather than function. An example of this is shown below. Companies using this approach also have the freedom to show two separate statements: an income statement and a statement of total comprehensive income.

Note that the two presentations give exactly the same answer. The only difference is in the way the costs are presented.

ABC plc
Statement of comprehensive income for the year ended
31 December 20X8

	£m
Revenue	56
Other income	2
Changes in inventories of finished goods and work in progress	3
Raw material and consumables used	(9)
Employee benefits expense	(16)
Depreciation and amortisation expense	(12)
Other expenses	(2)
Finance costs	(3)
Profit before tax	19
Income tax expense	(5)
PROFIT FOR THE YEAR	14
Other comprehensive income:	
Gains on property revaluation	1
TOTAL COMPREHENSIVE INCOME FOR THE YEAR	15

This text will use the first format throughout. That is partly because most companies choose to present their costs by function rather than by type of expense, and partly because it is more helpful to users to do so. Readers are often interested in, for example, the gross profit. If a company uses the alternative layout, then readers cannot see what the gross profit was.

A third statement provides an overview of changes in equity. This shows how the various components of equity have changed during the year:

ABC plc
Statement of changes in equity
for the year ended 31 December 20X8

	Share capital £m	Retained profit £m	Revaluation reserve £m	Total equity £m
Balance at 31 December 20X7	20	12	0	32
Profit for year		14		14
Dividend		(5)		(5)
Gain on revaluation			1	1
Balance at 31 December 20X8	20	21	1	42

Notes to the Accounts

We will look at a real set of financial statements in Chapter 3. When we do, you will see that a typical annual report comprises one page each for the main accounting statements, followed by dozens of pages of notes, most of which are cross-referenced to the financial statements themselves.

The notes have three main functions:

- They provide information about the manner in which the financial statements have been prepared and the specific accounting policies used.
- They disclose information required by accounting standards that is not presented elsewhere in the financial statements.
- They provide information that is not presented elsewhere in the financial statements but is relevant to an understanding of any of them. This might include information that is required by law rather than accounting standards, or it might be information that is necessary for a reader of the financial statements to have an adequate understanding.

From a teaching point of view, there is no possibility of your ever being asked to produce an annual report that runs to more than 50 pages of statements and supplementary notes. We will deal with some of the more commonplace notes in the course of later chapters of this text.

Preparing a Set of Financial Statements

Learning to prepare a set of financial statements in accordance with the IAS 1 formats and with all relevant notes is an important skill. If it is mastered properly, it can be seen as a problem-solving technique that can be applied to more complex problems, both accounting and non-accounting.

In essence, it involves the following steps:

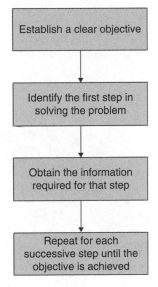

Establish a clear objective

Identify the first step in solving the problem

Obtain the information required for that step

Repeat for each successive step until the objective is achieved

Generally, the students who struggle with preparing financial statements do so because they are reactive. In other words, they do not break the task down into a series of manageable steps and quickly get bogged down in the detail of the question.

A typical question will provide you with a trial balance and a series of numbered paragraphs describing additional information that is to be taken into account. It might be necessary to process a great deal of data in order to arrive at the end product. That can be simplified by using the IAS 1 formats as a source of structure. Rather than setting out to prepare a statement of comprehensive income and a statement of financial position, it is better to start with the first line of the first statement and to work through each line in turn until the statements have been completed.

The following question is a typical example:

DFG Ltd
Trial balance as at 30 April 20X9

	Debit £000	Credit £000
Administrative wages	2 500	
Bank	600	
Delivery vehicle running expenses	700	
Delivery vehicles	2 400	

Inventory at 1 May 20X8	4 000	
Machinery	3 200	
Purchases	12 000	
Rent on factory	800	
Retained earnings		1 100
Returns from customers	500	
Sales		19 000
Selling expenses	1 200	
Share capital		8 400
Trade payables		1 400
Trade receivables	2 000	
	29 900	29 900

Inventory at 30 April 20X9 was valued at £4 200 000.

Required:
Use the above information to prepare a statement of comprehensive income for the year ended 30 April 20X9 and a statement of financial position as at that date.

Questions can run on for two pages or more, so this is a simple example. It does, however, involve processing each of the figures in the trial balance and making the correct adjustment for each of the additional pieces of information provided underneath.

The key is to start with the title of the first statement:

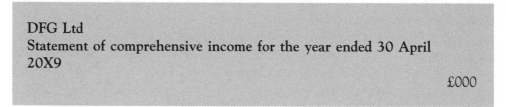

DFG Ltd
Statement of comprehensive income for the year ended 30 April 20X9

£000

Every accounting statement should have a proper title, and it should also state the currency that is being used. In this case, we are working in thousands of pounds sterling.

The next thing is to go back to the format and identify the first item that is to appear in this statement. In this case, it is revenue. Reading through the question from beginning to end, we can see that there are two numbers that are involved in arriving at this: sales for the year less returns from customers. We need to start a second sheet of paper for workings. We calculate revenue as follows:

Workings
<u>Revenue</u>

Sales	19 000
Returns from customers	(500)
	<u>18 500</u>

Going back to our first page, we insert the figure into the format and move on to the next line:

DFG Ltd
Statement of comprehensive income for the year ended 30 April 20X9

	£000
Revenue	18 500
Cost of sales	

Working through the statement line by line, preparing workings and any notes along the way, yields a full set of financial statements:

DFG Ltd
Statement of comprehensive income for the year ended 30 April 20X9

	£000
Revenue	18 500
Cost of sales	(12 600)
Gross profit	5 900
Distribution costs	(1 900)
Administrative expenses	(2 500)
PROFIT FOR THE YEAR	1 500
Other comprehensive income:	—
TOTAL COMPREHENSIVE INCOME FOR THE YEAR	1 500

As an alternative to showing a blank entry against other comprehensive income, it would be equally appropriate to call this an 'income statement' and to stop at the profit for the year. A note to the effect that 'There was no other comprehensive income for the year' would make it clear that you were aware of the requirement:

DFG Ltd
Statement of changes in equity for the year ended 30 April 20X9

	Share capital	Retained earnings	Total equity
	£000	£000	£000
Balance at 1 May 20X8	8 400	1 100	9 500
Profit for the year		1 500	1 500
Balance at 30 April 20X9	8 400	2 600	11 000

DFG Ltd
Statement of Financial Position as at 30 April 20X9

	Notes	£000
ASSETS		
Non-current assets		
Property, plant, and equipment	1	5 600
Current assets		
Inventories		4 200
Trade receivables		2 000
Cash and cash equivalents		600
		6 800
Total assets		12 400
EQUITY AND LIABILITIES		
Equity		
Share capital		8 400
Retained earnings		2 600
Total equity		11 000
Current liabilities		
Trade and other payables		1 400
Total equity and liabilities		12 400

Notes
1. Property, plant, and equipment

	£000
Machinery	3 200
Delivery vehicles	2 400
	5 600

Workings
Revenue

Sales	19 000
Returns from customers	(500)
	18 500

Cost of sales

Inventory at 1 May 20X8	4 000
Purchases	12 000
Rent on factory	800
Inventory at 30 April 20X9	(4 200)
	12 600

Distribution costs

Delivery vehicle running expenses	700
Selling expenses	1 200
	1 900

Administrative expenses

Administrative wages	2 500

Some Important Points About Preparing the Statements

There are one or two practical suggestions that can simplify this process.

Notes Versus Workings

The notes are part of the financial statements and so they are cross-referenced to the accounting statements themselves. There is only one note in the example given above. Readers have the opportunity to see how the total for property, plant, and equipment according to the balance sheet is made up.

The workings are not part of the statements and they would not be shown to anybody. An accountant preparing a set of financial statements in the real world would have working papers that are used to check the figures in the statements. Workings are extremely important for examination purposes because there is always a possibility that your examiner will be unsure where one or more of your figures come from. Providing a working to show, say, the calculation of the figure for revenue allows for differences of opinion as to the way that the figure is arrived at.

Workings should not be cross-referenced to the statements because that might create the impression that you would publish these rough calculations alongside the statements and notes.

Always have two separate sheets of paper for notes and workings. Never head up a single sheet of paper as 'Notes and workings' and leave the examiner to guess which is which.

If you are unsure whether something should go into the notes, then ask whether it ought to be disclosed to a reader, either in response to a disclosure requirement or because the information is necessary for an understanding of the accounts. If disclosure is necessary, then it should go in the notes. If not, then it should go in the workings. If you are unsure, then it is probably slightly safer to show it as a note on the basis that it is not in itself wrong to make unnecessary disclosures.

Work Neatly

Accountancy is about communicating information to inform decisions. Accounting statements are intended to be read and understood. It follows that the statements should be neat and tidy. That means that workings should be on a separate sheet and not scribbled in the margins of the statements. You should also avoid abbreviations.

Try to get into the habit of working neatly. It is easy to take shortcuts with the intention of working to a higher standard in the exam, but that is a rather naive approach. Generally, bad habits are more difficult to overcome while under exam conditions.

Working neatly is also a sign of a calm and methodical approach to the question. It would be unfair to claim that good answers are always tidier than poor answers, or that neat handwriting is enough to guarantee a good mark, but better answers are generally better presented in addition to having the correct numbers.

A Few Points About the IAS 1 Formats

The various headings and subheadings are not always defined in such a way that there can be no doubt as to what appears under any given heading. For example, the distinction between cost of sales, distribution costs and administrative expenses is a matter of deciding why a particular cost was incurred. Not everybody agrees on whether a factory manager's salary should be treated as part of the cost of sales or administration, and IAS 1 does not provide any guidance on this.

The best way of dealing with the ambiguity about the headings is to provide clear workings. Generally, examiners will accept any cost under almost any heading unless there is an instruction in the question as to how something should be treated or there can be no doubt that there can be only one place to show it (such as interest always appearing under finance costs).

There is no need to show zero figures for headings that are not relevant to a particular company. In our example above, DFG Ltd had no non-current liabilities and so there was no need to show anything.

Do not waste time trying to memorise the formats. Instead, work through as many questions as possible. After a while it becomes second nature to go through the formats from beginning to end.

Always use the IAS 1 formats as a guide so that you never have to worry about any more than a single figure at a time. It helps to work with four separate sheets of paper:

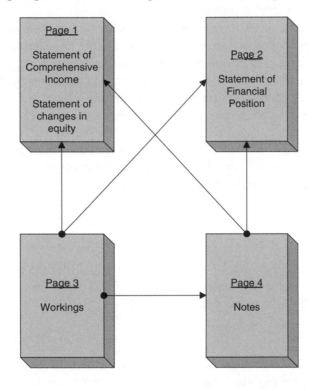

Summary

This text is about preparing financial statements, taking account of the rules laid down by the accountancy profession. This can be a complicated undertaking because history has shown that the directors of companies do not always wish to report truthfully to their shareholders. Hopefully, there are very few companies who publish distorted financial statements, but it can be difficult to distinguish the companies who report honestly from those who do not. The inability to distinguish good companies from bad undermines confidence in financial reporting and deters investment generally.

The rules published by the accountancy profession are intended to deal with some of the concerns that shareholders and other readers might have. Most cases of dishonest reporting have involved using gaps or ambiguities in the regulations. Presenting outright lies in the financial statements carries the risk of criminal penalties. 'Creative accounting' makes it possible to mislead readers while remaining within the rules.

The accountancy profession has been developing rules for many years. We saw one of those in this chapter. IAS 1 *Presentation of Accounting Statements* prescribes some of the content of a set of financial statements and lays down detailed formats for the main statements, including the statement of comprehensive income and the statement of financial position.

It is important to come to grips with the IAS 1 formats because they make it easier to deal with complicated questions with lots of adjustments. Working through the formats line by line means that you only ever have to think about a single figure at any one time. The easiest way to do this is to practise. It is also worth getting into good habits right from the start by working neatly and creating an organised workspace by having separate sheets of paper for each statement, the notes to the statements, and the workings.

Chapter 2 follows on from this one by exploring the manner in which accounting is regulated. Later chapters will look at specific topics in accounting and will deal with the application of the rules that have been devised for them.

Appendix

This section will revise one or two basics that should be familiar from the introductory stage, but which often get forgotten. Even if you are confident with the basics, it will do no harm to skim through this section.

Bookkeeping

It is important to be aware of the ways in which accounting records are maintained. If nothing else, the double-entry system can be used as one way to lay out a set of workings.

The 'balance sheet equation' lies at the heart of the bookkeeping system. This states that there should always be a clear relationship between assets, owners' equity, and liabilities. At any given time:

$$\text{Assets} = \text{capital} + \text{liabilities}$$

The logic behind this is that the assets controlled by the business must have been financed somehow. That finance must be provided by the owners (in the form of equity) or by third parties (in the form of liabilities).

It should never be a coincidence that the balance sheet equation holds true. In practice, bookkeeping records are organised so that it must do so.

Changes usually arise because of transactions. For example, a customer pays for goods that have been purchased on credit. Occasionally, accounting adjustments have to be made for less routine events such as a customer's balance being written off because it is irrecoverable.

Every transaction or adjustment affects two items in the records. For example, the customer's payment will increase the asset of cash and reduce the asset of trade receivables. If the balance sheet equation held before recording these adjustments, then it will still hold afterwards because one asset has increased and another has decreased by the same amount.

The bookkeeping system will keep track of each individual asset, equity, and liability balance. Each has its own record called an 'account'.

Any profit earned by the business belongs to the owners, and so income will effectively be added to the owners' equity and expenses deducted. Thus, income and expense accounts are effectively specialised equity accounts.

Thus, there are five categories of accounts:

• Assets • Expenses *If the balance sheet equation is to hold true, then an increase in an account on this side must be matched by a decrease in another account on this side . . .*	• Equity • Liability • Income *. . . or an increase in an account on this side.*

Accounting records are kept on computers and may be printed out from time to time in a manner that makes efficient use of paper. If you are working with double entry as a means of laying out some workings, you should revert to the old-fashioned convention of thinking of an account as being a sheet of paper that is ruled down the centre with a title at the top. The result is often referred to as a 'T' account because of the shape created by the intersecting lines:

Account name	
Debit side	Credit side

The left-hand side of each page is called the 'debit' side, and the right-hand side is called the 'credit' side. Inserting an entry on the left-hand side of an account is called 'debiting' the account, and making an entry on the right-hand side is called 'crediting'.

By convention:

- Increases in assets or expenses are shown on the 'debit' side of the accounts.
- Decreases in assets or expenses are shown on the 'credit' side.

Equity, liabilities, and income are the opposites of the above, so:

- Increases in equity, liabilities, and income are shown on the 'credit' side.
- Decreases in equity, liabilities, and income are shown on the 'debit' side.

Every transaction or adjustment affects two balances, so the rules of double entry can be summarised as follows:

	Increase	Decrease
Asset Expense	DEBIT	CREDIT
Equity Liability Income	CREDIT	DEBIT

This table will help you to enter the most complicated transactions and adjustments throughout the rest of your career. Even in computerised systems, instructions are given in terms of debits and credits.

It is not necessary to memorise the whole table. If you can remember that increasing an asset or expense is a debit, then it follows that a decrease is a credit and that entries for equity, liability, or income accounts are the opposite.

From time to time the accounts are balanced off to show the present state of affairs for asset, liability, and equity balances and the running totals for income and expenses.

In the above example, the company started off with £4000 paid for share capital:

Debit bank	£4000
Credit share capital	£4000

It paid £1000 for equipment:

Debit equipment	£1000
Credit bank	£1000

At the end of the month, we calculate the balance on this account by netting off

	Bank		
1/1/X4 Share capital	4 000	3/1/X4 Equipment	1 000
5/1/X4 Loan	7 000	12/1/X4 Wages	2 500
		21/1/X4 Rent	1 100
		31/1/X4 Balance c/d	6 400
	11 000		11 000
1/2/X4 Balance b/d	6 400		

the debits and credits. This company has a debit (asset) balance of £6400 because the debits exceed the credits by that amount. The £11 000 total is a double check that we have calculated the balance correctly. The fact that the two sides agree suggests that we have inserted the correct closing balance. That leaves an opening debit balance of £6400 at the start of the next period, and that will be adjusted for any transactions that take place thereafter.

The information in the various accounts can be summarised in the form of a trial balance.

The following trial balance was extracted from the books of HGK Ltd, a wholesaler, at 31 December 20X3:

	Debit	Credit
	£000	£000
Administrative expenses	325	
Bank	88	
Debenture interest	7	
Debenture loans		150
Distribution costs	185	
Dividend income		10
Dividends paid	75	
Fixtures and fittings	120	
Inventory at 31 December 20X2	340	
Investments	150	
Land and buildings	595	
Plant and machinery	220	

Purchases	970	
Rent income		90
Retained profit at 31 December 20X2		860
Sales		1 480
Share capital		625
Trade payables		215
Trade receivables	355	
	3 430	3 430

Note:

1. Inventories were physically counted at 31 December 20X3 and valued at £420 000.
2. The investments are to be treated as current assets.

This is a typical starting point for a preparation of accounts question. The trial balance can be rather more complicated and the notes far more extensive, but the trick of working through the IAS 1 formats from beginning to end imposes a structure and simplifies matters.

Each income and expense balance will be transferred into the statement of comprehensive income, and each asset, equity, and liability balance will appear in the statement of financial position. Each adjustment to those figures in response to the notes will affect two figures because of the rules of double-entry bookkeeping. It is a useful tip to score out trial balance figures that have been used as a check that nothing is entered twice or missed out altogether, and to tick the notes so that each is ticked twice by the end.

Think!

Take a few minutes to prepare a statement of comprehensive income, a statement of changes in equity, and a statement of financial position from the above information.

By the time you have done this, your question should look like this:

The following trial balance was extracted from the books of HGK Ltd, a wholesaler, at 31 December 20X3:

	Debit £000	Credit £000
Administrative expenses	325	
Bank	88	
Debenture interest	7	
Debenture loans		150
Distribution costs	185	
Dividend income		10
Dividends paid	75	
Fixtures and fittings	120	
Inventory at 31 December 20X2	340	
Investments	150	
Land and buildings	595	
Plant and machinery	220	
Purchases	970	
Rent income		90
Retained profit at 31 December 20X2		860
Sales		1 480
Share capital		625
Trade payables		215
Trade receivables	355	
	3 430	3 430

Note:

1. Stocks were physically counted at 31 December 20X3 and valued at £420 000. ✓✓
2. The investments are to be treated as current assets.

Your answer should be as follows:

Page 1

HGJ Ltd
Statement of comprehensive income
for the year ended 31 December 20X3

	£000
Revenue	1 480
Cost of sales	(890)
Gross profit	590
Other income (note 1)	100
Distribution costs	(185)
Administrative expenses	(325)
Finance costs	(7)
PROFIT FOR THE YEAR	173

There was no othre comprehensive income for the year.

HGJ Ltd
Statement of changes in equity
for the year ended 31 December 20X3

	Share capital	Retained profit	Total equity
	£000	£000	£000
Balance at 31 December 20X2	625	860	1 485
Profit for year		0	0
Dividend		(75)	(75)
Balance at 31 December 20X3	625	785	1 410

Page 2

HGJ Ltd
Statement of financial position as at 31 December 20X3

	£000
ASSETS	
Non-current assets	
Property, plant and equipment (note 2)	935
Current assets	
Inventories	420
Trade receivables	355
Investments	150
Cash and cash equivalents	88
	1 013
Total assets	1 948
EQUITY AND LIABILITIES	
Equity	
Share capital	625
Retained earnings	785
Total equity	1 410
Non-current liabilities	
Debenture loans	150
Current liabilities	
Trade and other payables	215
Total liabilities	365
Total equity and liabilities	1 775

Page 3

Notes
(1) Other income

	£000
Rent received	90
Dividend income	10
	100

(2) Property, plant, and equipment

	£000
Land and buildings	595
Plant and machinery	220
Fixtures and fittings	120
	935

Page 4

Workings

	£000
Cost of sales	
Opening inventory	340
Purchases	970
Closing inventory	(420)
	890

Property, Plant, and Equipment

The accounting issues associated with tangible non-current assets will be discussed in detail in Chapter 8. This section will briefly review the bookkeeping issues raised by these assets.

You should remember that items of property, plant, and equipment are recorded initially at cost. Thereafter, that cost is depreciated to reflect the fact that these assets have finite useful lives. Land is the only asset that is not normally depreciated because land is the only physical asset whose life is potentially unlimited.

We keep two separate accounts for each category of asset, one showing the cost and the other keeping track of depreciation. The notes attached to the statement of financial position show how the net balance is made up by subtracting total depreciation from cost.

From time to time, assets are disposed of, complicating the calculation of closing balances and depreciation.

There is also the possibility that assets will be revalued. In that case, depreciation is charged on the revalued amount.

Typically, questions state how depreciation has to be charged. In simple cases, it is sufficient to calculate the charge for the year and then to add that amount to the depreciation account.

For example, a company has a debit balance of £300 000 on vehicles at cost and a credit balance of £120 000 on vehicles at depreciation. Depreciation still has to be charged at 25% on the reducing balance basis. This means that we still need to charge depreciation based on 25% of the book value, which is (£300 000 − 120 000) × 25% = £45 000.

The statement of comprehensive income will show a charge for the year of £45 000 as an expense. This will be included under the appropriate heading associated with the use to which those assets were put. If they were delivery vehicles, then the depreciation charge will be a distribution cost.

The notes to the statement of financial position will show vehicles at cost of £300 000 and depreciation of £165 000, to give a net book value of £135 000. This will be included in the total for property, plant, and equipment, as shown on the face of the statement.

Disposals of assets can complicate these calculations, and it is sometimes worth investing a little time and effort in workings that simplify things.

In essence, the problem of adjusting for the disposal of an asset is a simple one. If an asset has been disposed of, then all trace of it must be removed from the company's records. This means that both the cost and the depreciation accounts must be adjusted. It is, however, extremely difficult to do this and to arrive at the correct figures for the statement of comprehensive income and statement of financial position without making use of T accounts.

There are three accounts involved, one for the asset at cost, one for depreciation, and a disposal account. The cost and depreciation are transferred to the disposal account to remove them from the other accounts. The proceeds of disposal are recorded in the disposal account. Any balance is then taken to the statement of comprehensive income as a gain or loss on disposal. The gain or loss is shown under the same heading as the depreciation charge for that asset. The terminology is slightly misleading because the gain or loss is actually the correction of a forecasting error. A gain on disposal suggests that the asset was depreciated too heavily throughout its life and was sold for more than anticipated, and a loss suggests that the depreciation charge was inadequate.

For example, a company shows a debit balance of £600 000 on machinery at cost and a credit balance of £200 000 on machinery at depreciation. There is a credit balance on the disposals account of £6000. Further investigations reveal that:

- During the year, an asset that had originally cost £40 000 and on which depreciation of £30 000 had been charged was sold for £6000. No entries have been made in respect of this transaction except for the credit of the proceeds to the disposal account.
- Machinery is to be depreciated at a rate of 20% per annum on the reducing balance basis. A full year's depreciation is charged on the year in which an asset is acquired, and none in the year of disposal.

The simplest way to draw this information together is by means of T accounts:

Machinery – cost

Balance b/d	600 000	Disposal		40 000
		Balance c/d		560 000
	600 000			600 000
Balance b/d	560 000			

Machinery – depreciation

Disposal	30 000	Balance b/d		200 000
Balance c/d	170 000			
	200 000			200 000
		Balance b/d		170 000
Balance c/d	248 000	Depreciation expense		78 000
	248 000			248 000
		Balance b/d		248 000

Machinery – disposal

Machinery – cost	40 000	Bank		6 000
		Machinery – depreciation		30 000
		Loss on disposal		4 000
	40 000			40 000

Adjusting the opening balances for the effects of the disposal results in balances of £560 000 on machinery at cost and £170 000 on machinery at depreciation. The charge for the year has yet to be calculated at 20% of book value, which is (£560 000 − 170 000) × 20% = £78 000. That is shown in the statement of comprehensive income as an expense, and the final balance on the depreciation account is £248 000, so machinery has a net book value of £560 000 − 248 000 = £312 000.

The disposal account shows the book value of £40 000 − 30 000 = £10 000 being offset against the proceeds of £6000. That means there is a loss of £4000, which will be shown as an expense in the statement of comprehensive income. If the disposal account had shown a gain, then that would also have been offset against the expenses in the statement of comprehensive income.

Property, plant, and equipment need not be shown at cost less depreciation. There are certain circumstances in which it is more appropriate to show the asset at a valuation. We will deal with those circumstances in detail in Chapter 8, so this brief note will deal with the bookkeeping adjustments only.

The key to accounting for a revaluation is to change the book value to the amount determined by the valuation exercise. That means setting the balance on the depreciation account to zero and adjusting the balance on the asset at cost account to reflect the valuation. If this results in an increase in the book value, then the amount of the increase is credited to a part of shareholders' equity called the revaluation account. We will deal with the effects of decreases in Chapter 8.

For example, a company has a factory that originally cost £500 000 and has been depreciated by a total of £200 000. The directors have had the factory revalued at £750 000 and wish to reflect this in the statement of financial position.

The balance on the factory at cost account (which will have to be renamed the factory at valuation account) will be increased by £250 000 to £750 000. The balance on the depreciation account will be decreased by £200 000 to zero. Both adjustments are debits, and the corresponding credit will be shown in the revaluation reserve:

Debit – factory at cost/valuation	£250 000
Debit – factory depreciation	£200 000
Credit – revaluation reserve	£450 000

The increase in the revaluation reserve will be shown in the statement of comprehensive income for the year, and the closing balance will be part of equity.

In the future, the factory's depreciation will be based on the £750 000 valuation.

Tutorial Questions

Question 1

Bring a set of financial statements to class. Analyse this to show the relative proportions of statutory and voluntary disclosures. Look at the presentation –

does it appear to have been professionally designed? Was it expensive to print?

- Why do companies publish so much material on a voluntary basis?
- Why is so much money spent on the actual document itself?
- Why are shareholders sometimes advised to read the accounts by starting at the back and working forwards?

Hint:
It is fairly easy to download annual reports from the Internet. Company websites often have a link with a title like 'investor relations', and that usually leads to the latest annual report.

Question 2

Use the following information to prepare a statement of comprehensive income, a statement of changes in equity, and a statement of financial position for HIJ Ltd:

HIJ Ltd
Trial Balance as at 31 December 20X1

	£000	£000
Administration expenses	160	
Bank		40
Cash	7	
Computer – cost	100	
Computer – depreciation		40
Debenture interest	12	
Debentures (10%)		120
Dividend paid	10	
Inventory at 1 January 20X1 – finished goods	186	
Inventory at 1 January 20X1 – raw materials	108	
Inventory at 1 January 20X1 – work in progress	34	
Land and buildings – cost	300	
Land and buildings – depreciation		40
Manufacturing overheads	120	
Manufacturing wages	550	
Ordinary share capital		400
Patents and trademarks – cost	270	
Patents and trademarks – amortisation		70
Plant and machinery – cost	160	
Plant and machinery – depreciation		70

Purchases – raw materials	760	
Retained earnings at 1 January 20X1		280
Sales		1 781
Selling and distribution costs	117	
Share premium		200
Trade payables		98
Trade receivables	195	
Vehicles – cost	75	
Vehicles – depreciation		25
	3 164	3 164

1. Inventories at 31 December 20X1 were as follows:

	£000
Raw materials	113
Work in progress	38
Finished goods	278
	429

2. Depreciation for the year has been charged and included in manufacturing overheads.

   Hints:
   There is a credit balance on the bank account. What does that mean?

- The company owns patents and trademarks. These are intangible non-current assets. Intangible assets are written off over their useful lives in the same manner as tangible assets. The only difference is that this is known as amortisation rather than depreciation.
- Share premium is part of share capital. Shares carry nominal values, but they can be sold for more than their face value. The difference between that face value and the selling price is called the share premium, and it is treated as part of share capital.

Question 3

Prepare a set of financial statements from the following:

TUV plc
Trial balance as at 31 December 20X7

	Debit £000	Credit £000
10% debenture loans		400
Administrative staff salaries	18	

Bank	105	
Computer – cost	250	
Computer – depreciation		50
Delivery vehicles – cost	230	
Delivery vehicles – depreciation		80
Directors' salaries	35	
Disposal		10
Dividend	30	
Inventory at 1 January 20X7	20	
Loan interest	20	
Machinery – cost	588	
Machinery – depreciation		180
Manufacturing wages	49	
Office heating and lighting	9	
Ordinary shares		560
Purchases of materials	250	
Rent – administrative offices	32	
Rent – factory	28	
Repairs to machinery	27	
Retained earnings at 1 January 20X7		220
Sales		1 000
Sales commission	68	
Trade payables		27
Trade receivables	84	
Vehicle running costs	80	
Warehouse – cost	700	
Warehouse – depreciation		96
	2 623	2 623

1. Inventory was counted on 31 December 20X7 and valued at £25 000.

2. The acquisition of a piece of machinery costing £12 000 has been posted incorrectly to the repairs account. No adjustment has been made in respect of the correction of this error.

3. The balance on the disposals account represents the proceeds of the disposal of a delivery vehicle that had originally cost £30 000 and that had been depreciated by £13 000. No other entries have been made in respect of this transaction.

4. Depreciation has still to be charged as follows:

  - machinery – 10% straight line;
  - computer – 20% straight line;
  - warehouse – 2% straight line;
  - delivery vehicles – 25% reducing balance.

5. The warehouse is to be revalued at £900 000 as at 31 December 20X7, after charging depreciation for the year.

6. The computer is used mainly for accounting and payroll purposes.

Hint:

  - The loan carries a 10% interest rate. How much should be shown as an expense? How should the unpaid element be treated?

Further Work

The answers to these end-of-chapter questions can be found at the back of the book.

Question 1

The following information was extracted from the financial statements of GHI Ltd:

GHI Ltd
Trial Balance as at 31 December 20X1

	£000	£000
14% debenture stock		500
Administration costs	2 700	
Audit fees	42	
Bank	600	
Debenture interest paid	35	
Distribution costs	3 200	
Dividend paid	160	
Fixtures and fittings – cost	1 500	
Fixtures and fittings – depreciation		400
Interest received from loan stock		220
Inventory as at 1 January 20X1	2 090	
Investments in loan stock	2 100	
Land and buildings – cost	4 500	

Land and buildings – depreciation		190
Manufacturing costs	10 880	
Ordinary share capital		5 000
Plant and machinery – cost	2 800	
Plant and machinery – depreciation		1 300
Rental income		160
Retained profit		2 900
Sales		20 467
Trade payables		870
Trade receivables	1 400	
	32 007	32 007

1. Inventories at 31 December 20X1 have been valued at £3 100 000.

2. Depreciation for the year has been charged and included in manufacturing costs.

3. Only half the debenture interest for the year has been paid. The remainder should be accrued.

Prepare GHI Ltd's statement of comprehensive income and statement of changes in equity for the year ended 31 December 20X1 and its statement of financial position as at that date.

Question 2

Prepare a set of financial statements from the following information:

NOP plc
Trial balance as at 31 December 20X4

	Debit £000	Credit £000
Bank	10	
Delivery vehicles – cost	360	
Delivery vehicles – depreciation		133
Disposal		13
Dividend	50	
Factory – cost	400	
Factory – depreciation		22
General reserve		100
Inventory at 1 January 20X4	15	
Machinery – cost	430	
Machinery – depreciation		90

Office equipment – cost	150	
Office equipment – depreciation		40
Purchases	200	
Retained profit		350
Sales		700
Share capital		200
Share premium		215
Trade payables		25
Trade receivables	60	
Wages – clerical staff	70	
Wages – production staff	50	
Wages – sales staff	93	
	1 888	1 888

1. Inventory was counted at 31 December 20X4 and was valued at £20 000.

2. During the year, a piece of machinery that had cost £30 000 and had been depreciated by £10 000 was sold for £13 000. No entries had been made in respect of this sale, apart from a credit to the disposal account in respect of the proceeds.

3. Depreciation is to be calculated as follows:

   • factory – 2% of cost;
   • machinery – 10% of cost;
   • office equipment – 20% of cost;
   • vehicles – 25% of book value.

A full year's depreciation is to be charged in the year of acquisition and none in the year of disposal.

Hint:
• Reserves can take lots of different forms and have a variety of different titles, but they are all part of equity.

References

Jones, M. (2009), *Creative Accounting, Fraud and International Accounting Scandals*, John Wiley & Sons, Ltd, Chichester, UK.

Smith, T. (1992), *Accounting for Growth: Stripping the Camouflage from Company Accounts*, Random House Business Books, London, UK.

AN OVERVIEW OF REGULATION

2

Contents

Learning Objectives

After studying this chapter you should be able to:

- explain why accounting standards are necessary;
- describe the standard-setting process;
- describe some of the forces that can affect the success or failure of the standard-setting process;
- describe the role of the external auditor.

Introduction

The very nature of accounting makes it necessary to have regulations in place to ensure that the figures can be relied upon. History shows that in the absence of regulation there will always be a risk that financial statements will be manipulated to suit the needs of the preparers.

This chapter will take an overview of the way in which accounting rules are set and enforced. It will deal with the reasons for regulating accounting and some of the problems that regulation can create. This is one of the most interesting areas of accounting because the rules and regulations are best understood by referring to problems that occur in the real world.

A Brief History

In Chapter 1 we saw that accountants have an unfortunate reputation for publishing misleading information. It is difficult to tell whether or not that reputation is deserved because much of it is based on suppositions and suspicions that are based on a few extreme cases.

One of the reasons that accounting scandals capture the public's attention is that they often have the ability to affect large numbers of people. Those affected may have had little or no prior warning of their fate, and some may lose their entire savings and financial security. That creates uncertainty in the minds of all users of financial statements because they too could end up losing a significant proportion of their wealth.

The basic problem is that in most cases the companies that cause these scandals are indistinguishable from the rest, and so those who were not involved start to worry whether they might be victims of a similar but unrelated scandal.

Accounting Scandals

The following examples are drawn from the United Kingdom. Other countries have had their own scandals, but it is easier to see how the system of regulation reacts when it is placed in a single national setting.

One of the most influential accounting scandals of modern times was associated with GEC's takeover of AEI in 1967. Prior to the takeover, AEI had forecast profits of £10 million for the year that was half-way through. In fact the company reported a loss of £4.5 million. Only £5.0 million of this difference could be explained by forecasting errors, and the remaining £9.5 million was due to differences of opinion over the correct accounting treatment for various items. This scandal caused a great deal of concern because there were no agreed benchmarks that could be used to resolve the disputed accounting choices. The resulting outcry was instrumental in the creation of the Accounting Standards Steering Committee, whose role will be discussed below.

The introduction of accounting regulations has not been sufficient to prevent scandals from occurring. We will discuss some of the reasons for this as the chapter develops, but standard-setters are hampered by the fact that they cannot foresee every possible misleading or distorting accounting treatment.

An intriguing paper, published in 1999, charts the extent to which accounting *causes célèbres* were reported during the period from 1962 to 1992 (Edwards and Shaoul, 1999). The paper lists 191 cases that occurred during that period. The frequency of occurrence is tabulated below:

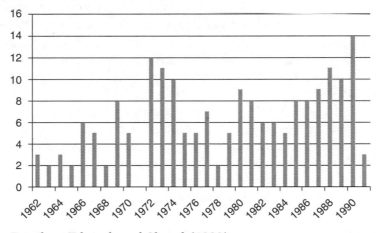

Source: Based on Edwards and Shaoul (1999).

One interesting point arising from this paper is that many of these cases were really business scandals, such as contested takeover battles between major corporations, where accounting was only marginally implicated in a much bigger debate. For example, a bidding company might wish to take over a target company whose directors wish to remain independent. Typically, the bidder would offer to exchange its shares for those of the target company. The directors of the bidding company would have an incentive to 'talk up' the value of their shares and 'talk down' the values of the shares of the target company, so that the target company's shareholders will view the offer as a generous one and give them a controlling interest. The board of the target company have the opposite agenda, so that the offer will appear inadequate and the bid will fail. In such cases, both sides will often publicly criticise one another over everything that they can think of, from the weaknesses in the other board's business strategy to its choice of accounting policy, and so it might be misleading to accept all of these cases as true 'accounting scandals'.

Standard-setting in the United Kingdom

In spite of the limited number of cases, it would appear that the investing public regards each and every scandal as a major cause for concern. The credibility of financial statements is clearly a significant aspect of investors' confidence, and anything that undermines that credibility has a wider impact than that on the investors who are directly affected. The accountancy profession's response is often to develop new and better ways of setting standards so that it can be more responsive to concerns.

In 1970, the Institute of Chartered Accountants in England and Wales (ICAEW) established the Accounting Standards Steering Committee (ASSC). The ASSC was effectively responsible for the earliest mandatory accounting requirements in the United Kingdom, other than those laid down by company law. Over time, the ICAEW was joined by the other members of the Consultative Committee of Accounting Bodies (CCAB),[1] and by 1976 the ASSC became the Accounting Standards Committee (ASC) and was effectively under the joint ownership of each of the bodies.

Essentially, the ASC's role was the publication of Statements of Standard Accounting Practice (SSAPs), each of which was intended to narrow the areas of difference in terms of accounting practice in a specific area. During its lifetime, it published many such standards. The precise number might be a matter of an accounting debate in itself. There were nominally 25 SSAPs in total, but some of those were revised during their lives, and so there were at least 30 standards issued.

Accounting for depreciation is one of the many areas that were visited by the ASC. This attracted attention because of inconsistencies in the approach taken by different companies, most notably over the depreciation of property. Prior to the publication of SSAP 12 in 1997, it was a matter of debate as to whether buildings ought to be depreciated. Thus, financial statements of different companies were not comparable because some charged depreciation

---

[1] The CCAB is a body that gives the six main accountancy bodies in the United Kingdom a collective voice. Its membership comprises: The Institute of Chartered Accountants in England and Wales (ICAEW), The Institute of Chartered Accountants of Scotland (ICAS), The Institute of Chartered Accountants in Ireland (ICAI), The Association of Chartered Certified Accountants (ACCA), The Chartered Institute of Management Accountants (CIMA), and The Chartered Institute of Public Finance and Accountancy (CIPFA).

on their buildings and others did not. The ASC followed its normal processes and:

- established a working party to identify the problem and suggest a solution;
- published an 'Exposure Draft' for public comment, so that all interested parties could make their views known on the proposed treatment;
- published an SSAP requiring that all non-current assets with finite useful lives should be depreciated.

The application of SSAP 12 identified some of the problems faced by standard-setters. It had to be amended in 1981, revised in 1987, and amended in 1992. In each case, the problem was that companies were reading the requirements of the SSAP in a creative manner that enabled them to justify disregarding the fundamental and easily understood principle that any asset, other than possibly land, had a limited life and should be depreciated over the course of that period. We will look at some of the specific problems associated with accounting for depreciation in Chapter 8. For now, it is sufficient to note that the precise wording of the standards does matter because it can establish the range of acceptable treatments.

The ASC made a significant contribution to the regulation of accounting in the United Kingdom, but the fact that it was essentially a joint venture between six separate accounting bodies was a source of friction. Each SSAP had to be accepted by the council of each of the six bodies before it could be formally issued. Even though that was only very rarely a problem, it became apparent that it would be better to have a more autonomous and better-resourced body that could fulfil that role.

The United Kingdom has made a major investment in the process for setting standards relating to financial reporting. An independent entity called the Financial Reporting Council has been established. The FRC is an independent body that draws its funding from a variety of sources, including large companies, professional accounting bodies, and the government. The FRC is responsible for the oversight of several areas associated with the preparation of financial statements and their audit. It is also responsible for the overview of the United Kingdom's system of corporate governance, which is a catch-all term for the mechanisms associated with the way in which companies are managed, such as the appointment of directors, their remuneration, and the ideal structure for the board. The FRC is also responsible for the standards affecting the actuarial profession, which is an occupation group that has some importance to accountancy.

Simplifying the structure created by the FRC in order to focus on the preparation of financial statements gives us the following:

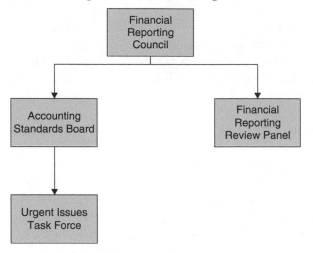

A more detailed plan can be found on the FRC's website.[2]

The FRC itself is responsible for the supervision of the whole process. For example, it appoints the members of the entities that report to it and is responsible for dealing with the highest-level dealings with stakeholders such as the government and professional accountancy bodies. That includes matters such as negotiating the funding arrangements and reporting to the outside world.

The Accounting Standards Board

The Accounting Standards Board (ASB) is responsible for issuing accounting standards. There are presently two series of standards in the United Kingdom. When the ASB was created, it adopted those SSAPs that were still in force as its own, and several of those remain. Any new standards issued by the ASB were entitled Financial Reporting Standards or FRSs. Some FRSs replaced SSAPs, while others were on new topics.

The ASB still has an important role to play in the UK context, but our focus in this text is on the work of the International Accounting Standards Board, which is largely responsible for setting accounting standards that affect all major companies throughout the European Union and most other countries.

The work of the ASB (and that of both the UITF and FRRP, which are described below) is described on its website, which is most easily reached by going to the FRC's site and clicking through the links on its homepage.

---

[2] www.frc.org.uk

The Urgent Issues Task Force

It has already been suggested that one of the problems affecting standard-setting is that preparers of accounts always have the initiative when it comes to finding loopholes in the rules. Furthermore, problems can arise unexpectedly. The Urgent Issues Task Force (UITF) is responsible for developing rapid responses to such cases. It publishes UITF Abstracts which are granted the status of the ASB's standards until such time as a more formal solution can be found, if necessary, in the form of a new FRS or the revision of an existing one. Thus, the UITF prevents the proliferation of unsatisfactory or conflicting interpretations of law or accounting standards.

As with the ASB, the UITF has an international counterpart in the form of the International Financial Reporting Interpretations Committee (IFRIC), which will be discussed when we get to the international standard-setting process.

The Financial Reporting Review Panel

The Financial Reporting Review Panel (FRRP) does not necessarily have an equivalent outside the United Kingdom, but its work illustrates some of the issues associated with enforcing accounting standards.

.The Companies Act 2006 makes it possible to apply to the courts to have a company restate and reissue its financial statements if they are deemed to be defective. The FRRP is authorised to seek such an injunction from the courts if it believes that a company that falls within the remit of this legislation[3] has published financial statements that depart from the requirements of the Companies Act or applicable accounting standards.

The FRC has equipped the FRRP with a sizeable 'war chest' in the form of a cash reserve that can be used to meet the legal fees associated with taking court action. In practice, though, it has yet to be necessary to pursue an action through the courts. It is normal practice for the FRRP to meet with potentially erring companies and then to reach an agreement as to a suitable course of action if it is found that there is a valid complaint. It may be deemed sufficient for the company to agree not to adopt the contentious accounting policy in future years.

In the first instance, any investigations conducted by the FRRP will be in confidence. If a material problem is discovered, then the FRRP will publish a report, which will be posted on its website and publicised by means of a press release. Thus, all interested parties should be warned that there is a problem even if the financial statements are left in their original state. .

---

[3] Generally, that it is a public company or a large private company.

International Standards

The UK system described has an international counterpart in the form of the International Accounting Standards Board (IASB), which publishes accounting standards for the international community. They have proved enormously successful in this regard:

- Since 2005, the European Union has required listed companies to prepare their financial statements in accordance with the IASB's International Financial Reporting Standards (IFRSs).
- The United States is working on a programme that will, eventually, lead to US listed companies reporting in terms of IFRSs.
- Many countries have adopted IFRSs as their own 'national' standards (e.g. Australia, Israel, Malaysia, Mexico, and New Zealand) or have adopted accounting standards that are substantially in line with IFRSs (e.g. China).
- Several other countries are working towards either adoption of or convergence with IFRSs (e.g. Brazil, Canada, Chile, India, Japan, and Korea).

The structure of the standard-setting process is as follows:

The International Accounting Standards Committee (IASC) Foundation is an independent entity that raises finance and appoints and supervises the members of the other bodies listed. The Foundation's trustees are drawn from a diverse range of geographical and professional backgrounds. Funding comes from institutions in the major industrialised countries around the world.

The IASB is responsible for setting the standards themselves. We will discuss the process adopted by the IASB in the next subsection.

The Standards Advisory Council (SAC) provides a forum for individuals and representatives of organisations to meet and provide some advice and input into the workings of the IASB itself. The membership of the SAC is widespread and diverse and comprises people who are interested in assisting the development of high-quality accounting standards. The SAC aims to hold three two-day meetings every year. This is a valuable resource for the IASB because the SAC members are one step removed from the standard-setting process and can offer suggestions on strategic directions that the IASB might consider.

The International Financial Reporting Interpretations Committee (IFRIC) performs a very similar role to that of the United Kingdom's UITF. IFRIC works in conjunction with various national standard-setting bodies to provide guidance on problem areas that are not yet the subject of an IFRS and also on areas where an IFRS is being interpreted in either differing or unacceptable ways. IFRIC identifies the appropriate accounting treatment and publishes an IFRIC Interpretation. Interpretations are approved by the IASB and have the force of an IFRS until such time as they are replaced by a standard.

The IASB's goal is to 'provide the world's integrating capital markets with a common language for financial reporting'. That is a potentially thankless task because the world's capital markets were not always as tightly integrated as one would imagine. For example, in the medium-term past, German companies tended to raise their long-term finance by borrowing from banks and did not rely heavily on equity invested by shareholders. Typically, a major company would have very close ties with a major bank and would grant direct access to regular management meetings and internal accounting reports. There is very little need for detailed financial statements in such an environment. Furthermore, the banks' preference was for highly conservative accounting statements that were best suited to measuring the security of the funds that had been advanced.

The Process of Setting a Standard

In essence, we saw the outline approach in our earlier discussion of the setting of a UK standard on the accounting treatment of depreciation. The process is as follows:[4]

- *Agenda.* While the process of standard-setting is necessarily reactive in the sense that the need for a new standard might be prompted by the actions of preparers, the IASB is also committed to working through a coherent pro-gramme that is intended to develop a series of high-quality standards that will enhance the overall quality of accounting statements. The IASB's agenda must, therefore, be kept under review and updated from time to time.
- *Project planning.* When the time comes to start work on a particular item on the agenda, the IASB must decide whether to work alone or to collaborate with another standard-setting agency. It may be, for example, that the IASB will work

---

[4] Further details can be obtained from the *IASB Due Process Handbook*, which is available for download from the IASB's website.

with the Financial Accounting Standards Board (FASB), the primary standard-setter in the United States. The IASB's senior staff will also have to designate staff to take responsibility for the project.

- *Discussion paper.* The IASB will often publish a discussion paper, as one part of the process of setting standards in an open and transparent way. A discussion paper can be used to explain the issue and to give interested parties an initial opportunity to comment and express their views. As the name suggests, discussion papers invite comment, and the comments that are received are made available to the members of the project team, with a summary being posted on the website.
- *Exposure draft.* Unlike discussion papers, exposure drafts are mandatory. An exposure draft is essentially a draft standard that is published so that any and all interested parties can make an informed comment on the proposed changes to the rules. The exposure draft is written by the IASB's staff. The document must be approved by the IASB before it can be issued for public comment. The comments themselves provide the IASB with feedback on the merits of their proposal. The comments are summarised on the IASB website.
- *IFRS.* The IASB will consider the information gathered during the consultation process, and the exposure draft may be amended prior to the publication of an IFRS. In some cases the IASB may decide to issue a revised exposure draft and seek further comments before the publication of an IFRS.
- *Monitoring.* The IASB keeps the operation of the standards in issue under regular review. It holds meetings with interested parties. This process may lead to the subject matter of a particular IFRS being placed back on the IASB's agenda and the foregoing cycle being repeated to develop an amended or revised IFRS.

This process is potentially both slow and expensive. Discussion papers and exposure drafts are normally made available for comment for 120 days each. Once a standard has been published, it will not normally come into effect immediately. The IASB has to allow for the impact of new rules and regulations on preparers and users alike. Some standards require the collection of additional information in order to prepare the financial statements in accordance with the new rules. Some readers will have to consider the implications. For example, contracts might contain clauses that use accounting figures. If the basis for preparing those figures changes, then that might have implications for both parties to the contract.

Think!

What problems might standard-setters encounter in practice?

Standard-setting in the Real World

In an ideal world, standard-setting would be a straightforward, analytical process that started with the identification of a problem and ended with the determination of the accounting treatment that best resolved the issue. In practice, standard-setting is rarely that simple. There are several reasons for this, some of which will be developed in Chapters 6 to 13 when we look at the regulation of particular areas in depth.

Regulatory Capture

Regulatory capture arises when regulators realise that they require the cooperation of those whom they are regulating in order to function. They may still be able to exert considerable influence, but they are constrained by the potential loss of credibility that might arise if their rules are not complied with. There was a very extreme case of this in the United Kingdom in the 1980s, when SSAP 16 was withdrawn owing to a widespread refusal to make the disclosures required by the standard.[5] This SSAP had always been unpopular with companies, partly because it was complicated and difficult to apply but mainly because it led to lower reported profits. Preparers tolerated the standard for a while, but eventually lost patience and started to ignore it altogether.

One of the most obvious ways in which standard-setters can be influenced is through lobbying on proposed changes. Lobbying can take many forms. The most obvious approach would be to submit comments on discussion papers and exposure drafts. The IASB would clearly welcome any such comment, whether positive or negative. It does, however, make any objections a matter of public record and may reflect badly on the entity making the comments.

---

[5] SSAP 16 was the ASC's second attempt to deal with the accounting implications of changing prices. Inflation was a serious problem in the 1970s, and that tended to render traditional historical cost financial statements misleading. SSAP 16 required the publication of an additional set of financial statements that was designed to correct for the distortions created by the changing price levels that affected the business. For example, the time lag between purchasing inventory and then selling it tended to overstate profit. For the sake of argument, suppose a tin of paint was purchased for £2.00 and sold eight weeks later for £3.00. Traditional historical cost accounting would say that the profit on this transaction was £1.00. If, however, the paint were replaced and the supplier charged £2.40 for the replacement, then the business would really be only £0.60 better off after it sold the paint than it had been before. SSAP 16 adjusted for the effects of such price changes. It also required an adjustment to the depreciation charge, which was based on historical costs that could be many years out of date. Given that prices generally rise, these adjustments meant that reported profit was reduced by SSAP 16.

Lobbying need not take place in public. A degree of anonymity can be obtained by pressing another party, such as a trade association or the entity's external auditor, to comment in a particular way. Directors and senior managers would also be able to make direct contact with IASB staff in order to make comments privately that might be embarrassing if expressed in public. The frequency of different approaches to lobbying in the United Kingdom is discussed in Georgiou (2004).

The effects of preparers' behaviour on the standard-setting process will be a recurring theme in later chapters of this text. There have been many occasions when standards have been withdrawn or heavily modified before or after their introduction in response to negative responses from preparers. An overview of some of these can be found in Zeff (2002).

Clearly, the preparers of financial statements benefit from having credible accounting standards in force. They will not necessarily press their ability to influence the IASB too far or they will struggle to convince readers that their financial statements have any relevance.

Economic Consequences

Economic consequences arise when readers of financial statements change their opinions or attitudes because of a change in accounting standards. For example, the publication of IFRS 2 *Share-based Payment* in 2004 had the effect of bringing additional costs into the income statement.[6] In fact, nothing 'real' had actually changed because of the new standard. The cash flows and the impact on owners' equity associated with issuing options were exactly the same after the new standard came into effect as before.

The intriguing thing is that a number of major multinational companies claimed that they would no longer give options as part of their rewards for board members. They claimed that the recognition of these additional costs under IFRS 2 was the reason for this.

This is not the first time that such arguments have been made about the implications of an accounting standard. IAS 19 *Employee Benefits* and its equiv-alent national standards around the world were used as a reason for the withdrawal of defined benefit pension schemes. In other words, companies claimed that the

---

[6] A detailed discussion of this IFRS lies outside the scope of this text. In essence, it had become commonplace for companies to give their directors share options as part of their remuneration packages. These were not generally accounted for in the financial state-ments unless and until the directors exercised their options. Adverse publicity associated with the whole area of directors' motivation led to a demand that the value attributable to these options should be estimated when they were granted and treated as an expense in the income statement.

changes in their accounting figures arising from this standard made it impossible to continue to provide employees with this type of pension. Again, that argument ignored the fact that the amounts of cash to be paid and the timing of those payments were completely unaffected by the new standard.

In a sense, economic consequences motivate much of the pressure from preparers of financial statements, which, in turn, causes regulatory capture.

Think!

Is it logical for corporate decisions and policies to be changed in response to new accounting treatments?

Arguably, there is no logic to arguments based on economic consequences. The manner in which a transaction or relationship is accounted for does not really affect the cash flows and legal rights and obligations that are associated with it. There are only two possible cases where that may not be true:

- Tax charges could be linked to accounting measures of profit. A new accounting standard that changes taxable profit will have a genuine impact on the company's cash flows.
- Bank loans are usually associated with lending covenants. A lending covenant is really just a contract that gives the bank the right to demand immediate repayment if the terms are breached. One common form of covenant is a limit on the ratio of debt to equity according to the published statement of financial position. If a new accounting standard requires the recognition of a liability that would not otherwise have been included or has the effect of reducing equity, then the company could, at least technically, be in breach of such agreements.

The effects of new standards can be difficult to predict and they may be illogical. For example, when the United States introduced new rules on the accounting treatment of post-retirement healthcare, many companies claimed that they could no longer honour a commitment to continue to pay for employees' medical care after they had retired.

In the United States, the provision of healthcare benefits is an important part of many employees' remuneration packages. Large corporations often agreed to continue to pay for healthcare for eligible employees after they had retired for the remainder of their lives. Before the FASB's Financial Accounting Standard 106 *Employers' Accounting for Post-retirement Benefits Other Than Pensions*

(FAS 106) came into force in 1992, the costs of this healthcare were simply treated as expenses as and when they were paid for. FAS 106 required that the value of the potential liability associated with providing pensioners with lifelong healthcare should be estimated and brought into the statement of financial position. This new rule added liabilities worth billions of dollars to reported liabilities. In some cases, this led to corporations writing to pensioners and telling them that their healthcare provisions had to be withdrawn, with the blame generally being directed at FAS 106 (see Baker and Hayes, 1995).

The important point to note is that FAS 106 had no impact on the cost of fulfilling the commitments that companies had made to their present and past staff. The standard did not require more money to be spent on healthcare, nor did it require anything to be paid sooner. The billions of dollars' worth of costs had already been incurred as part of formal and informal agreements arising from past employment contracts. They had not been accrued as liabilities before because the liabilities themselves were difficult to value accurately. Sometimes regulators have to make a difficult choice between excluding a potentially significant asset or liability and including that balance as an estimate that may be wildly inaccurate. FAS 106 reflected a situation where the regulators had decided that it was better to introduce an estimate than to exclude a major liability.

The adoption of new rules on accounting for pensions had a marked effect on the provision of pension benefits by major corporations. As with the changes brought about by FAS 106, the changes were about attaching different valuation and disclosure policies to cash flows and commitments that were otherwise un-affected by the new accounting rules. The following briefing point was extracted from a briefing note downloaded from the Canadian website of Ernst and Young (2009), a major international accountancy firm:

> The accounting changes described above also have a direct impact on the design and implementation of your pension and benefit plans.
>   Many employers may see IFRS as an additional incentive to . . . shift from defined benefit pension plans to defined contribution plans.

The difference between a defined benefit pension plan and a defined contribu-tion plan is a matter of risk. Under a defined pension scheme, the employer agrees to pay a pension that is based on a fraction of salary at the time of retirement. The cost of doing so varies as forecasts of salary levels change. IAS 19 *Employee Benefits* introduced a requirement to recognise these costs in the financial statements in a manner that made them far more prominent than before. This requirement had no effect on the 'real' economic cost of paying those pensions in terms of the amount or timing of any payments. As with FAS 106, the new rules simply changed the manner in which the problem was reported in the financial statements.

The alternative to a defined benefit is a defined contribution. Under such a scheme, the employer agrees to pay a percentage of each employee's salary into a pension fund. Pensions are then paid on the basis of the value of the fund's assets at the time of retirement, which varies according to the returns obtained on the investments. This shifts the risks associated with pensions from the employer to the employee. Under IAS 19 there are no changing commitments, and so no further costs can be recognised once the contributions have been calculated and paid.

In 2002, Ernst and Young was reported as closing its defined benefit pension scheme 'because of worries over the new accounting standard'.[7] Of course, the partners of Ernst and Young fully understood the significance of the fact that changes to accounting numbers do not necessarily affect the underlying commercial reality. However, the new standard did encourage many major corporations to switch from defined benefit to defined contribution schemes.

Think!

Should standard-setters take greater care over setting standards that might have such profound effects on companies?

One of the recurring themes in this section has been that the accounting standards themselves have not affected the costs borne by companies or the risks associated with doing business. New accounting standards may have made certain economic relationships more visible, and that may have encouraged company boards to change their policies.

It is debatable whether the accountancy profession could ever bring a major problem to light. For example, long before the publication of IAS 19, investors were aware of the costs and liabilities associated with pensions. They may have found it difficult to value those costs and liabilities accurately, although large investors and investment analysts can seek clarification from the company about such matters. We will discuss the role of the major investors in informing markets in Chapter 5.

If it can be proved that standard-setters are consciously setting standards in such a way as to bring about a particular social or economic end (e.g. fairer treatment of employees or higher share prices for investors), then there could easily be

---

[7] The standard referred to was the United Kingdom's FRS 17, although the requirements were virtually identical. These comments are attributed to Ernst and Young: 'Ernst & Young final salary dispute goes to arbitration', Telegraph.co.uk, 11 October 2002.

arguments that their actions are undemocratic because pursuing such goals usually involves making decisions about the respective rights of different stakeholders. Making employee pensions seem cheaper in order to mislead shareholders into paying their retired workers more clearly involves such a decision. If standards are set in accordance with 'good accounting' principles, without regard to economic consequences, then that concern can be addressed.

Firefighting

Standard-setters are at a disadvantage to those who wish to exploit loopholes in the system of regulation. New standards are often set in response to problems that have arisen in practice. Those problems are generally aimed at enhancing a specific aspect of reported performance, such as increasing profit. Resolving problems in one area simply encourages the guilty parties to look elsewhere for further opportunities.

It would be unfair to characterise the standard-setting programme as being entirely reactive. Indeed, Chapter 5 deals with attempts to develop a 'conceptual framework' that is intended to make the whole process rather more proactive. The fact remains, though, that standard-setters cannot predict or prevent each and every problem that might arise in financial reporting.

There was a remarkable event in the late 1980s, when a number of companies attributed a value to their brand names for balance sheet purposes. For example, Rank Hovis McDougall plc capitalised its brands at £678 million in 1988, and several other major companies followed suit. This event raises two major issues relating to the regulation of accounting:

- This event was unforeseen by regulators. Companies were able to recognise massive revaluation reserves and reduce their gearing ratios dramatically without being hampered by rules about how brands should be valued (if at all).
- The influx of brand values into balance sheets led to disagreement and debate as to the purpose of financial statements. Some of the companies who had capitalised brands argued that the statement of financial position was supposed to reflect the value of the company as a whole. Other commentators argued that financial statements were prepared for stewardship purposes and that capitalising brands was not helpful and was even potentially misleading.

One of the problems facing standard-setters is that preparers will always have the initiative if they wish to search for gaps or inconsistencies in the rules. The work of the IFRIC will deal with problems more quickly than was possible in 1988, but it is virtually impossible to ensure that every potential form of 'creative accounting' is eliminated.

The External Auditor

It is undoubtedly useful to have standards, but they will always have limited value unless there is some system in place to measure the extent to which companies put those standards into practice when preparing their financial statements.

The role of the external auditor is to form an opinion on the financial statements and to express that opinion in the auditor's report. A typical audit report, based on International Standard of Auditing 700,[8] concludes with the following 'opinion paragraph':

> In our opinion, the financial statements give a true and fair view of (or 'present fairly, in all material respects,') the financial position of ABC Company as of December 31, 20X1, and of its financial performance and its cash flows for the year then ended in accordance with International Financial Reporting Standards.

The external auditor checks the accuracy of the figures in the bookkeeping records and then checks that the financial statements based on those bookkeeping records comply with all applicable rules and regulations before expressing such an opinion. If the financial statements do not comply with the rules, then the auditor can discharge this responsibility by describing any material concerns in the audit report. Thus, the external auditor is one of the most important safeguards in ensuring compliance with IFRS.

Auditors rely heavily on the accounting standards when they are coming to an opinion. That is not just because the standards are useful. Auditors are forced to be defensive because anyone who loses money through investing in or lending to a company may claim that they did so because the auditor expressed an invalid opinion. If they can make a case that the auditor caused them to suffer some loss, then they can seek compensation through the courts. Audit firms are required to have healthy levels of insurance cover in order to meet any such claims, and so the auditor is a potentially lucrative target.

Summary

Financial reporting has to be regulated because history shows that there will always be disagreements and uncertainties when preparers are left to prepare accounts

---

[8] ISA 700 *The Independent Auditor's Report on a Complete Set of General Purpose Financial Statements.* International Standards of Auditing (ISAs) are published by the International Auditing and Assurance Standards Board.

without constraints and guidance. Codified accounting standards give readers much more confidence in the figures. The fact that there is a system in place should also protect the accountancy profession's reputation by reducing the number of accounting scandals, although these appear to be an ongoing fact of life for accounting regulators.

There is a global standard-setting system in place that is rapidly easing national standard-setting bodies to one side in the interest of having consistency from country to country. The IASB is responsible for setting standards that govern the preparation of financial statements for major companies in many countries, including the European Union.

The process of setting accounting standards is as much a political exercise as a technical one. Standard-setters require the cooperation of the preparers who are subject to these standards.

Tutorial Questions

Question 1

A retailer owns many large buildings in prime city-centre sites. It maintains those buildings to a very high standard. Over time it has seen the market value of these buildings rise. *Assuming that there are no rules governing depreciation of buildings*, write two arguments:

- one setting out the case against depreciating these buildings;
- the other setting out the case for depreciation.

Discuss the problems that your ability to develop conflicting arguments might create for preparers and users of financial statements. (*Note: there are rules in place that resolve this dilemma. We will discuss them in Chapter 8.*)

Question 2

Go to the websites of both the IASB and the national standard-setter for your home country. Identify the aims and objectives of both bodies. Explain why it might be relevant to have a national standard-setter even if there are international standards in force.

Question 3

Go to the IASB website and find an ongoing project that is under way. (*Hint: try to find one that seems reasonably straightforward and understandable.*) Prepare a summary of the issues.

Question 4

Discuss the problems faced by the IASB in reading the comment letters submitted in response to an exposure draft.

Question 5

Should the IASB hold itself responsible if a new standard has adverse consequences for any particular sector of business or society?

Question 6

Obtain a real annual report and find the external auditor's report. Express the various assurances that the auditor makes in your own words.

Question 7

Obtain the latest annual report from the FRRP (obtained via the FRC's website) and summarise the issues that have come to light in the previous year's activity.

Further Work

There are no questions with answers in this chapter. If you wish to do some further work, then you should explore the IASB's website and read the summaries of some of the accounting standards that can be found there. You should also explore the website of your own country's standard-setting body.

References

Baker, C. and Hayes, R. (1995), The negative effect of an accounting standard on employee welfare: the case of McDonnell Douglas Corporation and FASB 106. *Accounting, Auditing and Accountability Journal*, **8**(3), 12–33.

Edwards, P. and Shaoul, J. (1999), Reporting accounting? *Accounting Forum*, **23**(1), 59–92.

Ernst and Young (2009), *Pensions and Benefits Under IFRS.* [On-line]. Available: www.ey.com/Global/assets.nsf/Canada/IFRS_PensionsBenefits/$file/ IFRSPensionsBenefitsJan09.pdf

Georgiou, G. (2004), Corporate lobbying on accounting standards: methods, timing and perceived effectiveness. *Abacus,* **40**(2), 219–237.

Zeff, S. (2002), 'Political' lobbying on proposed standards: a challenge to the IASB. *Accounting Horizons,* **16**(1), 43–54.

READING A SET OF PUBLISHED ACCOUNTS

3

Contents

Learning Objectives

After studying this chapter you should be able to:

- describe the content of a typical annual report;
- describe the role of 'soft' narrative disclosures and 'hard' quantitative information;
- calculate some broad measures of performance and financial position.

Introduction

This chapter is a slight departure because it asks you to obtain a set of financial statements for a real company and to work through a short exercise that is designed to make you familiar with the content and also the process of interpreting the results.

Do not be put off by the fact that financial statements are full of complex technical terminology that is unfamiliar. All that you need to do is focus on the broad content and the way in which it is presented.

Preparing Financial Statements in the Real World

The best way to understand what is involved in the preparation of a set of financial statements in the real world is to look at a few real examples. There are two very easy ways to obtain sets of accounts. Many companies post their annual reports on their corporate websites. The trick is to look for a link with a title like 'investor relations'. Alternatively, there are sites that provide free access to readers who wish to browse and download company financial statements. For example, the homepage of the *Financial Times* (www.FT.com) has a link to 'UK annual reports'. Clicking on that offers immediate access to a host of company reports from the United Kingdom and from a very wide range of other countries.[1]

This section will look at the 2007 annual report published by Domino's Pizza UK & IRL plc. You should download at least one annual report for yourself and work through it in the same manner as will be described below.

The first thing to notice is that the document runs to 100 pages, although this includes the front and back covers (the report is available in printed form as well as electronic) and an extensive list of branches. Even ignoring this material, the annual report covers almost 90 A4 pages.

Soft Information

Most annual reports follow a very similar pattern. They tend to start with softer, narrative reports that are intended to give an overview of the business. Some of that material is required by regulators. For example, the local stock exchange is likely to require a narrative statement by the company chairman and the chief

---

[1] The FT's site requires you to register before you can access reports, but doing so has been free of charge for several years and remains free as at the time of writing.

executive. These mandatory disclosures are normally supplemented by descriptive material that is intended to give a flavour of how the business operates, both in terms of creating wealth for shareholders and also in terms of impact on the environment and on society.

Working through this section of Domino's annual report reveals the following:

- Two pages of 'financial highlights', which show sales, profits, earnings per share, and dividends per share for the present year and the four preceding years as bar charts.
- Two pages of 'performance highlights', which show performance indicators such as sales volume, e-commerce sales, store openings, and delivery statistics for this year and the four preceding years.
- One page is devoted to the executive chairman's statement. This is a very brief overview of the business, with almost as much space devoted to changes to the composition of the board of directors as to the business itself.
- The next six pages consist of the chief executive's report.[2] This provides a series of comments on the company's success during the previous year and indicates confidence in the future.
- Two pages deal with the chief financial officer's review. This consists of both a commentary on some of the key figures in the financial statements themselves and a discussion of some of the decisions taken by the company in terms of raising finance.
- Two pages deal with the company's statement of corporate social responsibility. This deals with those aspects of the business that demonstrate that Domino's is a good corporate citizen.
- Two pages list the company's directors, giving a brief résumé of their backgrounds, and the key advisors who serve the company.
- Two pages provide a very detailed description of the directors' remuneration. This information gives the shareholders a very clear appreciation of the

---

[2] You may be aware that many companies are managed in such a way that no single individual has outright control. Typically, there are two types of company director. Executive directors are full-time employees of the company and they are involved in and responsible for the ongoing management. Non-executive directors are members of the board, but they do not normally work for the company on a full-time basis. Non-executives act as a deterrent to any malpractice or dishonesty on the part of the executive directors because they can oversee major decisions and examine areas such as executive pay and accounting decisions. The chief executive is normally a full-time director and is responsible for the direction of the company. The chairman is normally a non-executive director and is normally responsible for the management of the board of directors.

amounts that are being paid in terms of salaries, share options, and other forms of reward.

- Three pages provide a series of specific disclosures that are required by UK company law and other sources of regulation. This is headed up as the directors' report. Companies in other countries may present similar facts and figures under this heading, or there may not be a direct equivalent.

Apart from the directors' report, most of these disclosures would be found in the annual reports published by companies in many countries around the world. There are frequently pressures to volunteer information even though it is not specifically required by law. For example, companies may choose to provide extensive disclosures on their environmental performance because it can be good for business to demonstrate that a business is not especially harmful to the environment.

Hard Information

By now readers have read through more than two dozen pages without seeing many numbers. That changes when the annual report starts to deal with the financial statements themselves.

At first glance, the accounting statements themselves can be quite off-putting. The basic statements are designed to be read in conjunction with a series of notes. The statements themselves often list items that are difficult for even an expert reader to understand. This subsection is designed to provide a 'user-friendly' route through the accounts.

Domino's financial statements run on for approximately 50 pages. Most of that is taken up with the notes.

Before we look at the financial statements themselves, we need to clarify the concept of group financial statements. Chapter 12 will provide an introduction to the process of preparing group accounts, so this description is purely a taster to enable you to read an annual report. Very few of the businesses that you will encounter in the real world are organised as wholly independent entities, and so you will have to read group accounts if you are going to read accounts at all.

Groups usually comprise a holding company and a number of subsidiaries. The holding company controls the other group members, usually by holding shares in the subsidiary companies.[3]

---

[3] There are other models for the creation of business groups. There is a Japanese model that has a rather more complicated structure than the one described here. The holding company/subsidiary company model is commonplace throughout most of the world, including Europe and America.

A simple group is shown below:

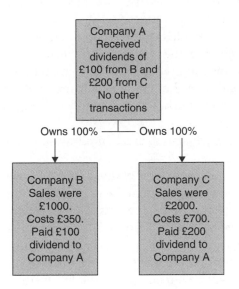

Company A owns 100% of each of Companies B and C. A shareholder in Company A would not learn a great deal from its income statement because the only transactions are in the form of dividends received from the two subsidiaries. That does not necessarily tell the shareholder anything about the success or otherwise of the group members.

The process of preparing group accounts involves presenting the group of companies as a single economic entity. That involves cancelling transactions between group members and combining the remaining figures.

For example, the Company A Group made total sales of £3000 and incurred costs totalling £1050. That suggests that it made a profit of £1950. This information is likely to be far more relevant to the readers of the financial statements because it presents the activities of the real business as opposed to the legal entity in which they own shares.

The same logic can be applied to the group statement of financial position (or balance sheet). Combining the balance sheet figures of the individual group members to show the overall investment of the group in terms of wealth-creating assets is far more useful than the holding company's balance sheet, which might show nothing more than the holding company's investment in the subsidiary company shares.

Domino's group financial statements comprise the following:

- One page devoted to the statement of directors' responsibilities. The purpose of this is essentially to advise readers that the responsibility for the preparation of the financial statements rests with the directors. The statement identifies the rules and regulations that have been adhered to in the preparation of Domino's financial statements. This statement provides a very subtle warning that readers should be aware of the subjectivity inherent in preparing financial statements in accordance with the rules (this will be a recurring theme in several chapters of this text).
- There is a page for the independent auditor's report. The external audit is conducted by an independent firm of accountants. The end result is the expression of an opinion on the truth and fairness or the fair presentation of the financial statements. An audit is a major undertaking and auditing is normally taught as a separate course in its own right.
- The group financial statements (income statement, balance sheet, statement of changes in equity, and cash flow statement) are given a page each.
- The foregoing information is supplemented by roughly 35 pages of notes. Most of these are cross-referenced to the main financial statements and provide additional detail to those who are interested in going into more depth. It is important to bear in mind that the notes are there and to use them to ensure that any information taken from the main statements has not been distorted by combining two or more figures to give a total that may not be particularly helpful. For example, at 31 December 2007, Domino's had a total of over £10 million showing as 'trade and other receivables'. If you wish to know how this figure was made up, then you can go to a note that analyses the total into four separate subtotals. This type of analysis may make all the difference between calculating a meaningful ratio and making a sensible comment about performance or financial position and calculating or stating something illogical.
- After the group accounts there are four pages dealing with the holding company financial statements. These are unlikely to be of any real use to many readers, but are available if required. We will discuss the possibility that group financial statements may be misleading in Chapter 12.

• Finally, the statements conclude with a matrix summarising key financial statistics over the past five years and a list of Domino's stores in the United Kingdom and Ireland.

Avoiding Headaches

There is a danger that you could be intimidated by reading a real set of accounts at this stage in your studies. There will almost certainly be items in the financial statements that are unfamiliar, and many of the notes will deal with issues that you have not yet encountered. The secret is to accept that most real companies have to account for complicated transactions and balances that will not be covered until a later stage in your studies. The best way of dealing with this is to accept before you start that some of the information will be of very little use to you.

You should not be too disappointed if the financial statements are prepared in accordance with an earlier version of IAS 1 *Presentation of Financial Statements*. It will take a few years for the new titles for the main statements and the new presentation requirements to be adopted by all of the companies that you are likely to encounter.

A Few Simple Suggestions

Having a logical approach to reading the accounts will help enormously.

Flip through the whole package of materials that you have downloaded. This will be easier if you have a paper copy or if you have printed out the document that you downloaded, but even an electronic copy can be flicked through on screen. Make sure that you have an overview of the quantity of information in the various sections, particularly the introductory materials before the financial statements themselves and the information in the notes.

Make sure that you know what the company actually does. This should be clear from the annual report, but you can also look at the company's website or do an Internet search for business news relating to the company.

Look at the figures in the income statement (or statement of comprehensive income) and establish the following:

• revenue for this year and last;
• gross profit for this year and last;

- profit before interest and tax for this year and last (it may be necessary to add the finance charge back to profit before tax in order to arrive at this figure);
- capital employed for this year and last (take the totals for equity and non-current liabilities).

Once you have that information, you can think about the company's performance:

- Is revenue growing from year to year?
- Are costs under control? (Calculate gross profit as a percentage of revenue.)
- What rate of return did the company earn on the funds invested? (Calculate profit before interest and tax as a percentage of capital employed.)

Once you have done this, you have already obtained a good overview of the performance for the year. Any additional analysis that you undertake will be more concerned with elaborating on these broad impressions. You will find this more interesting if you draw your own conclusions as to whether the company's performance is improving or declining.

You should look at the figures for equity and non-current liabilities. If the company is heavily dependent upon debt, then it will be perceived as being more risky.

You might also consider the liquidity position by comparing the figures for current assets and current liabilities. Unfortunately, these figures change so rapidly that any conclusions you draw in this area will probably be out of date before the statements are even published.

Use the notes to the financial statements to answer a few simple questions. For example, look at the accounting policies relating to property, plant, and equipment to see how depreciation is calculated. Look at the note on property, plant, and equipment to see how the total in the statement of financial position is made up. There might be sufficient information for you to form an opinion as to whether the company's accounting policies are too optimistic or pessimistic.

Finally, look through the notes for details of any contingent liabilities. We will discuss these in more detail in Chapter 11. Contingent liabilities cannot be recognised in the statement of financial position because there is too much doubt about the likelihood or the amount of any payment. For example, a customer might have lodged a substantial compensation claim that is working through the courts. These contingent liabilities can be sufficient to bring down the company, so they must be taken into account in any analysis of the company's position.

Once you have worked through these steps, you will have obtained almost as much benefit as is possible from reading the financial statements as an outsider. Hopefully, you will be slightly frustrated because there is not sufficient information to answer every question that occurred to you. For example, the accounting policies' note on depreciation might not provide much real detail about the assumptions used to calculate depreciation. Such frustrations are quite common because companies do not always wish to give away too much information that might prompt embarrassing questions from the shareholders or give away too much useful information to the competitors.

If nothing else, reading the statements with a view to understanding how the business is progressing will help you to understand the pressures that the directors face when preparing accounts. Readers are interested in the figures for profit and capital employed, and yet it is very easy to lose track of that fact when learning how to prepare the statements.

It is worth looking at the layout of the statements and the associated notes. Most companies use experts in typesetting to ensure that the figures are as clear and easy to read as possible. Reading the statements will help you to remember the disclosure requirements and will give you some ideas about the importance of clarity.

Summary

This short chapter is designed to give you the confidence to read through a real set of financial statements. You will find it helpful to read some annual reports because it will help you to become familiar with the presentation requirements. It will also help you to appreciate the fact that accounting is a practical discipline and that the accounts are read by shareholders and others with a view to making decisions.

Many companies make their financial statements available electronically, and others will supply printed copies on request. It is possible to acquire several sets without going to any great trouble.

Tutorial Questions

Question 1

Bring a set of financial statements to class. Analyse this to show the relative proportions of statutory and voluntary disclosures. Look at the presentation – does it appear to have been professionally designed? Was it expensive to print?

• Why do companies publish so much material on a voluntary basis?

- Why is so much money spent on the actual document itself?
- Why are shareholders sometimes advised to read the accounts by starting at the back and working forwards?

Question 2

Find the directors' signatures on the annual report. How long did it take after the year end for the accounts to be approved? Does this surprise you?

Question 3

Describe the content of two major notes to the financial statements and explain why each might be useful to the readers of the accounts.

Further Work

There are no questions with answers in this chapter. If you wish to explore further, then look at a number of annual reports. You might select two or three companies from the same industry and attempt to compare their performance.

ACADEMIC RESEARCH AND THE STUDY OF ACCOUNTING

Contents

Learning Objectives

After studying this chapter you should be able to:

- describe the sources of information about accounting matters;
- describe the various types of research that are conducted by accounting academics.

Introduction

This chapter is a slight departure from much of the rest of the book because it looks at the potential role that accounting research might have to play in informing and enlightening interested readers in pursuit of knowledge. It also provides an overview of some of the alternative sources of information that might be drawn upon by anyone investigating a topic.

Sources of Information and Understanding

There are many different sources of information and comment on accounting matters. The process of conducting the search might have changed with the development of on-line archives rather than being forced to dig through dusty volumes on a library shelf, but the basic choices of sources have been unchanged for many years.

Think!

Where would you start if you were trying to obtain information about an aspect of accounting?

Current Events

The most obvious source of information is to be found in the business pages of the 'quality' press. Business columns will report and analyse the implications of accounting developments and will aim to put these into print as quickly as possible, while the issue is still deemed newsworthy.

The biggest problem with newspaper coverage on any topic arises from the reliability of the sources that journalists are forced to use. Generally, journalists rely upon press releases and 'contacts' in order to stay abreast of breaking news. If, for example, the IASB decides to develop a new standard on a particular topic, then it will issue a press release at each stage in order to demonstrate that work is under way and that the organisation is active. All organisations are careful to present themselves in the best possible way when they release information to the press.

Newspapers are generally worth reading as a source of information about how a particular matter is being presented and, perhaps, understood by society. There is no guarantee that the journalists who write the business pages are themselves particularly well qualified to evaluate the information that is being presented to them (although it would be fatal to generalise over this). Certainly, press coverage is designed to keep readers abreast of recent events.

Newspapers will also offer informed comment from interested parties. For example, the *Financial Times* has a long-running accountancy column that carries comments from senior practitioners, regulators, and those who are critical of the accountancy profession. These columns give a valuable insight into the thoughts and the opinions of decision-makers, even though their views will always be affected by their backgrounds and positions.

Professional Perspectives

There are vast numbers of magazines that are written for practising accountants. Their role is to inform and update the reader on matters such as changing regulations, advice on implementing existing rules, and an accounting perspective on recent news. These magazines are often associated with a specific accounting body. For example, the ACCA, a global accountancy body based in London but with an international membership, publishes a digital magazine called *AB* that is accessible via its website (www.ACCAGlobal.com) and has editions for the Asia Pacific region, Malaysia, the United Kingdom, and the rest of the world.

Magazines may claim to take an independent and unbiased position on the matters that they cover, although it is often very clear that their target readership is made up of qualified accountants who are sympathetic to their profession's aims and objectives.

The content of these magazines is often far more useful than the discussion in newspapers. The articles are written by staff writers, who are often qualified accountants, and by external consultants, who are often senior members of the profession. The fact that the magazines specialise also means that the articles are much longer than the newspaper coverage of the same events, and they usually go into far more depth than the articles based on press releases. The coverage may be ultimately sympathetic to the accountancy profession, but these publications will often point out the shortcomings of particular rules and regulations or current techniques.

Refereed Journals

Accountancy is a relatively recent arrival on the university campus. The first professional accounting body came into being in 1854. Universities did not offer programmes in accounting until the early part of the twentieth century. Compare this to the legal profession, which can trace its presence in academia back through several centuries.

All academics are paid to do research, to teach, and to administer their courses. It has long been recognised that research is by far the most important activity in terms of promotion and career advancement. Academic research is measured largely in terms of the publication of papers in refereed journals.

A refereed journal is one whose content is subjected to a rigorous review process by a system of peer assessment. Draft papers are sent to acknowledged experts in that field and they comment on their strengths and weaknesses. Papers are not published unless those experts inform the editor that they meet the journal's quality criteria and that any major shortcomings that they have identified have been addressed and dealt with.

The starting point is that the author or team of authors writes a paper and submits it to the editor. The editor makes a decision as to the paper's suitability in principle and, assuming that it is considered worthy of review, will send it to two referees. Most journals operate a system of anonymous refereeing whereby the author's name is withheld from the referees and the referees' names are withheld from the author. Anonymity reduces the risk of bias due to preconceptions of the quality of the work done by a particular named author. It also grants the referees a little more freedom to report their findings honestly. The referees will only rarely recommend that a paper be published in its present state. They will usually indicate areas for improvement and ask for those to be addressed. The author is then given the opportunity to address those comments before resubmitting. There may be several iterations of review and resubmission before the paper is finally accepted.

There is a great deal of strategic thinking and planning involved in developing an academic research plan. Many journals specialise in a specific field of research within accounting, and so there is some logic in writing a paper with a particular journal or group of journals in mind. Different journals vary in terms of perceived quality, and so an author has to be realistic in deciding which journal to submit to. The risk in sending a paper to a very high-quality journal is that there is much more competition for space, and so the standard expected by referees is that much higher. Less prestigious journals are still worth publishing in, but they do not carry the same degree of recognition as a publication in a journal with a higher rank. This is important both for the author and for his or her institution. The quality and quantity of research publications are important factors in assessing any academic's CV and will also be major factors in determining the overall strength of an academic department.

The Internet

There is no doubt that the Internet has had a profound effect on virtually every aspect of human life. One of the most useful aspects of the Internet is that many of the publications and information sources listed above are accessible on-line. In some cases it is necessary to pay for a subscription, but many publications are available free of charge.

University libraries often have paid electronic subscriptions to newspapers, magazines, and refereed journals. Registered students can usually obtain a password to gain access to those subscriptions. All university students should make the greatest possible use of those facilities if they are available.

Most accountancy bodies have a presence on the Internet. These are well worth consulting, although professional bodies often restrict access to much of their content to members and student members. Professional accountancy firms also provide a host of useful material on their websites, and not just material to promote their services. There is often a lot of useful news and analysis, as well as some detailed study and reference material that is available for download.

In many respects, electronic access is more convenient than referring to paper copies of publications. On-line searches often locate particular articles or papers that would be difficult to find using paper indices, and electronic copies are readily available, unlike paper copies which can be lost or out on loan to another reader.

The credibility of an electronic copy of a traditional publication is exactly the same as for the publication itself. That is an important point about the Internet because many lecturers complain that student essays cite some very dubious sources without any consideration of the author. In some respects, the low cost of publishing electronically is both a strength and a weakness because authors do not need to convince a publisher that a document is worth printing or depend on it selling in economic quantities.

By way of illustration, two websites that are well worth visiting could not be more diametrically opposed in terms of their view of accounting and accounting institutions. Invariably, any comment about either will leave the author of this text open to accusations of bias, so it is recommended that anyone who visits either site does so with an open and enquiring mind. Neither is a commercial site, and both are open to any interested reader:

- The eStandardsForum is owned by The Financial Standards Foundation, which claims to support activities that facilitate the creation and maintenance of a global economic and financial system, based on private sector-led market economies, responsible private investment, and a liberal foreign trade regime.
- The Association for Accountancy and Business Affairs (AABA) claims to be working to advance the public interest by facilitating critical scrutiny of commercial and non-commercial organisations.

For our purposes, the most notable point about these two sites is that they are based on diametrically opposed views of accounting and the work of the accountancy profession. In the broadest possible terms, the eStandardsForum appears to be based on the premise that capital markets create wealth and that accounting exists to serve and support the markets in that process. In contrast, the AABA site seems to regard capital markets as exploitative and harmful and accounting as implicated in the apparatus of protecting the interests of the wealthy. Neither site is necessarily more or less credible than the other, but an Internet search that alighted on just one might leave the reader with a rather biased view.

The Accounting Literature

In academic circles, only the refereed journals count as 'literature'. This material is often not given a great deal of prominence in undergraduate degree programmes because of the need to cover technical accounting material in order to meet the requirements of professional accounting bodies for exemption purposes.

One of the distinguishing characteristics of an academic paper is that it is rooted in a theoretical framework and demonstrates this by drawing on prior research in order to show that the paper is a contribution to the literature that has gone before it. The author(s) may not necessarily agree with past findings because it is possible to contribute by highlighting shortcomings in the prior literature or by presenting a dissenting interpretation of events or observations. The theoretical framework is important because a theory provides a view of the world that makes it possible to explain observations in a logical and coherent way. Observations are far less meaningful unless they can be presented in relation to a theory.

The structure of an academic paper normally contains the following elements:

Introduction	The paper commences with a brief statement of the authors' intent. It states what they have set out to achieve and gives an indication of their findings.
Literature review	Academic papers are never written without regard to a theoretical framework (although that may be implicit in the text rather than clearly stated in the paper). The authors' review of prior literature shows how they believe their paper fits into the body of prior research and contributes to it. It also demonstrates that the paper deals with a topic that is of interest to an academic audience. The fact that papers have already been published in that area indicates that others are interested in it. The literature review is more than just a passive summary of the literature. The authors draw out connections between

	different strands of the literature and identify the advantages and disadvantages of different research approaches to the topic under consideration.
Findings/ analysis	Depending on the style of the paper and the nature of the journal, this might be several sections or just one extensive discussion. For example, a statistical paper might have one or more sections for the presentation of figures and associated test results and others for the analysis of the implications of those observations.
Conclusion	The conclusion summarises the authors' views on the contribution that they have made.
References	Every paper cited in the article will be listed in a standard format so that it can be found easily. That imposes a discipline on authors because misquoting or taking another author's words out of context can easily be uncovered.

One of the distinguishing characteristics of a refereed journal article is that there will not be any unsupported assertions. If the authors state something, then that statement will be supported by a reference to another paper that has already established that point or they will provide evidence of their own that they have gathered.

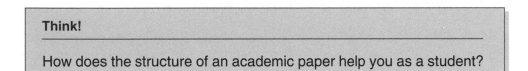

Think!

How does the structure of an academic paper help you as a student?

An academic paper can easily be several thousand words long and may involve many pages of complex arguments and analyses. It is important to read the introduction and conclusion carefully. If you are considering using a paper in writing an essay, then the introduction and conclusion will help you to establish very quickly whether the paper is, in fact, relevant. It is also worth returning to the introduction and conclusion while reading the detail in the body of the paper, just to be reminded of the purpose of the article.

The literature review and the references are also an important resource. There is no guarantee that the authors will have cited every relevant paper in their article, but their expertise and that of the referees suggests that they are unlikely to have overlooked any important papers that were in print when the work was being done.

If you are writing an essay or a dissertation, it is also worth remembering that some journals specialise in particular areas or styles of research. If a particular journal falls into a relevant category, then it is worth skimming through the contents pages (which are likely to be published on-line) for the past four or five years of publication and listing titles that are worth looking up. In the same way, if a particular author seems to have specialised in that area, then he or she might be worth seeking out using a search engine.

Branches of Accounting Literature

There are many accounting journals and finance journals that publish accounting papers. This section offers the briefest glimpse into some of the broad categories.

Think!

Should academics devote their research to resolving the problems faced by preparers and users of financial statements?

It has already been mentioned in passing that accountancy is a relative new-comer to the university campus. Early writings were 'normative'. They attempted to solve real-world accounting problems, such as the best way to account for depreciation or deal with the effects of changing prices, in order to propose the 'norms' for good accounting. The problem with such research is related to the subject matter of Chapter 5. It is very difficult to make a case for a particular accounting technique unless there is clear and explicit agreement on the objectives of accounting. The main difficulty faced by authors who wish to enable 'better' accounting is that there are rarely benchmarks that can be used to measure the success or failure of a paper.

Normative research continues and undoubtedly has its supporters, but large numbers of academics have sought out alternative approaches that have the advantage of offering criteria for establishing whether a paper has achieved the aims that it has set for itself.

The two branches that are to be described in the greatest depth in this section are markets-based 'positive' accounting and the far more diffuse 'critical' accounting school. If nothing else, focusing on those two branches of the literature highlights the broad range of research that is conducted in accounting.

Positive Research

Positive research is essentially about observing and reporting on the world as it is, rather than the normative approach of reporting on the world as it should be. Positive accounting research takes many forms, but at its most basic it attempts to measure the impact of accounting information on the capital markets. If the publication of a piece of accounting information affects share prices, then, by definition, the market finds that information useful.

Think!

What are the advantages of positive research from the point of view of the researcher?

Positive research is by no means easy, but it has the advantage of offering a clear-cut result. The researcher starts with a series of observations, subjects those observations to a statistical analysis in order to generate test results, and, provided those results are interesting, generates a publishable finding.

For example, a research paper could investigate whether the capital markets find a particular voluntary disclosure useful. The authors could measure the extent to which the capital markets react to the financial statements of companies that make this disclosure compared with those that do not. If there is a significantly bigger reaction to those who disclose, then the capital markets do find information in the disclosure.

Positive research takes economics as its starting point. It works on the basis that market participants will wish to maximise their economic utility. Economic utility is normally expressed as a function of two further factors: risk and return. Generally, these are summed up by the returns offered from investing in a particular security. If the returns obtained from a particular investment are significantly different from expectations during a period when a piece of information was released, then the markets must have revised their impression of risk and/or return. If the study was designed properly, then the result isolates the effect of that piece of information.

The starting point is to think about how the stock market works. Generally, share prices fluctuate in response to changing expectations about risk and return. The current share price is essentially an unbiased and fair reflection of the real worth of the underlying shares allowing for these factors. If share prices differ from their 'real' values, then market forces will correct that because skilled investors will see an opportunity to earn a higher return. If, for example, investors started to notice that share prices were artificially depressed on days when the weather was bad (and so investors felt more pessimistic), then they would buy shares on cold, wet days and then resell them at a profit when it was warm and sunny. Soon, there would be sufficient notice being taken of the effects of the weather on share prices for the opportunity to make an easy profit to disappear.

The fact that the stock market reacts in this way to incorporate all available information is called the efficient markets hypothesis (EMH). The EMH suggests that all relevant information is incorporated into the share price at any given time and that there is no real way to make more than a 'fair' return from investing. The word 'efficient' relates to the market's efficiency at processing information as and when it becomes available. Studying the manner in which the market reacts will indicate the ways in which accounting information is used by the markets, and that will highlight the relevance of financial statements.

Two examples sum up the broad approach that is being taken in this type of study. The starting point is to use a model to relate the returns offered on a variety of securities with a statistic that measures their risk. All securities should offer a 'normal' return that can be explained in terms of risk. If returns are significantly more or less than expected, then the markets have given an 'abnormal' return, which is usually interpreted as meaning that the share price has reacted to a piece of news, such as the release of the annual report.

In their famous study, Ball and Brown (1968) looked at capital market returns over a twelve-month period for two groups of companies. One group had reported profits at the end of the year under study that were greater than those published in the previous year, and the other reported lower profits. Perhaps not surprisingly, the returns obtained from the companies whose profits had improved were high compared with the market as a whole, and those of the companies whose performance had declined were lower. The real surprise was that tracking the returns month by month from the beginning of the year to the end revealed that most of the change occurred during the year and before the annual reports were published. In fact, only 20% of the movement occurred during the month in which the financial statements were published. A diagram showing a simplified version of these results is shown below:

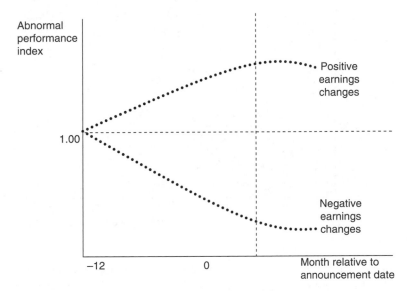

One possible interpretation of this result is that the capital markets are able to predict much of the information that will be found in the annual report. Arguably, that suggests that financial statements are less important than one would expect.

The Ball and Brown findings do not necessarily mean that published financial statements are useless. Rather, they indicate that the capital markets revise their perceptions whenever new information becomes available. For example, share prices of car manufacturers might decline if the number of new cars sold falls unexpectedly. A decline in sales volume is likely to result in a decline in reported profit, and so many of the signs that one might expect to see in the annual report can be predicted. It may be that the markets rely heavily on accounting information in less obvious ways. For example, they might use the results published by one retailer to update their expectations for the reported profits of other retailers whose accounts are yet to be published. The fact that there is still some evidence of a price correction during the month of publication indicates that there is some useful information in the annual report.

A related form of study, again published in 1968, involved calculating abnormal returns at around the time of the report itself. This study was conducted by Beaver (1968), who gave his name to the 'Beaver blip'.

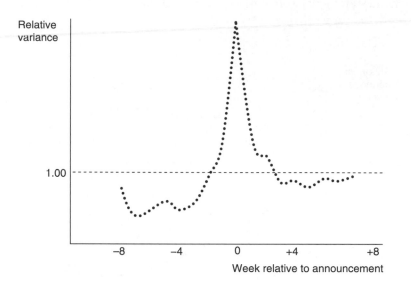

The relative variance is a measure of abnormal returns. Beaver found that it averaged 1.00 throughout most of the year, except for the period immediately around the publication date for the annual report. In other words, the markets do find useful information in the financial statements, as evidenced by the spike in abnormal returns that occurs at that time (Beaver ignored the direction of the return, so the 'blip' measures the extent of both positive and negative abnormal returns).

This approach to research began during the 1960s, when advances in the availability of stock market data and affordable computer power made it possible for academics to design and conduct basic positive research. There are now several highly regarded journals that publish papers drawing on this approach, including (but by no means restricted to) *Journal of Accounting and Economics*, *Journal of Accounting Research*, and *The Accounting Review*.

The early Ball and Brown and Beaver blip studies, groundbreaking though they were, have long since been overtaken by far more sophisticated papers with far more specific objectives. For example, a paper by Leuz (2003) examined market returns on the German New Market (Neuer Markt), comparing those who chose to report under IAS rules with those who reported under US Generally Accepted Accounting Principles. The logic underlying this study was that differences between the reporting requirements in the two sets of rules might have implications for share prices. The paper's main finding was that there were no significant differences in the returns, and so the markets did not find one set of rules more transparent than the other.

> **Think!**
> ———————————————————————
>
> Academics with an interest in positive research often claim that their research benefits from being objective and free of any political bias. Are those claims fair?

There is no great benefit to be had from claiming that one style of research is somehow more useful or worthy than another, but people often claim that their preferred football team/city/choice of music is better than everyone else's, and that often happens with approaches to research also.

One possible danger with positive research is that it tends to restrict itself to capturing the effects of accounting information on the stock market. Information is only deemed useful if it affects the behaviour of those who can influence share prices and market returns. There is no harm in conducting research that is aimed at the information needs of those readers, but that does involve an implicit value judgement because it excludes other stakeholders who have a legitimate interest in accounting information.

There are other potential dangers associated with the underlying evidence-gathering and statistical processes that go into this research.

Event window	One of the biggest problems is in deciding what timeframe to study. For example, should we examine market returns on the day that the annual report is published, or the week? The choice of event window can affect the results, and, indeed, choosing one period could yield a publishable result, while choosing a longer, shorter or different period could render the results statistically insignificant. Papers generally do not state that the authors ran the statistics on the basis of several credible event windows, each of which gave a more or less convincing result.
Confounding events	Accounting figures may be published in conjunction with the release of other information. If the financial statements come out on the day that the dividend is announced, then the market could be reacting to the dividend rather than the profit figure.

| Statistical anomalies | Many statistical tests are sensitive to assumptions about the underlying figures and the distribution of the data. If those assumptions are invalid, then the results may be misleading. |
| Design issues | Researchers often eliminate some observations because they are distorting the results ('outliers'). The decision to include or exclude certain observations could affect the results. |

It should be borne in mind that published articles have been through a refereeing process, and so the reader should be reasonably confident in the results. Having said that, an afternoon spent reading a large number of papers on market reactions to a particular event can prove frustrating if the object of the exercise is to establish whether markets react to a particular event or not. It is not unusual for some papers in reputable journals to report positive findings and equally prestigious journals to carry papers that found none. That can happen because the studies have used different research designs.

For example, Chapter 1 discussed the Enron scandal briefly. Many papers were published about the market credibility of the audit firm that was implicated in this case. One of the accusations that came out at the time was that the auditor had shredded working papers in order to destroy potentially incriminating evidence that might be used against it. Whether or not that accusation was true, there is a testable hypothesis that it would undermine the market's confidence in the figures published by the audit firm's other clients, and so their share prices would drop. One published study (Chaney and Philipich, 2002) found just such a market reaction, which implies that the markets are interested in the credibility and integrity of auditors and is therefore an interesting result. A subsequent study by a different team of researchers found that other relevant information, which had nothing to do with the audit firm or the shredding of documents, had been published during the event window of the original study. This alternative study (Nelson *et al.*, 2008) found that the negative market reaction was actually due to the other information rather than the shredding. Neither paper is necessarily incorrect, but a reader should always take care when reading the results of a small number of research papers.

Our discussion has focused on some of the work done on financial reporting, but the same approach has been used on other important topics, such as the market's reaction to particular corporate governance factors. Positive researchers do not necessarily restrict themselves to accounting statements or financial reporting.

Critical Research

The term 'critical theory' is generally associated with the Frankfurt School, a group of German philosophers, sociologists, and economists who were active from the 1920s through to the 1930s. Their starting point was essentially Marxist, but critical theory now encompasses a whole range of philosophical or sociological theories that take a critical view of society.

In many respects, critical accounting research is worlds removed from positive accounting research. It does not require vast amounts of data or computing power to process it. It is, however, a more recent branch of accounting research, with general agreement that much of the early groundwork took place at the University of Sheffield in the 1970s. The development of this branch of research is discussed in much greater detail in Roslender (2006).

There is no single approach to conducting critical research, and so the following paragraphs are really only intended to provide the briefest glimpse into the literature. There is a journal called *Critical Perspectives on Accounting* that focuses on critical papers. There are other journals that are very receptive to critical work, notably *Accounting, Organisations and Society, Accounting Forum and Accounting, and Auditing and Accountability Journal.* Given the range of critical literature, it would be difficult, and possibly misleading, to apply anything other than the elephant test to setting out the boundaries (the elephant being a creature that is difficult to describe, but you know one when you see it).

In terms of size and interest, the critical research community is large and growing. There are several conferences devoted solely to the discussion of critical research. The 2008 Critical Perspectives on Accounting Conference in New York attracted approximately 250 delegates from around the world. That conference rotates on a three-year cycle with the Interdisciplinary Perspectives on Accounting Conference (IPA), hosted in the United Kingdom or another European country, and the Asia Pacific Interdisciplinary Research in Accounting Conference (APIRA), hosted in the Pacific Rim. These conferences are supplemented by a number of smaller national and international conferences.

The one theme that draws the critical literature together is that critical researchers use their chosen theories to describe the practices of accounting in a manner that highlights the limitations of accounting and the harm that it can sometimes cause. Critical researchers rarely offer specific solutions to the problems that they encounter in their exploration of accounting, but the same is true of positive accounting research. Unlike positive research, most critical studies portray accounting as a force that reinforces inequalities or other negative forces or relationships within business or society at large.

An example of this thought process can be found in a paper by Burchell, Clubb, and Hopwood (1985) that examines the history of reporting value added. Value added statements are an alternative means of reporting performance. They present the enterprise as a partnership between the stakeholders who contribute to the generation of wealth:

- employees, whose labour 'adds value' to the inputs;
- shareholders, whose equity funds the facilities required to add that value;
- government, whose infrastructure – ranging from roads to law and order – makes it possible to generate wealth.

A simple example will suffice. The following summarised income statement was prepared by a business:

VA
Income statement for the year ended 31 December 20X9

	£m
Revenue	30
Bought in goods and services	(9)
Wages	(11)
Profit before tax	10
Tax	(3)
Profit after tax	7

This is the traditional method of measuring success or failure. There are, however, alternative approaches:

VA
Value added statement for the year ended 31 December 20X9

	£m
Revenue	30
Bought in goods and services	(9)
Value added created	21
Value added applied:	
To employees	11
To government	3
To shareholders	7
	21

This statement presents exactly the same figures in a different way. Expressing performance in this way makes a major conceptual difference in its treatment of staff costs. The traditional income statement views the workforce as an expense and highlights the manner in which the shareholders benefit from the profits created by the business. That presents staff in a negative light as a cost that ought to be minimised. The value added statement stresses the wealth that is created and shared by all parties. It is debatable whether presenting performance in this manner would eliminate poor employee relations, but at least it demonstrates that there are different ways of thinking about accounting.

Burchell, Clubb, and Hopwood (1985) examine the upsurge in interest in reporting value added that emerged briefly in the 1970s. One of the key points they make, which underlines this brief insight into the critical accounting literature in general, is summed up by the following quote:

> In such a context accounting is seen as a means of vision. A change in accounting implies a change in what is seen and hence a change in action.

Critical accounting research often focuses on the nature of accounting as it is viewed from a particular perspective. The authors' intention is generally to highlight this sense that accounting shapes and changes the world by virtue of the things that it makes visible and the manner in which it presents them.

The underlying theoretical framework is generally much more visible in critical research, if only because there is a wide range of approaches that might be taken. The following discussion is necessarily too brief to do more than indicate some of the areas that might be pursued in greater depth, perhaps in pursuit of a starting point for an honours dissertation.

Marxism is inextricably linked with the critical research literature, which is hardly surprising given that critical theory came out of the work of the Frankfurt School. In essence, Marxism starts with the premise that there are two factors necessary for the creation of wealth: capital, in the form of the means of production (factories, etc.), and labour. In capitalist societies the means of production are owned by an elite group whose privileged position endows them with the means to extract virtually all of the wealth created by labour. Employees receive sufficient to enable them to feed and clothe themselves and their families (those families being the source of labour in the future). Marx believed that the capitalist society was inherently unstable because it embodied a host of economic contradictions in addition to the inequalities implied by the diversion of wealth. One of the ways in which capitalist society would sustain itself would be by creating false realities so that the interests of capital were always protected.

Many accounting papers start from the basis that accounting serves the needs of capital and is part of the whole apparatus of sustaining the capitalist society.

A special issue of *Critical Perspectives on Accounting* that was devoted to Marxism and accounting conceptual frameworks[1] provides a good starting point.[2]

Foucault was a French philosopher whose work on 'disciplinary power' has inspired a host of accounting studies. These generally focus on the manner in which people are made 'governable'. Foucault's history of the exercise of power in Western societies in the context of the penal system (Foucault, 1991) has been used to theorise studies of the effects of power in a variety of contexts. Generally, accounting researchers use Foucault to theorise papers in management accounting, looking at the manner in which behaviour is affected by budgets, standard costing, and similar techniques. For an overview of some of these papers, see Armstrong (1994).

Feminism provides yet another perspective, or, more properly, collection of perspectives, that can be used to theorise accounting research. Feminist research can focus on gender equality, which is clearly an important matter in itself. Indeed, there have been studies that look at the extent to which the accountancy profession admits women and promotes them to senior levels. A useful overview can be found in Haynes (2008). There is, however, a more fundamental feminist perspective arguing that more is required than merely admitting women to particular occupations and granting them the same opportunities for advancement. There are certain masculine traits and attitudes that may well have negative effects. For example, the dogged pursuit of a single objective is a particularly male-oriented outlook that might be replaced by a more feminine ideal that aims to pursue a wider range of outcomes, including a sense of care and nurture. Some of these discussions are summarised in Chioni Moore (1992).

Mainstream Research

Positive research and critical research are by no means the only approaches that are taken to the investigation of accounting. There are many journals that publish papers on accounting that rely on neither the detailed analysis of stock market statistics nor the underpinning of a philosophical framework.

---

[1] Conceptual frameworks are the fundamental statements of the nature and purpose of accounting that are developed by standard-setters to provide the roots for coherent and valid accounting standards. We will discuss these in Chapter 5.
[2] See *Critical Perspectives on Accounting*, **10**(5), October 1999. This comprises a Marxist critique by Bryer, several comments on his paper, and a response to these comments.

Journals such as *The European Accounting Review, Accounting and Business Research, Abacus,* and *Accounting Horizons* carry both empirical[3] and normative[4] papers.

Rightly or wrongly (probably wrongly), the positive and critical streams are regarded as a little more prestigious. Refereed journals are ranked in various ways by various authorities, but it is clear that the highest ranked generally belong to one or other stream. For example, the *Financial Times* ranks the research of business schools around the world by their research output in 40 'high-quality' journals, of which four are accounting journals:

- *Accounting, Organisations and Society;*
- *Journal of Accounting and Economics;*
- *Journal of Accounting Research;*
- *The Accounting Review.*

The first of these is heavily associated with critical accounting, and the other three are essentially positive in outlook.

It should be stressed that journal rankings can never truly represent the quality of the research that they publish. Perceptions of quality are affected by a host of factors, but they can become somewhat self-fulfilling. If academics believe that they stand more chance of being promoted if they publish in a particular journal, then they are more likely to write papers that are designed to appeal to that journal's editors. That will increase competition for space in that journal and will reinforce the perception of quality.

Academic journals are not the only source of mainstream research papers. Many professional accountancy bodies provide funding for research projects. The resulting research reports are often available for download. It is always worth looking for a link to research in any accountancy body's website.

Summary

This chapter discussed some of the sources of information and ideas that might assist you in your study of accounting. As with any information-gathering exercise, it is important to consider the source of anything that you read or download before deciding how far it can be relied upon.

---

[3] Empirical research basically reports observations that have been obtained from experiment and observation.

[4] Normative research aims for a norm or an ideal standard, perhaps the pursuit of 'better' accounting.

Accountancy supports a wide-ranging publishing industry of its own, ranging from newspapers and magazines through to academic journals written by and for academics.

Tutorial Questions

Question 1

Go to the IASB website and download a recent press release. What information does it contain? Does the language sound positive?

Question 2

Search the on-line archives of a major newspaper in order to see how the matter dealt with in your press release from the first question has been covered. How much of the reporting seems to have come from the press release itself?

Question 3

Find the website of a professional magazine and download the contents page of the latest issue. What topics are covered? How much of the coverage relates to financial reporting?

Question 4

Use a search engine to locate the web pages of the eStandardsForum, the Association of Accountancy and Business Affairs, and at least two other sites that offer views and comments on accountancy. Summarise the positions of each of these organisations.

Question 5

Study the contents pages of the most recent issues of several refereed accounting journals. Download the abstract of an article that interests you. Describe the style of research, the approach taken to the research, and the findings. How useful do you think this paper would be to an accounting practitioner or standard-setter?

Further Work

There are no questions with answers in this chapter. If you wish to develop the material covered, then spend some time on-line or in the library and become more familiar with the content of the various newspapers, magazines, websites, and journals that are available.

References

Armstrong, P. (1994), The influence of Michel Foucault on accounting research. *Critical Perspectives on Accounting*, **10**(5), 25–55.

Ball, R.J. and Brown, P. (1968), An empirical evaluation of accounting income numbers. *Journal of Accounting Research*, **6**, 159–178.

Beaver, W.H. (1968), The information content of annual earnings announcements. *Journal of Accounting Research* **6** (Empirical research in accounting: selected studies), 67–92.

Burchell, S., Clubb, C., and Hopwood, A. (1985), Accounting in its social context: towards a history of value added in the United Kingdom. *Accounting, Organisations and Society*, **10**(4), 381–413.

Chaney, P.K. and Philipich, K.L. (2002), Shredded reputation: the cost of audit failure. *Journal of Accounting Research*, **40**, 1221–1245.

Chioni Moore, D. (1992), Notes towards feminist theories of accounting: a view from literary studies. *Accounting, Auditing and Accountability Journal*, **5**(3), 92–112.

Foucault, M. (1991), *Discipline and Punish: The Birth of the Prison*. Penguin Books, London, UK.

Haynes, K. (2008), Moving the gender agenda or stirring the chicken's entrails? *Accounting, Auditing and Accountability Journal*, **21**(4), 539–555.

Leuz, C. (2003), IAS versus U.S. GAAP: information asymmetry-based evidence from Germany's New Market. *Journal of Accounting Research*, **41**(3), 445–472.

Nelson, K.K., Price, R.A., and Rountree, B.R. (2008), The market reaction to Arthur Andersen's role in the Enron scandal: loss of reputation or confounding effects? *Journal of Accounting and Economics*, **46**, 279–293.

Roslender, R. (2006), Critical theory, in *Methodological Issues in Accounting Research: Theories and Methods*, edited by Hoque, Z. Spiramus Press, London, UK.

THE CONCEPTUAL FRAMEWORK

Contents

Learning Objectives

After studying this chapter you should be able to:

- discuss the concept of truth and fairness;
- describe the importance of the conceptual framework project;
- discuss the IASB's *Framework for the Preparation and Presentation of Financial Statements*.

Introduction

Many countries lay down a strict requirement that financial statements give a true and fair view. Truth and fairness is a vague and complicated concept to discuss in abstract terms, and is an even more difficult concept to put into practice.[1]

One of the ways in which the accountancy profession deals with this problem is by defining the nature and purpose of accounting by producing a conceptual framework for financial reporting. The IASB has a conceptual framework in place for the development of future standards.

Accounting and Force of Habit

Up until the recent past, accountants used some very basic, but useful, rules of thumb to solve problems. There was an established way of dealing with most matters, and so these rules of thumb were only rarely called into play.

There were lots of accounting choices built into the manner in which accounting was practised, although they were largely taken for granted. For example, accruals-based accounting was used in place of cash-based accounting, which meant that revenues were recognised when they were earned and expenses when they were incurred. That was not necessarily a bad thing, although it did introduce quite a lot of scope for subjectivity in measuring performance, whereas the financial position in the statement of financial position was made as objective as possible by relying heavily on reporting assets at cost or cost less depreciation.

There is no harm in having a consistent set of settled procedures and processes for accounting, provided users of financial statements are satisfied with the information that they are given. The problem is that there is no clarity about the precise limits of the conventions that have been established. If a board of directors is keen to use a novel accounting practice that has never been considered before, they will invariably ask their auditors 'where does it say that I cannot do that?' before arguing that their preferred method is both innovative and superior to past practices.

The role of accounting scandals in the development of accounting standards was touched upon in Chapter 2. This chapter will look at some of the attempts to underpin the standard-setting process with a coherent statement of principles.

---

[1] In the early 1990s, the BBC broadcast a documentary about financial accounting. Four respected commentators were asked to state what was meant by 'a true and fair view'. The first three, senior partners from major accountancy firms, choked or giggled but said nothing. An investment analyst with no direct links to the profession described a true and fair view as 'a guess'.

Initially, the standard-setting process was often directed at resolving specific problems that were undermining the credibility of financial reporting. That meant that there simply was no time to resolve the 'bigger' questions about the nature and purpose of accounting statements.

Truth and Fairness and Fair Presentation

The move towards international accounting standards has reduced the emphasis on differences between different countries' accounting practices.

One notable export that has travelled around the world is the United Kingdom's requirement that financial statements give a true and fair view. This is a statutory requirement that has been carried forward through various revisions and updates of UK company law since it first appeared in the Companies Act 1947. The Companies Act 2006 states that the directors of a company must not approve accounts unless they are satisfied that they give a true and fair view of the assets, liabilities, financial position, and profit or loss. The external auditor is bound by similar requirements when expressing an opinion on the financial statements.

The requirement for the financial statements to give a true and fair view comes before anything else. For example, a company will have to disclose additional details, over and above the minimum requirements laid down in the Act, if those details are necessary in order to give a true and fair view. There could even be very rare circumstances in which a specific treatment laid down by law would result in the financial statements being misleading. In that case the accounts can use an alternative to the treatment required by law, provided that is being done in order to give a true and fair view. The ability to set aside specific statutory requirements under those circumstances is known as the 'true and fair override'.

The European Union's Fourth Directive governs the statutory requirements relating to financial reporting in all member states. Before the directive came into force, most countries outside the United Kingdom and Ireland did not have an equivalent to the true and fair view. The requirement to give a true and fair view was incorporated into the Fourth Directive at the United Kingdom's insistence.

Think!

Try to define a true and fair view.

Neither the UK Companies Act 2006 nor the Fourth Directive defines 'true and fair'. This would suggest that the phrase should be understood in terms of its normal, everyday English usage. There have been suggestions that this might mean that truth and fairness are related but distinguishable concepts, with the former meaning that the accounts are factually correct and the latter that they are unbiased. There is, however, a more compelling argument that the phrase should be regarded as a hendiadys, in other words, that it is a complex idea expressed as two words coupled with 'and' (Parker, 1994).

A number of attempts have been made to explore the meanings of truth and fairness. Many of these come back to the view expressed by Flint (1982):

> The fact that a 'true and fair view' is a philosophical concept and not susceptible to definition by a comprehensive set of detailed rules is, in fact, its most fundamental and characteristic feature.

Flint's justification for regarding truth and fairness as a philosophical concept follows on from the way in which it combines elements of two almost contradictory approaches to the regulation of financial reporting. On the one hand it imposes a general requirement for directors to prepare financial statements that meet the needs of shareholders and other users. This is an overriding requirement and one that places a great deal of emphasis on the ability and integrity of the accountants who prepare and audit the financial statements. On the other hand the system also prescribes the form and content of financial statements in considerable detail and normally requires compliance with a detailed body of rules. These rules are designed to reduce the need for subjective judgement, thereby reducing the scope for distortion and also rendering the statements produced by different businesses more comparable.

The relationship between truth and fairness and accounting standards is a complicated one. If standards define acceptable practice in the context of the areas that they cover, then compliance with standards should imply that the financial statements are acceptable (and give a true and fair view). However, the fact that there is a true and fair override that permits the standards to be set aside in order to give a true and fair view implies that it is a quality that may have a meaning of its own, beyond the confines of the standards.

The UK Financial Reporting Council commissioned the opinion of a senior lawyer ('Counsel's Opinion') on the meaning of true and fair.[2] This is a sophisticated

---

[2] Martin Moore QC's opinion on 'The True and Fair Requirement Revisited' was published in 2008 and is available on the Financial Reporting Council's website.

and detailed analysis that considers the requirement in terms of both UK and EU law.[3]

One potentially significant element of the Counsel's Opinion is that the requirement to 'present fairly', which is the overriding requirement of IFRSs,[4] is 'not a different requirement to that of showing a true and fair view, but is a different articulation of the same concept'.

Counsel's conclusions also indicate that compliance with relevant accounting standards is 'highly likely' to result in financial statements that show a true and fair view or present fairly, but that is not enough in itself to guarantee it. The application of standards requires judgement, and the directors must pay attention to the financial statements as a whole as well as to the individual figures and disclosures.

Counsel is of the opinion that the freedom to depart from accounting standards in order to avoid a misleading result is available, but that the scope for arguing that financial statements will give such a misleading result is very limited.

The phrase 'present fairly' also appears in US company law, although there is also an explicit reference to 'conformity with generally accepted accounting principles' (GAAP). US accounting standards are undergoing a process of change, with a shift from rules-based to principles-based accounting. A series of commentaries was published in the March 2003 issue of *Accounting Horizons* on the changes that are taking place in the United States. A European perspective on those same changes can be found in Nobes (2005). One notable difference between the United States and the European Union is that the United States does not, at present, have a true and fair override. If a rule is part of GAAP, then it must be adhered to.

Think!

How do standard-setters know what constitutes a true and fair view?

---

[3] This analysis is not necessarily relevant to reporting regimes outside the European Union, although the logic running through the opinion is probably applicable to most countries that have chosen to adopt IFRSs.

[4] See, for example, paragraph 15 of IAS 1 *Presentation of Financial Statements*, which states that 'financial statements shall present fairly the financial position, financial performance, and cash flows of an entity'.

Companies who prepare financial statements in accordance with IFRSs and/or in compliance with company law in the European Union are required to give a true and fair view (or present fairly). An accountant who wishes to prepare a set of financial statements that gives a fair presentation can rely heavily on IFRSs for guidance. That imposes a significant duty on the standard-setters, who must consider the implications of any new rules that they develop.

Having said that, one of the arguments for accounting standards is that they define truth and fairness.

A Very Simple Example

IAS 10 *Events After the Reporting Period* deals with a question that could easily lead to distorted financial statements. If information becomes available to the directors after the year end, then there could be two lines of thought:

• The financial statements are supposed to reflect all available information.
• The financial statements are supposed to reflect the position as it was understood at the year end.

In the absence of a clear statement of acceptable practice, the statements could be distorted by the exclusion of 'bad news' that only became available after the year end.[5]

IAS 10 clarifies the treatment by distinguishing 'adjusting events' from 'non-adjusting events'. Adjusting events provide evidence of conditions that existed as at the year end, such as the sale of inventory for less than cost to establish that it should have been written down to its net realisable value. Non-adjusting events are conditions that arose after the year end, such as a fire damaging a major factory.

The IAS imposes a duty to recognise events that occur after the reporting date and up to the date when the statements are authorised for issue. That reduces doubt as to what should happen if information becomes available well after the reporting date.

Finally, the IAS requires that adjusting events be reflected in the financial statements (so the inventory would be written down to its net realisable value) and that non-adjusting events be disclosed in the notes to the financial statements (so the fire would be described in the notes, but the property would remain in the statement of financial position at its book value and the loss would be recognised during the accounting period in which it actually occurred).

---

[5] Such as discovering that a receivable that had been considered recoverable as at the year end has become uncollectable afterwards.

What is a Conceptual Framework?

Chapter 2 described the origins of the standard-setting process. It was essentially a much-needed response to the criticisms that followed on from a series of high-profile accounting scandals. The standard-setters were forced to devote most of their time and energy to resolving individual problems and much of their time and energy to reacting to creative accounting schemes rather than developing an agenda that would improve the quality of accounting.

One of the techniques used by preparers of financial statements who wish to stretch the rules to breaking point is to question some of the fundamentals of accounting. For example, Chapter 2 mentioned the short-lived phenomenon of companies attaching values to their brand names and recognising them as non-current assets. At the time there were no rules to prevent this practice, and the amounts involved were substantial, with assets valued at hundreds of millions of pounds being recognised. The most worrying outcome was that the process of dealing with this was delayed because an argument broke out about the purpose of accounting statements. Some of the supporters of capitalisation argued that it was necessary to inform the capital markets of the value of these assets that were otherwise being ignored.[6] Critics of the practice argued that financial statements were prepared for stewardship purposes and that attempting to reflect market values in the accounts was a distraction rather than a help.

There are many potential readers of a set of financial statements, and each reader's interests may differ from those of the others. For example, investors in equity are largely interested in the company's ability to generate profits, whereas lenders are more interested in the security of their loans. Their differing interests might affect their preferences for accounting standards. Lenders would prefer to see a slightly pessimistic view so that the shareholders are deterred from taking large dividends and also so that they have the 'worst case' when reviewing non-current asset values in the balance sheet. Equity investors might prefer a little more optimism so that their shares are worth as much as possible. Standard-setters would undoubtedly benefit from clarity as to whose information needs the financial statements are expected to meet.

Once the user group (or groups) has been identified, the standard-setters also need to make some difficult decisions about the characteristics that their

---

[6] There was never any convincing evidence that the capital markets ever used this information to revise prices. Certainly, share prices did not leap up when companies published these valuations for the first time. Presumably, the markets were well aware that brands generated valuable cash flows long before companies started capitalising slightly spurious valuations.

information will have. For example, it is almost self-evident that accounting information has to be reliable, but how important is reliability? It may be that greater reliability can be obtained if more is spent on gathering and checking the figures. How much additional cost should be imposed on companies for the sake of greater reliability? It may be that greater reliability requires the postponement of publication until some of the uncertainties affecting figures are resolved. For example, the provision for doubtful receivables can be determined with far greater reliability six months after the year end than immediately after.

The point of a conceptual framework is to set out the purpose of financial reporting and to clarify the characteristics that accounting information should have. It will not eliminate the need for accounting standards, nor will it prevent problems from arising. A conceptual framework will provide a starting point for the development of any new standards that are necessary, and the resulting standards should be consistent with one another.

Problems

It is very difficult to develop a clear and useful conceptual framework without attracting criticism. That is because the drafting process forces the architects of the framework to make clear and explicit statements about contentious areas that will undoubtedly lead to complaints from several quarters.

Stating the purpose of financial statements will, almost by definition, identify a primary group of users. If a conceptual framework attaches priority to the needs of one group of users, then the others might claim that they are being let down and could lobby for change.

Identifying users and their needs is an important starting point because many other decisions follow on from that. One major issue in particular is the choice of measure to use in calculating and reporting capital and profit.

For example, a shop sells simple woodworking tools. On 1 January, at the start of the year, it purchased a hammer for £10.00. During the year, the general rate of inflation was 5%, but the price of woodworking tools increased by 8%. On 31 December, at the end of the year, the hammer was sold for £11.00. That gives us three potential profit figures on the sale of the hammer:

- *Historical cost* – the hammer cost £10.00 and was sold for £11.00, so the profit was £1.00. That is of interest to shareholders who are interested in stewardship (because they want to know that the directors have not stolen or lost the £11.00 from the sale of the hammer) and to the tax authorities (because they will use that series of transactions as the basis for charging tax).

- *Current purchasing power* – the hammer cost £10.50 (31 December £) and sold for £11.00 (31 December £), so the profit is £0.50 (31 December £).[7] That is of interest to shareholders who are interested in the real returns that their investment can generate, after allowing for the impact of inflation.
- *Replacement cost (or current cost)* – the hammer cost £10.80 to replace at the time of its sale and was sold for £11.00, so the profit is £0.20.[8] That figure is of interest to management for pricing purposes, and also to shareholders who have invested in the long term and are interested in whether the business can maintain its productive capacity in terms of its ability to replace inventory and other assets out of revenues.

Any asset can be valued in a variety of different ways:

Historical cost	How much did it cost?
Current purchasing power cost	How much did it cost after restating its historical cost for the effects of inflation?
Replacement (or current) cost	How much would it cost to replace that asset if it were sold or consumed?
Net realisable value	How much could the asset be sold for on the open market, after allowing for any costs that would have to be borne in the process?
Net present value	How much are the cash flows that the asset will generate worth, after allowing for the time value of money?

A detailed discussion of each of these models is outside the scope of this text. The important thing to note is that each could form the basis of the accounting

---

[7] This calculation restates all £ units so that they are consistent in terms of their buying power. If inflation is 5%, then £10.00 tied up at the start of the year would have to be worth £10.50 at the end of the year or the shareholders would have suffered a loss in their buying power.
[8] Inflation is a measure of average prices in the economy, but specific prices can change by more or less than that average. In this case, the replacement cost of tools has gone up by more than the general rate of inflation, and so the adjustment to historical cost has had a greater effect.

system. Each user would have different preferences. For example, a statement of financial position based on net realisable value would be very useful to a lender who wished to have an up-to-date analysis of the value of the assets that had been pledged as collateral.

In 1975, the United Kingdom's Accounting Standards Steering Committee published The Corporate Report, a discussion paper on financial reporting (ASSC, 1975). That took the needs of different user groups as its starting point and concluded that the best way to meet all of their needs to the fullest extent possible was to replace the traditional financial statements with a more comprehensive set showing the results under each of the different bases. The statements could even be laid out with a separate column for each measurement basis. This groundbreaking paper highlighted the danger of thinking through a conceptual framework from scratch. If it is too radical, then it will generate discussion and debate, but it is very unlikely to be implemented.

Generally, preparers of financial statements are resistant to change because it is always difficult to predict how changes to the reporting regime will affect the behaviour of users. For example, virtually all of the alternatives to historical cost accounting will have the effect of reducing reported profit figures.[9] Preparers are often reluctant to risk trusting the readers of financial statements to adjust their expectations to take account of the effects of a revised approach to measurement.

The IASB Framework

The IASB's *Framework for the Preparation and Presentation of Financial Statements* (the Framework) was adopted in 2001. The purpose of the Framework is to set out the concepts that underlie the preparation and presentation of financial statements. It will, therefore, guide standard-setters in the development of consistent and coherent standards.

The Framework may well be helpful and useful to preparers who wish to know as much as possible about standards and the standard-setting process, but the document does not have the force of an IFRS. It is theoretically possible that there will be occasions where an IFRS conflicts with the Framework, in which case the IFRS should be followed.

---

[9] Historical costs are generally out of date by the time that revenues are recognised. Most prices rise over time, so correcting for that lag in prices will almost always increase recognised costs and thereby lower reported profits.

The Framework deals with the following issues:

- the objective of financial statements;
- underlying assumptions;
- qualitative characteristics of financial statements;
- the elements of financial statements;
- recognition of the elements of financial statements;
- measurement of the elements of financial statements;
- concepts of capital and capital maintenance.

The Objectives of Financial Statements

The Framework lists a range of users of financial statements and discusses their interests in the financial statements in turn:

- investors;
- employees;
- lenders;
- suppliers and other trade creditors;
- customers;
- governments and their agencies;
- the public.

This listing avoids controversy by giving virtually every user having a legitimate interest in the financial statements and by avoiding any explicit ranking of their interests.

The Framework states that the objective of financial statements is 'to provide information about the financial position, performance, and changes in financial position of an entity that is useful to a wide range of users in making economic decisions'.

Rather than identifying a primary group of users, the Framework asserts that users' economic decisions are largely concerned with the generation of cash and cash equivalents. They wish to ascertain whether the company can generate cash and, if so, when and with what degree of certainty.

It is certainly possible to argue that a single set of financial statements cannot serve the needs of all potential users to the same extent. However, the identification of users is only one aspect of the accounting choices that are implicit in the development of a conceptual framework and a standard-setting programme. Those choices are constrained by political considerations in terms of obtaining the support of the preparers and also by economic considerations in terms of the costs and benefits of alternatives. Those constraints, which will be discussed throughout the remainder of this section, may well mean that the Framework could not meet every possible information need of, say, investors.

At a pragmatic level, the financial statements that are presently published are used by all of the groups identified by the Framework, and so it might be argued that they must be useful to all.

Underlying Assumptions

The Framework identifies two underlying assumptions:

- accruals basis;
- going concern.

Both of these should be familiar from earlier studies.

The accruals basis means that transactions are recognised when their effects occur rather than when cash flows arise. This should mean that measures of performance and financial position are more useful and relevant to readers.

The going concern assumption is essentially a justification for showing assets at a value other than the amounts that might be realised under conditions of duress. That has the effect of justifying carrying inventory at cost rather than the prices that would be obtained in a liquidation, which is a more realistic valuation method for most decisions. Paradoxically, going concern also means that certain errors and inaccuracies can be overlooked because they do not really matter. For example, valuing non-current assets at cost less depreciation means that readers do not really know what the assets would be worth if they were sold on the open market. If the business is a going concern, then that does not really matter if only because the assets have to be retained for use in the business and will be written off during their lives.

Qualitative Characteristics of Financial Statements

The Framework identifies four principal characteristics, some of which are supported by secondary characteristics:

Understandability	*Relevance*
Financial statements need to be understandable or they will not be of any use. The Framework states that	Relevance is judged in terms of decisions made by users. Arguably, most decisions involve looking ahead

users are expected to have a reasonable knowledge of accounting and business and should be prepared to read the financial statements with reasonable care.	rather than backward. The Framework states that historical information is often a valid basis for predictions. • materiality
Reliability Information is reliable if it is free from material error and bias. • faithful representation • substance over form • neutrality • prudence • completeness	*Comparability* Comparability requires that figures are comparable over time for any given company and also between companies. That requires consistency of accounting policies from year to year and also clear disclosure of the major policies in use.

Materiality is an important aspect of judging relevance. Information is material if 'its omission or misstatement could influence the economic decisions of users'. Materiality judgements involve the nature of the information as well as quantitative factors such as size as a percentage of profit or revenue. For example, directors' remuneration is likely to be material because it could have implications for the decisions taken by the board, and so even very small errors or omissions could have serious implications for readers.

If a matter is not material, then it can be omitted or ignored without any consequences for readers. Indeed, the accounts can be made easier to read if immaterial figures are combined so that readers are not distracted by excessive detail.

Faithful representation is an important quality, but one that is often compromised in accounting. For example, the statement of financial position should represent faithfully all of the assets that the business controls. Unfortunately, there are a great many assets that cannot be represented because of problems with recognition. One example would be goodwill, which is a vitally important asset, and one that companies often spend a lot of money on maintaining through marketing and customer service, but which cannot be recognised because of the immense measurement difficulties that it creates.[10]

Substance over form is an important basis for many standards. It requires that the financial statements reflect the economic substance of transactions or relationships rather than their legal form. This involves the famous 'duck test'.[11] In the

---

[10] The problems of accounting for goodwill are discussed in Chapter 9.
[11] If something looks like a duck and quacks like a duck, then it is a duck.

past it was often possible to report the legal form of a transaction so that the resulting figures were technically correct but nevertheless misleading. For example, Chapter 11 discusses long-term leases which give the user of an asset all of the risks and rewards of owning it and exactly the same commitment in terms of lease payments as would exist if the asset had been purchased with a loan. IAS 17 *Leases* requires that such leases be accounted for as if the assets had been purchased outright with a loan, which is the economic reality of the arrangement but not its legal form.

Neutrality implies that the financial statements are free from bias.

Prudence arguably contradicts neutrality by requiring a degree of caution in preparing the financial statements. Whenever there is any doubt, the lowest reasonable figure should be chosen for assets or revenues and the highest reasonable figure for expenses and liabilities. The emphasis is, however, on the word 'reasonable. There is a significant difference between prudent accounting and understating profits.

Completeness requires that figures should be complete, but only to the extent that is consistent with materiality and cost.

The Framework emphasises the need for professional judgement when using these characteristics in practice:

- There can be internal conflicts between the characteristics. Sometimes a more reliable figure is less relevant, and vice versa. For example, historical costs are generally more reliable than estimates of market value, but valuations are generally more relevant to most decisions.
- Timeliness can also come into play. Publishing later means that the information in the statements is less current, but there may be fewer estimates because problems like doubtful debts will have resolved themselves one way or the other.
- There can also be a trade-off between costs and benefits. It can be difficult to decide whether it is worth paying extra for higher-quality information.

The Framework does not give any characteristic priority over the others, so each case has to be decided on its own merits.

It is claimed that putting the principal characteristics into operation will normally result in statements that give a true and fair view (or present fairly). While there is no reason to disagree with that assertion, it is difficult to be sure that the qualities implied by each of these characteristics are present in sufficient quantity.[12]

---

[12] That may not be a bad thing. Accountancy would be much less of an intellectual challenge for its practitioners if there were no scope for professional judgement, and it might be a far less lucrative occupation as well.

The Elements of Financial Statements

The five elements of financial statements are:

Assets	Resources controlled by the entity as a result of past events and from which future economic benefits are expected to flow to the entity
Liabilities	Present obligations of the entity arising from past events, the settlement of which is expected to result in an outflow from the entity of resources embodying economic benefits
Equity	The residual interest in the assets of the entity after deducting all its liabilities
Income	Increases in economic benefits during the accounting period in the form of inflows or enhancements of assets or decreases in liabilities that result in increases in equity, other than those relating to contributions from equity participants
Expenses	Decreases in economic benefits during the accounting period in the form of outflows or depletions of assets or incurrences of liabilities that result in decreases in equity, other than those relating to distributions to equity participants

These definitions are vitally important because they will underpin the development of all future accounting standards. Figures will only appear in the financial statements if they fall within these definitions and the recognition and measurement criteria. These definitions may also prove very significant in setting clear and consistent accounting standards.

The definitions of assets and liabilities are by far the most important because they are the basis of the other three definitions. One thing that is quite noticeable about both is that they do not really reflect their everyday usage. For example, most individuals would link the concept of an asset to ownership and that of a liability to a legal obligation. The history of accounting has shown that the definitions of assets and liabilities have to reflect the economic substance of assets and liabilities rather than their legal form.

Much of the material in Chapters 8 to 11 is devoted to expanding on these definitions of assets and liabilities and putting these definitions into practice in the context of specific assets and liabilities.

Income and expenses are defined in terms of increases and decreases in assets and liabilities. Some changes in asset values go straight to equity rather than to income or expense. Accounting for revaluations is dealt with in Chapter 8.

Recognition of the Elements of Financial Statements

There are two basic criteria for recognising any given item under one of the five definitions listed above:

- It must be probable that any future economic benefit associated with the item will flow to or from the entity.
- The item must have a cost or value that can be measured reliably.

The word 'probable' crops up fairly frequently throughout IFRSs. It is best to regard something as probable if it is more likely to happen than not, or has a greater than 50% chance of happening. Inevitably, some items will be difficult to classify in terms of this criterion, and so there will always be some scope for professional judgement.

Evaluating reliability can be far more difficult. Accounting statements invariably involve estimates and assumptions. The decision as to whether a particular figure can be estimated with sufficient reliability is clearly a matter of professional judgement.

Measurement of the Elements of Financial Statements

The Framework lists four of the measurement bases that are available:

- historical cost;
- current cost;
- realisable value;
- present value.

These have been discussed earlier in this chapter.

The Framework makes no attempt to claim that any one measure is superior. It is stated that historical cost is the most common, but that some figures are based on alternatives. For example, inventory is valued at the lower of cost and net realisable value, and pension commitments are often valued at their net present value.

The assertion that historical cost is the most common basis is slightly disingenuous because many entities show non-current assets at their valuations rather than historical costs.

Concepts of Capital and Capital Maintenance

Capital can be defined and measured in a variety of different ways. One important distinction is between financial capital and operating capital.

The concept of capital maintenance is essentially about deciding whether a business has made a profit, a loss, or has just broken even. If capital remains unchanged after adjusting for any additional inflows or distributions, then the company has broken even. An increase implies a profit and a decrease implies a loss.

Financial capital values capital in money terms and is of particular interest to shareholders who regard their stake as purely financial. The business has made a profit if net assets are greater at the end of the period than at the beginning.

Financial capital can be measured in terms of either historical costs or units of purchasing power. Historical costs can be converted to units of purchasing power by using an index, such as the UK government's Retail Price Index, to restate figures at a consistent price.

Physical capital maintenance values capital in terms of physical productive capacity and is of particular interest to those who are interested in the company's long-term survival, such as managers and employees and also shareholders in family businesses whose interest goes beyond personal wealth.

The effects of these different capital maintenance concepts have been discussed briefly, with a simple exercise, earlier in this chapter.

Intriguingly, having pointed out that there are alternatives to the traditional historical cost concept of capital maintenance, the Framework states that it does not intend to prescribe any concept in particular. That leaves the way open to moving away from historical cost at some stage in the future.

Summary

Users of financial statements expect that the information they have been provided with gives a true and fair view. That is a difficult concept to pin down. There is a legal argument that readers expect the financial statements to have been prepared in accordance with the codified accounting standards, so compliance with IFRSs should enable the statements to give a true and fair view.

Standard-setters bear an enormous responsibility because they have the ability to set the boundaries of acceptable accounting practice. They have a duty to prepare standards in a coherent and consistent manner. One way to do that is to develop a clear statement of the objectives of accounting statements. Identifying the users, their information needs, and the characteristics that accounting statements will have in response to those needs ensures greater clarity as well as consistency.

The IASB has a detailed Framework that can be used to evaluate existing IFRSs and develop future standards.

Tutorial Questions

Question 1

Max is a manufacturing company. The following trial balance was prepared at the company's latest year end:

Max
Trial balance at 30 September 20X2

	$m	$m
Administration salaries	64	
Bank	98	
Cost of goods sold	1 142	
Distribution costs	148	
Dividend	300	
Interest paid	104	
Inventory as at 30 September 20X2	45	
Loans (repayable 20X8)		1 450
Plant and machinery – cost	762	
Plant and machinery – depreciation to date		324
Property – cost	4 456	
Property – depreciation to date		611
Provision for cost of sales		500
Retained profit brought forward		1 617
Share capital		600
Trade payables		27
Trade receivables	980	
Turnover		2 970
	8 099	8 099

(i) Plant and equipment that had cost $125 million and had been depreciated by $78 million was sold during the year. New plant and equipment was purchased for $160 million. These transactions have been included in the above figures. There were no other transactions involving fixed assets.

(ii) Depreciation for the year has still to be charged as follows:

- Property   2% of cost
- Plant and equipment   25% reducing balance

A whole year's depreciation is charged in the year of acquisition and none in the year of disposal.

(iii) Max's largest customer placed an order during September 20X2 for all of the goods that it is likely to require during the year ended 30 September 20X3. Max invoiced this customer for these goods during September 20X2. A total of $800 million was debited to trade receivables and credited to revenue in respect of this invoice. A provision for $500 million was created in respect of the estimated cost of manufacturing the invoiced goods.

(iv) Max's customer agreed to place the order referred to in (iii) above only after receiving a number of written assurances from Max's directors. The goods themselves would be delivered at times and in quantities decided by the customer. The customer would pay for the goods in accordance with Max's normal credit terms after delivery. The customer could cancel the order without penalty at any time, and any remaining balance on the invoice would be cancelled immediately.

(v) Max's external auditor has examined the documentation referred to in (iii) and (iv) above and disagrees with the directors' decision to treat this as a sale.

Prepare Max's statement of comprehensive income for the year ended 30 September 20X2 and its statement of financial position as at that date.

Explain whether Max is justified in treating the transaction described in notes (iii) and (iv) as a sale. Use the definitions of the elements of financial statements as a starting point.

Question 2

Discuss the advantages and disadvantages of offering companies the option of departing from the detailed requirements of standards in order to achieve a fair presentation.

Question 3

The external auditor responsible for the audit of G was dismayed to discover that the company had been taken over after the publication of the most recent annual report. The auditor is concerned that the company's buyer will complain that the financial statements were misleading and will seek substantial damages from the audit firm. Explain why the auditor might have such concerns even though no claim has been initiated.

Question 4

Discuss the limitations of historical cost accounting and suggest reasons for its continuing use.

Question 5

A company's chief accountant is considering the role of the IASB Framework with a view to amending the company's accounting policies if they do not reflect best practice. The company's policy of providing for future warranty costs raises some concerns in respect of the need to provide information that is both relevant and reliable. The finance director is concerned that this estimated balance might not be sufficiently reliable for inclusion in the financial statements.

(i) Describe the role of the Framework within the system of regulation and briefly explain whether it would be useful to the company for reviewing accounting policies.

(ii) Explain why there may be a conflict between relevance and reliability. Your answer should refer to the issues affecting the relevance and reliability of the provision for future warranty costs.

Further Work

There are no questions with answers in this chapter. If you wish to develop the material covered, then spend some time skimming through the technical summaries of IFRSs on the IASB website and try to find ways in which the Framework can be seen in operation.

References

ASSC (1975), The Corporate Report. Accounting Standards Steering Committee, Discussion paper.

Flint, D. (1982), *A True and Fair View in Company Accounts*. Gee & Co., London, UK.

Nobes, C. (2005), Rules-based standards and the lack of principles in accounting. *Accounting Horizons*, **19**(1), 25–34.

Parker, R.H. (1994), Finding English words to talk about accounting concepts. *Accounting, Auditing and Accountability*, **7**(2), 70–85.

ACCOUNTING FOR TAX

6

Contents

Learning Objectives

After studying this chapter you should be able to:

- account for current tax;
- account for deferred tax and explain the reasons for having deferred tax in the financial statements;
- discuss some of the implications of the changing treatment of deferred tax for the regulation of accounting.

Introduction

This chapter deals with the accounting treatment of tax. The discussion of current tax deals with the mechanics of the various adjustments that have to be made in respect of the annual tax bill. These are straightforward, even though the associated negotiations with the tax authorities can be quite complicated.

The chapter goes on to discuss the accounting treatment of deferred tax. Deferred tax arises when transactions are recognised for accounting purposes in one period and for tax period in another. That can lead to tax being charged in the 'wrong' accounting period. The deferred tax adjustment corrects for this potential distortion.

The historical background to the development of rules relating to deferred tax is interesting because it illustrates the problems for standard-setters when rules are unpopular.

Some Basic Tax Rules

Most countries make companies pay tax based on their profits. Some countries calculate this charge as a straightforward percentage of the profit figure in the financial statements. Many countries adjust the accounting profit in order to arrive at a taxable profit and this sum is then multiplied by the tax rate to arrive at the tax charge for the year.

> **Think!**
>
> Why would a government require the accounting profit to be adjusted before the calculation of tax?

The government might wish to encourage certain types of behaviour and discourage others, so it might treat certain types of transaction in a very favourable way. For example, there could be tax benefits associated with investing in certain types of fixed asset in order to encourage investment in physical plant and so expand employment opportunities and make the economy more competitive. Similarly, certain costs might not be allowable for tax purposes. For example, fines levied by the criminal courts might be disallowed for tax purposes as an additional disincentive to breaking the law.

The tax system will also be easier to manage if there is a degree of uniformity and consistency. Thus, many countries do not permit businesses to treat depreciation as an expense for tax purposes. Instead, the company might be entitled to an alternative form of tax relief on its non-current assets.

So, a tax computation would look like this:

> Accounting profit
> Less any income that is not subject to tax
> Add any expenses that are not allowable for tax purposes
> Less any allowances that are deductible for tax but not shown in the income statement
> Equals taxable profit

Tax is not an exact science. The various adjustments can often involve a great deal of discussion, debate, and negotiation with the tax authorities. The company might read a particular piece of tax law in such a way that an expense is allowed for tax purposes, but the tax authorities might believe the opposite. This can mean that the tax charge calculated at the end of the financial year is an estimate.

In most countries the tax charge is payable within a year and should be treated as a current liability.

Dealing with Forecasting Errors

In the simplest possible case the company will predict the tax payable accurately and will agree its tax charge with the tax authorities without any difficulty.

Example – the Simplest Possible Case

T's profit before tax during the year ended 31 December 20X3 was £500 000. It was estimated that tax of £60 000 would be paid on this amount. The previous year's estimate had proved to be acceptable to the tax authorities.

The following extracts would appear in T's financial statements:

Income statement	
	£
Profit before tax	500 000
Tax	(60 000)
Profit after tax	440 000

Statement of financial position – current liabilities	
	£
Tax	60 000

This case is simple because the tax charge was agreed without adjustment. That may not always be the case.

Under- and Overprovisions

The tax authorities may accept the tax calculations prepared by the company without any problem, but they may disagree with some of the logic. For example, the company might have spent a large amount on the refurbishment of some property and could have treated that as a repair cost in the income statement. The tax authorities may refuse to accept that this was an expense and insist on capitalising the cost. That would have the effect of pushing up the taxable profit beyond the company's estimate.

It is more difficult to imagine the tax authorities demanding less tax than the company had planned to pay, although the accounting estimate could have been based on the possibility that a dubious expense would not be permitted as an expense for tax purposes and so the final tax bill could be smaller than was expected if the expense is given.

Any under- or overprovision will leave a balance in the bookkeeping records after the bill has been settled. That balance will have to be eliminated, otherwise it will be misleading.

Returning to our example of T, during 20X4 it was agreed that the tax charge for the year ended 31 December 20X3 should be £55 000 rather than the £60 000 originally provided.

The estimated charge for the year ended 31 December 20X4 was £72 000, out of a profit before tax of £700 000.

The following extracts would appear in T's financial statements:

Income statement

	£
Profit before tax	700 000
Tax (see note 1)	(67 000)
Profit after tax	633 000

Statement of financial position – current liabilities

	£
Tax	72 000

Note 1 – tax

	£
Charge for year	72 000
Less: overprovision brought forward	(5 000)
Tax expense for year	67 000

The reason for this adjustment arises because the settlement of the previous year's estimated charge will leave an unnecessary credit balance on the tax account. When the balance was first created, the company would have created a credit balance of £60 000 in the tax account. Paying the bill for the £55 000 that was actually payable would reduce that balance to £5 000, but nothing is actually owed. The easiest way to cancel this is to debit the tax account and make the corresponding credit entry to the tax expense in the income statement.

It might seem like a distortion to cancel last year's forecasting error through this year's income statement, but there is an important principle that all expenses should flow through the income statement rather than, say, transferring them to retained earnings on the grounds that they relate to a previous period. Otherwise, companies could overstate the reported profit after tax every year by deliberately underproviding for tax.

A Word of Warning

Sometimes the accounting treatment for these tax adjustments takes a little while to sink in. One thing that often causes confusion is that the tax expense in the income statement is often different from the tax liability in the statement of financial position. That is normally due to adjustments such as the one that we have just discussed.

It can help to think of the tax figures in the statement of comprehensive income and the statement of financial position as two separate calculations. The tax expense can have several elements or adjustments, whereas the tax liability is normally the estimated amount payable in respect of this year's taxable profit.

IAS 12 *Income Taxes*

Companies must recognise the tax charged on the profit for the year in the statement of comprehensive income, unless the tax relates to items that are credited or charged directly to equity (e.g. some capital gains or losses – see Chapter 7).

We will discuss the disclosure requirements in IAS 12 after we have discussed the topic of deferred tax. Essentially, IAS 12 requires that the tax charge be broken down so that the tax effects of unusual transactions can be seen. For example, if the company closes down part of the business, then it must show the tax charge or relief associated with any gain or loss on closure separately.

Deferred Tax

The problem of deferred tax only arises in those countries where it is possible to earn profit in one period and be taxed on it in a different one. That is the case in the United Kingdom and Ireland.

For example, a company has paid in advance for an advertising campaign that will run early in the next financial year, just prior to the launch of a new product. That company operates in a country where it is permissible to treat the payment as an expense for tax purposes because it has been paid for, even though the cost will be carried forward as a prepaid expense in the statement of financial position and will not be recognised as an expense for accounting purposes until next year. Such a treatment would be acceptable in the United Kingdom and in many other countries.

If we assume that the company's profit before advertising costs and tax was £2.0 million and that it pays tax at a rate of 33%, then the following figures would appear in both the financial statements and the tax computation:

Year 1	Income statement	Tax computation
Profit before advertising	£2.000 m	£2.000 m
Advertising costs	0	(0.400 m)
Profit	2.000 m	1.600 m
Tax (33%)	(0.528 m)	£0.528 m
Profit after tax	£1.472 m	

The company does not recognise the advertising costs because the campaign will not run until next year. That does not prevent it from claiming the cost as an expense for tax purposes. The tax charge for the year is 33% of £1.6 million or £0.528 million.

Next year the profit before advertising and tax was £3.0 million. The company would be required to treat the cost of the advertising as an expense for accounting purposes, but it has already claimed tax relief, so the profits for accounting and tax purposes are as follows:

Year 2	Income statement	Tax computation
Profit before advertising	£3.000 m	£3.000 m
Advertising costs	(0.400 m)	0
Profit	2.600 m	3.000 m
Tax (33%)	(0.990 m)	£0.990 m
Profit after tax	£1.610 m	

The important point to note is that the total profit before tax in the income statement for the two years = 2.0 + 2.6 = £4.6 million. That is exactly the same as the total taxable profit according to the tax computation = 1.6 + 3.0 = £4.6 million.

The different treatments of the advertising cost have not affected the *amount* of profit in either the tax computation or the income statement, but they have affected the *timing* of the recognition of that profit.

One way to look at this pattern of recognition is that the tax system has delayed the payment of tax on £400 000 of profit that was earned in year 1 but that did not become taxable until year 2. If we accept that argument, then the delay in the payment of tax could be thought of as a 'timing difference'.

One Argument for the Accounting Treatment of Timing Differences

It could be argued that the accounting system recognises transactions in the 'correct' period and that timing differences arise because the tax system is designed to simplify the collection of tax or to impose an artificial degree of consistency between taxpayers. If that is the case, then all tax should be recognised in the period in which the associated 'real' costs are incurred and profits earned. In other words, all of the tax that will eventually be paid on year 1 profits should be matched against the pre-tax profits for year 1 and shown as a liability in the statement of financial position at the end of that year.

The 'deferred tax' liability at the end of year 1 would be £400 000 × 33% = £132 000.

The tax note to the income statement would be as follows:

	£
Charge for year	528 000
Increase in provision for deferred tax	132 000
	660 000

This would be deducted from the profit before tax of £2.0 million to give a profit after tax of £1.34 million.

The liability of £132 000 would appear as a non-current liability in the statement of financial position because it will not be paid until the settlement of year 2's tax charge, which will be paid some time in year 3.

We have already seen that the current tax charge is £528 000, and that will be shown as a current liability because it is anticipated that this amount will be paid during the following financial year.

During year 2 the company would be taxed on £400 000 of profits that had been earned in an earlier period.

The balance on the deferred tax account would be transferred back into the income statement:

	£
Charge for year	990 000
Decrease in provision for deferred tax	(132 000)
	858 000

The deferred tax liability would be discharged, and so the balance in the deferred tax account would be zero.

The cancellation of a timing difference is called a 'reversal'. Reversals may occur many years after the 'originating timing difference'.

Another Argument for the Accounting Treatment of Timing Differences

An alternative argument is that there is no liability until the company is actually assessed and asked to pay tax. One possible justification for this is the possibility that the company might never actually pay the tax on these timing differences if, for example, it has a series of losses for tax purposes and no tax ever becomes payable on that £400 000 timing difference.

If that argument is accepted, then the liability for deferred tax will always be zero and there will never be any adjustment for deferred tax in the tax expense in the statement of comprehensive income.

Yet Another Argument for the Accounting Treatment of Timing Differences

Finally, it can be argued that there is a compromise between our two previous positions. It could be argued that companies could consider the likelihood of paying their deferred tax within the foreseeable future. If the tax is likely to be paid, then it should be provided. If not, it can be ignored.

Thus, there are three possible treatments, each of which can be justified in terms of accounting arguments:

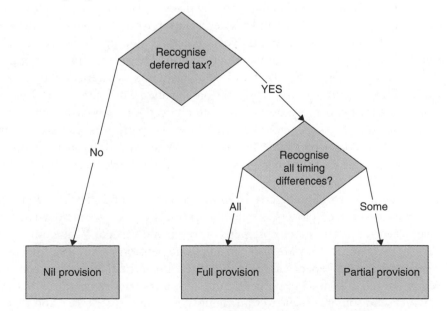

The full provision method is consistent with the argument that tax should always be recognised in the period in which the associated profit is deemed to have been earned. Under this approach, all deferred tax balances are recognised in full.

The nil provision approach deems that tax should only ever be recognised in the period in which it is charged. In other words, deferred tax should never be provided and the balance is always nil.

The partial provision approach deems that deferred tax should only be recognised in respect of timing differences that are likely to reverse within the foreseeable future. Any amounts that are not deemed likely to reverse should be ignored.

A Word About Timing Differences

Timing differences can arise for a number of reasons, but there are two in particular that can have a significant impact on the deferred tax balance.

Accelerated tax depreciation arises when the tax system permits non-current assets to be written off more quickly for tax purposes than for accounting purposes. Typically, the rate of depreciation for tax purposes will be set so that the rate used is effectively uniform for all businesses, regardless of the subjective judgements made for accounting purposes. Governments often permit a rapid rate of depreciation, partly so that businesses feel that the tax system gives them an incentive to invest in new assets.

The problem is that the total amount to be written off over the asset's life cannot exceed its original cost. So, any rapid tax depreciation when the assets are new will only lead to a larger tax charge in later years. For example, suppose a company has plant and machinery that originally cost £1 million. These assets have a net book value for accounting purposes of £600 000 and a tax written down value of £450 000. This means that the company has claimed £600 000 − 450 000 = £150 000 more for tax depreciation than it has charged for accounting purposes. If we apply the full provision approach, then the company will pay tax on this additional £150 000 at some time in the future when the difference eventually reverses. If we assume that the tax rate is, say, 30%, then the deferred tax liability is 30% × £150 000 = £45 000.

It is also possible to have deferred tax assets. For example, IAS 19 *Employee Benefits* requires that employers accrue the pension costs associated with their employees' service at the time those pension rights are earned. While employees are earning their salary, they are also earning some pension rights, and the cost of those is accrued as an expense as and when they are earned. Those costs are not allowed as an expense for tax purposes until the associated payment is actually made, which can sometimes mean waiting until the employees retire and receive their pensions.[1] Thus, a 20-year-old employee could be entitled to pension benefits for the work done during the present year, and these will be charged immediately to the statement of comprehensive income. The tax relief associated with this pension cost will not be received until the employee reaches retirement age at 65, which is 40 years or more in the future. Arguably, this deferred tax relief creates an asset in the same way that an accelerated tax depreciation charge creates a liability.

The History of Deferred Tax in the United Kingdom

The accounting treatment of deferred tax has gone through a full circle in the space of 25 years or so.

In 1975, the United Kingdom's Accounting Standards Committee published Statement of Standard Accounting Practice (SSAP) 11 *Deferred Tax*. This standard required the use of the full provision. At that time the UK economy was going through a period of massive inflation, and that was creating problems for companies because their profits were being overstated because of the effects of rising prices distorting historical cost profits. The government eased the potential tax burden by allowing companies to write off 100% of the cost of plant and equipment in the year of purchase and introduced some other measures that had the effect of temporarily depressing taxable profit.

The fact that the tax relief granted was theoretically temporary created a problem because SSAP 11 required the recognition of massive deferred tax liabilities. There was such an outcry from preparers of financial statements that the Accounting Standards Committee withdrew the standard before it came into force.

SSAP 11 was replaced in 1978 with SSAP 15 *Accounting for Deferred Tax*. SSAP 15 permitted the use of the partial provision basis, with companies having to recognise a deferred tax liability on those timing differences that were expected to reverse within the foreseeable future, which was generally taken to be within the next five years or so. Many of the reliefs granted by the government tended to roll over from year to year, and so only a small proportion of the potential charge was expected to reverse within the period under consideration. This made the standard far more acceptable to companies because it reduced their liability for deferred tax.

Arguably, SSAP 15 gave the directors a huge amount of discretion over the amount that they were going to charge because their predictions concerning the reversal of timing differences depended entirely upon their forecasts and

---

[1] Accounting for pensions is beyond the scope of this book. The accounting treatment depends on the nature of the pension scheme.

intentions concerning capital expenditure. If they planned to make ongoing investments, then the forecasts would have indicated increasing originating timing differences and no reversals, so no liability would be necessary. It would have been dishonest to have distorted forecasts and budgets in order to understate the deferred tax liability, but it would have been possible to get away with doing so and simply claiming that any subsequent difference between actual and planned investments was due to a change of circumstances.

Fortunately, the problems with the UK economy were tackled, and so the provisions that had led to the potential deferred liabilities were withdrawn. That created a new source of pressure on the standard-setters. The use of the partial provision meant that deferred tax assets arising on pension costs were not recognised because the timing differences that had created them were unlikely to reverse within the time period set out in SSAP 15. In 1992, SSAP 15 was revised and supplemented with an interpretation from the standard-setting board's Urgent Issues Task Force which left the partial provision basis in force for all timing differences except those in respect of post-retirement costs, such as pensions. That meant that very few deferred tax liabilities were recognised but that potentially massive deferred tax assets were coming into the statement of financial position.

This anomaly was finally resolved in 2001 when the standard-setting body, now known as the Accounting Standards Board, published Financial Reporting Standard 19 *Deferred Tax*. This standard required the full provision method for all deferred tax balances, whether assets or liabilities.

Document	Accounting treatment	Effect
SSAP 11 (ASC, 1975)	Full provision basis.	Would have required the recognition of massive liabilities for deferred tax.
SSAP 15 (ASC, 1978)	Partial provision basis.	Reduced recorded liability and granted some discretion over the recognition of deferred tax liabilities.
SSAP 15 revised (1992)	Partial provision remains in force for all timing differences, except those in respect of post-retirement costs, such as pensions.	Reduction in liabilities remains, but there is now scope for recognising deferred tax assets on pension costs.

FRS 19 (2001)	Full provision method required.	There is now no discretion over the recognition of liabilities, although the economic background means that liabilities will be relatively small. Some companies will be able to accrue tax relief on pension costs and so create large deferred tax assets.

The worrying thing about this story is that the changes have not really been driven by accounting arguments. Rather, the preparers of financial statements have lobbied ferociously on the need to change the regulations in order to achieve an 'acceptable' provision for deferred tax. This was particularly obvious when there was an inconsistency in the methods used for pension costs and other timing differences. Timing differences on accelerated tax depreciation are likely to reverse far more rapidly than timing differences on pension costs. Combine that observation with the traditional tendency for accounts to be prepared in a prudent way, with higher recognition thresholds for assets than liabilities, and it becomes quite difficult to justify this collection of practices. Indeed, the inconsistency of treatment was one of the factors that drove the development of FRS 19.

It is also worth noting that the accounting treatment of deferred tax has no impact whatsoever on the underlying economic reality. The same amounts of tax will be paid at exactly the same time regardless of whether a provision is created for deferred tax or how any such provision is calculated.

IAS 12 and Deferred Tax

IAS 12 effectively requires the use of the full provision method.

Calculating Deferred Tax

The trick to calculating the figures for deferred tax is to start with the cumulative differences between the recognised costs and revenues for tax and accounting purposes. Multiplying these cumulative differences by the relevant tax rate gives the closing balance on deferred tax. The closing balance is shown in the statement of financial position, and the increase or decrease goes to the tax expense for the year.

Ideally, the relevant tax rate should be the rate that will be in force when the timing difference reverses, although that is virtually impossible to predict and so the current rate of tax is used instead, on the basis that the current rate is the best estimate of the rate that will apply in the future.

For example, at the end of last year, a company's non-current assets had a net book value of £500 000 and a tax written down value of £300 000. The tax rate in force at the time was 28%.

At the end of this year, the assets had a net book value of £480 000 and a tax written down value of £260 000. The tax rate has increased to 30%.

Last year's closing balance on deferred tax would have been the cumulative timing difference of £500 000 − 300 000 = £200 000 multiplied by the tax rate of 28% to give a balance of £56 000.

This year's closing balance will be larger, partly because there has been an additional originating timing difference and partly because the tax rate has increased. The timing difference at the year end will be £480 000 − 260 000 = £220 000, and multiplying that by the latest tax rate of 30% gives a closing balance of £66 000.

Thus, at the end of this year the tax expense will include an increase in deferred tax of £66 000 − 56 000 = £10 000, and the statement of financial position will show a closing balance of £66 000.

The increase can be analysed to show that part was due to the year's originating timing difference of £220 000 − 200 000 = £20 000. Multiplying by 30% to give the tax value gives £6000. The remainder is due to the 2% increase in the tax rate applied to the existing cumulative total of £200 000 to give an additional liability of £200 000 × 2% = £4000.

Deferred Tax Assets

The treatment of deferred tax assets is exactly the same, although deferred tax assets are recognised only if their recovery is regarded as more likely than not.

If a company has both deferred tax assets and liabilities, then the two can be offset against one another provided two conditions are met. These are not particularly onerous and are unlikely to pose problems provided the assets and liabilities relate to taxes levied by the same tax authority on the same entity. This provision in IAS 12 contrasts with that of IAS 1, which normally requires that the offsetting of balances be avoided. Arguably, the asset and liability figures are the result of recognising tax expenses in the correct accounting period, which is the period in which the taxable profits are earned.

Any deferred tax asset will be shown in the statement of financial position as a current asset. The amount will almost certainly have to be shown separately if it is material because readers should not treat this as a liquid asset when analysing the working capital position.

A Comprehensive Example

On 1 January 20X1, S had a credit balance of £1 500 000 on its deferred tax account. This was increased to £1 700 000 at 31 December 20X1.

The company also had an opening debit balance of £4000 on its taxation account after settling the liability for the year ended 31 December 20X0.

S expects to pay £900 000 corporation tax on its profits for the year ended 31 December 20X1.

Organising this information in a logical sequence:

- The current tax charge on this year's profits is £900 000.
- There is a debit balance of £4000, which means that there was an underprovision last year.
- The deferred tax balance has increased by £200 000.

The tax expense note would be:

	£000
Charge for year	900
Underprovision brought forward	4
Increase in provision for deferred tax	200
	1 104

The statement of financial position will show two liabilities for taxation:

Non-current liabilities	
Deferred tax	£1 700 000
Current liabilities	
Tax	£900 000

Presentation Requirements

IAS 12 sets out a variety of detailed requirements for the presentation of tax, both current and deferred. The components of the tax expense that we have listed so far in examples should be shown separately in the tax expense note. Any movements in deferred tax should be broken down to show the extent to which they were caused by originating or reversing timing differences or changes in tax rates altering the liability on existing timing differences.

Tax expenses or income associated with a specific element of the performance figures for the year should be reported separately. These include:

- Tax relating to each separate component of comprehensive income.
- Any current or deferred tax that relates to items that are charged or credited directly to equity (there are examples of these in Chapter 7).
- In respect of discontinued operations, the tax expense relating to:
  (i) the gain or loss on discontinuance;
  (ii) the profit or loss from the ordinary activities of the discontinued operation for the period, together with the corresponding amounts for each prior period presented (see Chapter 7).

Companies are also required to publish a reconciliation of the tax expense and the product of accounting profit multiplied by the applicable tax rate. The purpose of this reconciliation is slightly disturbing in many respects. Some analysts ignore the reported profit figure according to the statement of comprehensive income and divide the tax expense by the tax rate to arrive at the figure for taxable profit. The taxable profit figure is designed to charge tax in a consistent way rather than to support business decisions, but the analysts who use this approach do so because they are reassured by the additional consistency that they find.

For example, the British retailing group Kingfisher reported a profit before tax of £450.5 million in its 2006/07 annual report. Multiplying that figure by the tax rate of 30% gave a tax charge of £135.2 million. That differs from the recognised tax expense of £112.1 million. The company published the following reconciliation of the reasons for this difference:

	£ million
Accounting profit multiplied by the tax rate	135.2
Share of post-tax results of associates and joint ventures	(5.1)
Expenses not (taxable)/deductible for tax purposes	(8.8)

Losses not recognised	0.2
Foreign tax rate differences	2.1
Adjustments in respect of prior years/attributable to change in tax rates	(11.5)
Tax expense	112.1

The point of this reconciliation is that readers can be reassured that Kingfisher's reported profit is credible, if only because it can be reconciled back to the company's profit for tax purposes. If the company's accounting policies were really questionable, then they might have to be adjusted before the calculation of the taxable profit, and that would have been highlighted in the above reconciliation.

The tax expense is calculated in exactly the same way as for the hypothetical companies in this chapter:

	£ million
UK corporation tax	
Current tax on profits for the year	35.7
Adjustment in respect of prior years	(0.3)
	35.4
Double taxation relief	(5.5)
	29.9
Foreign tax	
Current tax on profits for the year	80.7
Adjustments in respect of prior years	(2.3)
	78.4
Deferred tax	
Current year	12.7
Adjustment in respect of prior years	(8.9)
Attributable to changes in tax rates	—
	3.8
Income tax expense	112.1

These disclosures are commonplace in other companies' annual reports. For example, the Danish pharmaceutical group Novo Nordisk provided its shareholders with a detailed narrative explanation of its effective tax rate for its 2007 results:

The effective tax rate for 2007 was 22.3%, a decrease from 29.6% in 2006. The significantly lower effective tax rate for 2007 primarily reflects a non-recurring reduction of around 3 percentage points from Novo Nordisk's divestment of its ownership of Dako's business activities as well as a non-recurring effect of close to 2 percentage points from the re-evaluation of the company's deferred tax liabilities as a consequence of the reduction in the Danish corporation tax rate to 25% introduced in 2007.

The realised effective tax rate for 2007 was in line with the previously communicated expectation of a tax rate of 'around 22%' for the full year of 2007.

The details provided by the group are not so interesting in themselves, but they do provide some comfort that the underlying figures are credible.

Summary

The accounting treatment of tax is generally far less complicated than the underlying tax calculations themselves. The difficult part is generally reaching an agreement with the tax authorities as to an appropriate tax charge for the year.

The story of deferred tax is one of the less appealing illustrations of the effects of lobbying and dissent on the standard-setting process. The accounting treatments adopted changed over time to accommodate the wishes of users for reporting the smallest reasonable tax expense year by year. Changes in the underlying economy affected various factors that affected the tax expense, and the accounting standards varied in line with this.

Tutorial Questions

Question 1

Bring a set of financial statements to class. Highlight the figures in respect of current and deferred tax. Identify the ways in which the statements ensure that the tax implications of the company's business have been disclosed in a clear and relevant manner.

Question 2

G made a profit before tax of £450 000 during the year.

1. Tax on total profits has been estimated at £136 000. A rate of 35% has been assumed.
2. There is a credit balance on G's trial balance of £9000. This represents the difference between the previous year's estimate and the amount actually paid.

Prepare extracts from G's income statement and statement of financial position, and the notes to the accounts, to show how profit for the financial year and the tax liability as at the end of the year would be calculated.

Question 3

The chief accountant of H is in the process of drafting the annual report for the year ended 31 October 20X1. He is currently preparing the note in respect of deferred tax.

The deferred taxation account had a credit balance of £1.5 million at 31 October 20X0. This a net amount comprising a deferred tax asset of £1.2 million in respect of pension costs and a deferred tax liability of £2.7 million in respect of accelerated capital allowances. The company has consistently made taxable profits and fully anticipates the recovery of the deferred tax asset.

During 20X0, the company charged £18.0 million in depreciation and claimed £20.8 million in capital allowances. There was no net change in the position concerning timing differences on pensions.

Assume a corporation tax rate of 30% throughout.

Required:
(a) Explain the purpose of deferred taxation.
(b) Prepare a note in respect of deferred taxation for H. This should be in a form suitable for publication.

Question 4

IJ plc
Trial balance as at 31 December 20X1

	£000	£000
16% Debentures		50
Administrative expenses	16	
Audit fee	2	
Bank overdraft		12

Cash	2	
Corporation Tax		4
Debenture interest paid	4	
Deferred tax		15
Distribution costs	9	
Inventory at start of year	47	
Land and buildings – cost	250	
Land and buildings – depreciation		30
Machinery – cost	30	
Machinery – depreciation		18
Provision for bad debts		1
Purchases	240	
Retained earnings		29
Sales		353
Share capital – ordinary shares of £1		175
Trade payables		26
Trade receivables	30	
Vehicles – cost	15	
Vehicles – depreciation		7
Wages and salaries (manufacturing)	75	
	720	720

1. Inventory was valued at £52 000 on 31 December 20X1.

2. The following accruals have to be taken into account:

   • Wages and salaries   £1000
   • Administrative expenses   £3000

3. Depreciation is to be charged as follows:

   • Land and buildings   2% of cost (manufacturing cost)
   • Machinery   20% of cost (manufacturing cost)
   • Vehicles   20% of cost (distribution expense)

4. The estimated corporation tax charge on the profits for the current year is £18 000.

5. It is IJ's policy to adjust the provision for bad debts to 10% of debtors at the year end.

6. The balance on the corporation tax account represents the amount remaining after settling the balance in respect of the year ended 31 December 20X0.

7. The deferred tax figure should be increased by £4000 because of changes in the tax rate, and by a further £2000 because of originating timing differences.

Required: Prepare a set of financial statements for IJ plc.

Further Work

The answers to these end-of-chapter questions can be found at the back of the book.

Question 1

You have obtained the following information from the records of R:

1. The company made a profit before tax of £300 000 during the year. The tax charge for the year, based on a rate of 35%, has been estimated at £80 000.

2. At the end of the previous year the company estimated that its tax liability would be £70 000. In fact, £76 000 was paid.

Prepare extracts from R's income statement and statement of financial position, and the notes to the accounts, to show how profit after tax and the tax liability as at the end of the year would be calculated.

Question 2

Prepare a statement of comprehensive income, statement of changes in equity, and balance sheet in a form suitable for publication from the following information:

WV
Trial balance as at 31 December 20X1

	£000	£000
Administration costs	200	
Bad debts	22	
Bank		140

Commissions received		490
Deferred taxation		55
Dividends paid	18	
Dividends received		3
Investments (short term)	14	
Manufacturing overheads	370	
Opening stocks – finished goods	320	
Opening stocks – raw materials	185	
Opening stocks – work in progress	205	
Overdraft interest	17	
Plant and machinery – accumulated depreciation		285
Plant and machinery – cost	1 575	
Plant and machinery – disposal		12
Property – accumulated depreciation		220
Property – cost	600	
Provision for doubtful debts		10
Purchases of raw materials	640	
Retained earnings		208
Sales		3 500
Selling and advertising	240	
Share capital		300
Share premium		100
Taxation	7	
Trade payables		160
Trade receivables	290	
Wages – administration	210	
Wages – distribution	170	
Wages – manufacturing	400	
	5 483	5 483

1. Stocks at 31 December 20X1 were valued at:

	£000
Raw materials	260
Work in progress	170
Finished goods	410

2. Plant and machinery is to be depreciated by 20% of cost. Property, which consists largely of the factory, is to be depreciated by 2% of cost.

3. The balance on the disposal account represents the proceeds from the sale of a machine that had cost £30 000 when it was purchased four years ago. No further entries have been made in respect of this transaction. WV charges a full year's depreciation in the year of acquisition and none in the year of disposal.

4. Just before the year end, the company had its property valued at £800 000. The directors have decided to bring this valuation into the balance sheet.

5. The provision for doubtful debts is to be increased by £2000.

6. The balance on the tax account comprises the amount remaining after the settlement of the previous year's assessment.

7. The balance on deferred tax is to be increased by £17 000.

8. Corporation tax of £460 000 is to be provided for the total taxable profit earned during the year.

Question 3

The following information has been extracted from the bookkeeping records of Halflife, a manufacturing company, as at 30 September 20X9.

	£000	£000
Bank	19	
Deferred tax		800
Delivery vehicles – cost	120	
Delivery vehicles – depreciation		78
Disposal		10
Dividend paid	200	
Factory – cost	8 000	
Factory – depreciation		260
Interest	180	
Inventory as at 30 September 20X8	610	
Long-term loan		1 200
Manufacturing equipment – cost	1 800	
Manufacturing equipment – depreciation		540
Purchases of raw materials	6 800	
Retained earnings		974
Sales revenue		15 000
Share capital		1 500
Sundry administration costs	40	
Sundry distribution costs	72	
Sundry manufacturing costs	190	

Tax	7	
Trade payables		720
Trade receivables	1 700	
Trade receivables provision		20
Trade receivables written off	14	
Wages – administration	160	
Wages – manufacturing	980	
Wages – selling and distribution	210	
	21 102	21 102

You have also been provided with the following information:

1. Inventory was counted and valued at £730 000 on 30 September 20X9.

2. On 1 October 20X8 the directors had the factory professionally valued. According to the valuer's report, the factory was worth £12 million as at that date. The directors agreed to incorporate that valuation into the financial statements, but they have not yet done so.

3. During the year, a delivery vehicle that had been purchased in August 20X6 for £30 000 was sold for £10 000. No entries have been made in the books for this disposal, apart from recording the £10 000 received.

4. Depreciation is still to be charged for the year on the following bases:
   • Factory – 2% of cost or valuation
   • Manufacturing equipment – 10% of cost
   • Delivery vehicles – 25% of book value
   A full year's depreciation is charged in the year an asset is acquired or revalued, and none in the year in which it is disposed of.

5. The directors have decided that a further £100 000 of trade receivables should be written off and that the trade receivables provision should then be adjusted to 3% of the outstanding balance.

6. The external auditor's fee for the year has been estimated at £80 000.

7. The balance on the tax account is the result of an underprovision for the year ended 30 September 20X8.

8. The corporation tax charge for the year has been estimated at £150 000.

9. The provision for deferred tax can be reduced to £750 000.

Prepare a statement of comprehensive income and a statement of financial position for Halflife.

REPORTING EARNINGS AND EARNINGS QUALITY

7

Contents

Learning Objectives

After studying this chapter you should be able to:

- discuss the problems associated with reporting and interpreting trends in accounting figures;
- explain the various ways in which the totals in the financial statements can be analysed in order to make them more useful to readers;

Introduction

Accounting information is intended to be useful and helpful to the readers of the accounts. Unfortunately, the directors who are responsible for preparing the accounts are not always keen to report clearly and honestly, either because they wish to make their management of the company seem more impressive than it really is or because they are reluctant to provide their competitors with information that might be used in order to compete against them.

History suggests that accounting regulations must be left with the least possible discretion. Detailed and prescriptive rules might not always lead to the best accounting practices, but at least the resulting figures have a greater uniformity than if the preparers are provided with general guidance and left to interpret that for themselves.

Earnings Per Share and Some Dubious Algebra

A great deal of attention has been paid to the calculation of the earnings per share ratio. Indeed, there is a whole IAS devoted to it (IAS 33 *Earnings per Share*). The actual calculation of this ratio can become very complicated, but those complications do not fall within the scope of this text.[1] Essentially, earnings per share can be calculated as

$$\frac{\text{Earnings attributable to ordinary shareholders}}{\text{Number of ordinary shares in issue}}$$

Think!

How useful is the earnings per share figure?

At first glance, it is debatable whether the earnings per share figure has any relevance whatsoever. The earnings figure is clearly important, but dividing by the number of shares in issue generates a result that is almost a random number because the number of shares in issue has no particular significance of its own. For example,

---

[1] Essentially, the complications arise when the number of shares changes during the period for some reason, or when there are financial instruments in issue that can be converted into shares and that might affect the present shareholders' right.

suppose two identical companies each have earnings of £10 million and issued share capital of £20 million. The only difference is that one has issued 20 million £1 shares and the other has issued 200 million £0.10 shares. The first company will have an earnings per share figure of £20 million/20 million = £1.00 per share, while the second will have a figure of £20 million/200 million = £0.10 per share. They differ by a factor of 10, even though the results are actually identical.

The earnings per share figure is not intended for use on its own. Instead, it is used as the basis of the price/earnings ratio:

$$\frac{\text{Current share price}}{\text{Earnings per share}}$$

The price/earnings (or P/E) ratio expresses the current share price as a multiple of the most recent earnings per share. If the P/E ratio is relatively large, then investors are more willing to pay a larger multiple of earnings. That can mean several things, but the most likely explanations are that:

- The company is viewed as a relatively safe investment, and so shareholders are being asked to pay more for a given annual earning potential.
- Future earnings are expected to grow significantly, and so the past results are too small a denominator in the P/E ratio.

For example, on 6 November 2008, Marks and Spencer had a P/E ratio of 4.49 and Nokia a P/E ratio of 8.90. Clearly, the two businesses are in such different lines of business that their accounting performances are not directly comparable, but on that particular date the stock markets were prepared to value Nokia at a substantially higher multiple of earnings than Marks and Spencer.

How Not to Use Mathematics

There is a tendency among business people to use very simple algebra to rearrange the formula for the P/E ratio:

$$\text{P/E} = \frac{\text{current share price}}{\text{earnings per share}}$$

Multiplying both sides by earnings per share leads to

$$\text{Current share price} = \text{P/E} \times \text{earnings per share}$$

In other words, they believe that increasing the reported earnings per share number will increase the share price.

> **Think!**
>
> Does this analysis make any sense?

The formula used by management is perfectly logical, but it ignores the reality of the relationships.

The current share price can never be the dependent ratio in this equation because that implies that the capital markets would be willing to take the earnings per share at its face value and the P/E ratio as given. In fact, the markets read the financial statements with a view to extracting useful information, but they read the figures in an intelligent way in the knowledge that the figures could easily have been distorted. It is difficult to imagine that the P/E ratio could ever be set or fixed in such a way that it drove share prices, rather than share prices moving and changing the P/E ratio.

The extent to which markets can be misled by accounting information is difficult to determine. Statistical studies would require researchers to be able to identify companies whose financial statements were misleading or distorted to different extents and then to compare their market returns with those whose financial statements were not misleading. There have been many attempts to study the impact of accounting choices on share prices, but these are unlikely to yield categorical findings to the effect that management can or cannot manipulate the share price using the flexibility inherent in accounting. Certainly, a major study based on US data (Francis *et al.*, 2005) found that companies with poor accruals quality[2] tended to have higher cost of capital than firms with good accruals quality.

A Spanish study investigated the intriguing role that graphs in the annual report might play in affecting share prices (Muiño and Trombetta, 2009). The advantage of this approach is that graphs are designed to present and summarise information that is already in the financial statements in some other form. There are a number of well-known techniques that can be used to create a false impression using graphs.

---

[2] Accruals quality is essentially, a measure of the extent to which accruals are affected by intentional and unintentional estimation errors. Large errors equal poor quality.

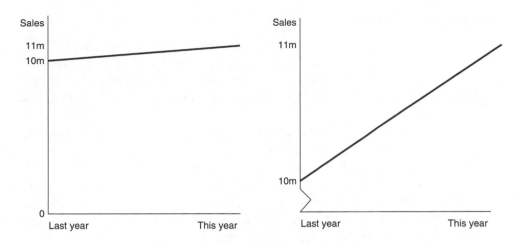

For example, the two graphs shown above are identical except that the one on the left has the sales axis starting at zero and the one on the right has it starting at £10 million. The effect on the eye when comparing the two impressions of trends is quite startling.

There are many other tricks that are generally well known but nevertheless effective. For example, businesses that sell products by volume of liquid have discovered an interesting variation on the traditional histogram:

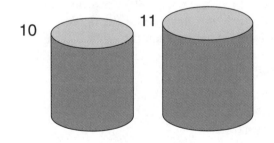

The point is that the can on the right is 10% taller and wider than the can on the left, but the eye is drawn to the volumes of both cans. Volume is related to the square of the radius, so a small increase in the width creates a much larger increase in the volume.

This study uncovered an interesting anomaly. It turns out that the use of distorted graphs has no real impact on the company's cost of capital, apart from the period immediately after the publication of the financial statements. That might imply that the market can be misled slightly in the short term, but it soon settles down.

Some Ancient History

In the late 1980s and early 1990s, a UK company called Polly Peck International discovered a loophole in the accounting rules as they stood at that time. The company raised cash by borrowing at a low rate of interest in strong currencies and used the cash raised to make deposits in weak currencies on which a high rate of interest was paid.

Very simple economics can be used to explain that the differences between interest rates in different currencies are actually an illusion. The total cost of borrowing in a foreign currency includes the movements in the underlying currency. If the currency strengthens, then it will cost the borrower more to repay the loan. This means that banks making loans in strong currencies that are expected to rise have to offer lower rates to attract borrowers because the capital value of the loan will increase along with the currency.

The same arguments work for deposits made in weak currencies that are expected to decline. Banks have to offer high rates of interest to compensate for the expected loss in the value of the sum deposited that will be incurred when the value of the currency falls.

There was no commercial logic for Polly Peck's back-to-back scheme to borrow and then deposit those same funds. The scheme was attractive because the company's managers had noticed that the standards in force at that time permitted the interest received to be treated as income and the interest paid as a finance charge, but the capital losses associated with the increases in the value of the debt and the losses in the value of the deposit went straight to reserves as a deduction from retained earnings. The way in which the figures were stated meant that the income statement looked healthy even though the company was suffering capital losses that were being disclosed elsewhere in the financial statements.

The scheme worked as follows:

- Borrowed £100 in a 'rising' currency at 2%.
- Deposited £100 in a 'falling' currency at 30%.
- Income statement extract:
  Interest received £30
  Finance charge £2
  'Profit' £28
- But:
  - the sum borrowed has now increased to £115 (capital loss = £15);
  - the sum deposited has now fallen to £80 (capital loss = £20);
  - total capital loss = £35, offset against retained earnings and not shown as a cost in the income statement.

Any reasonably informed reader of these financial statements would have seen that the company was worse off as a result of these transactions, but not all readers have sufficient understanding to spot such problems. Furthermore, it is always in the interests of the more informed shareholder quietly to sell the securities to someone who is not quite as well equipped to appreciate that the reported performance is misleading. One of the noticeable lessons from the Polly Peck disaster was that there were no major investment institutions holding shares in the company by the time that it failed.

Some More Ancient History

Once upon a time, accounting standards permitted companies to distinguish 'extraordinary items' from other transactions. For example, IAS 8 *Unusual and Prior Period Items and Changes in Accounting Policies*, issued in 1978 and subsequently revised, defined extraordinary items as ' . . . gains or losses that derive from events or transactions that are distinct from the ordinary activities of the enterprise and therefore not expected to recur frequently or regularly'.

Extraordinary items were accounted for separately from other transactions. Profit or loss was calculated before extraordinary items. The earnings per share ratio was calculated using profit before extraordinary items. The logic behind this was that any event that was defined as extraordinary should probably be ignored in deciding how the entity was performing.

> **Think!**
>
> Could the definition of extraordinary items have been abused? What problems might have arisen?

Unfortunately, many companies decided that the best way to enhance their reported earnings per share figure was to classify as many expenses as possible as extraordinary. Not surprisingly, very few companies treated revenues as extraordinary. The effect of this was to undermine the credibility of financial statements because it soon became apparent that earnings per share had to be restated in order to incorporate the effects of the overstatement due to 'extraordinary' items that were anything but extraordinary in nature.

IAS 1 and Some Solutions

IAS 1 *Presentation of Financial Statements* has a few things to say about ensuring the quality of the information relating to earnings.

All items of income and expense are to be recognised in the profit or the loss for the period unless a specific requirement of an IFRS requires them to be taken to equity. There are very few cases where profits or losses can be recognised outside the income statement or statement of comprehensive income.

IAS 1 also expressly forbids the treatment of any items of income or expense as extraordinary, whether in the statement of comprehensive income or in the notes to the financial statements.

Think!

Are these requirements of IAS 1 overreactions? Do they undermine the credibility of the standard-setting process?

It might be argued that IAS 1 is making accounting inflexible in its treatment of these specific issues. There may well be occasions when it would be reasonable to adjust equity rather than taking an adjustment to the statement of comprehensive income, or to treat a cost or revenue as extraordinary.

The problem is that history has shown that any freedom or flexibility in standards is open to abuse if it has the potential to increase reported earnings. Even if this abuse is visible and easily corrected by readers, it is difficult to justify the publication of financial statements that have to be restated before they can be used properly.

Clearly, there will be very rare occasions when transactions should be highlighted in the notes to the accounts as being out of place in the calculation of profit for the year without some separate consideration. In those cases, the directors will have to leave it to the readers to decide whether or not to compensate for that when they base any decisions on the reported profit figure.

IAS 1 does require the separate disclosure of items of income or expense that are material. An item is material if knowledge of it would affect a decision taken by the users of the financial statements. This goes some way towards dealing with the problems created by the unusual circumstances described above. If, for example, a company suffered a massive loss because of the closure of a factory, then that loss could be highlighted as a separate item on the face of the statement of comprehensive income or in the notes to the financial statements. It would still be included in the calculation of profit and of EPS, but readers could decide for themselves whether to set that event aside in reaching a conclusion on the company's performance.

For example, the 2007 annual report of the Greencore Group, an Irish food manufacturer, had three separate columns in its income statement for the year ended 28 September 2007. The first column showed figures before exceptional items, the second the exceptional items themselves, and the third the total. Total operating profit from continuing activities for the year, after allowing for cost of sales and other operating costs but not finance income and costs, came to €91.041 million. The group sustained an exceptional cost of €5.923 million when it terminated some leases on property that had become surplus to requirements and it had to pay a penalty to the lessors. This left a total operating profit of €85.118 million. Earnings per share were calculated on the total column, with no adjustment for this unusual charge, but readers can decide for themselves how to interpret the company's overall performance.

IAS 8 and Some Further Clarifications

IAS 8 *Accounting Policies, Changes in Accounting Estimates and Errors* deals with some specific issues and expands upon some of the ideas that we have seen in IAS 1.

Accounting Policies

IAS 8 provides some general guidance that is intended to 'fill in the gaps' if a policy needs to be developed in the absence of a specific accounting standard.

Firstly, the broad concepts of relevance and reliability should be adopted as selection criteria:

Relevant	Reliable
• Supports decision-making	• Represents faithfully • Reflects economic substance • Neutral/free from bias • Prudent • Complete in all material respects

If it is not possible to determine the most appropriate accounting policy from this guidance, then the next step would be to consider whether it is possible to identify a suitable treatment by referring to an accounting standard that deals with a parallel or broadly similar problem.

If there is no inspiration to be had from reviewing accounting standards, then the preparer is advised to refer to the Framework for the Preparation of Financial Statements.

Finally, the preparer can look to the following:

Other standard-setting bodies that use a similar conceptual framework to the IASB in developing accounting standards	Other accounting literature	Accepted industry practices
. . . but only to the extent that this does not lead to a policy that conflicts with the principles of the IFRS or the Framework		

Think!

Why does the IASB need to have a standard dealing with matters that are not the subject of an IFRS?

It may seem slightly superfluous to have a standard that deals with topics that are not deemed important enough to be the subject of an IFRS. One justification for providing this detailed hierarchy of steps to be taken when dealing with gaps in the rules is the threat of creative accounting. Accounting regulators are always nervous of the realisation that a particular matter is not the subject of an accounting standard and that it will lead to a public scandal when companies abuse the loophole in the rules. At least IAS 8 requires that the principles that are already established in the existing standards must be followed in these circumstances.

Changes in Accounting Policies

IAS 8 requires consistency from one year to the next, so changes are only permitted when an IFRS is introduced that requires a change or in situations where it is felt that a change is necessary in order to provide more relevant or more reliable information.

Changes in accounting policy are, in fact, very rare. They should not be confused with corrections or revisions to accounting estimates. If, for example, a company decides that switching from straight-line depreciation to reducing balance would improve the quality of its accounting information, it is unlikely that this would be seen as a change in accounting policy in terms of IAS 8.

If a change in accounting policy is brought about by an IFRS, then there may be some transitional arrangements in the new standard. These will give clear guidance as to how any changes should be reflected in the financial statements.

If there are no specific transitional arrangements or the change has not been prompted by a new IFRS, then IAS 8 requires that it should be applied retrospectively, which means that:

- comparative figures should be restated and
- opening balances should be restated for cumulative effect

unless it is impracticable to determine either the period-specific effects or the cumulative effect of the change.

For example, suppose that a change in accounting policy would have reduced the opening balance on property, plant, and equipment by £10 million if the new policy had been applied from the very start, and suppose that last year's depreciation charge would have been £1 million higher. Under IAS 8, the opening balances on property, plant, and equipment and retained earnings would both be restated by reducing them by £10 million, and the comparative figures for depreciation would be increased by £1 million.

Think!

What is the logic of applying changes in accounting policies retrospectively?

A retrospective change has the effect of removing the effects of switching policies from the reported earnings for the year. Taking them straight to the balance sheet enables users to see the performance for the year on the basis of the revised accounting policies. These figures can also be measured against the comparatives in a consistent and meaningful way.

Change in Accounting Estimates

Financial statements are full of estimates. For example, the statement of financial position shows trade receivables at the estimated value of the amount that customers are likely to pay.

It is inevitable that many of the assumptions used to prepare financial statements will change whenever new information comes to light. When there is a change in an estimate, then it will be recognised in the calculation of profit in the period in which the change occurs. If the change relates to future periods, then it will be recognised in the period affected by the change.

The carrying value of any asset or liability in the statement of financial position may also have to be adjusted for the revised estimate.

The nature and amount of any change must be disclosed.

Correcting Errors

When it is discovered that previously published financial statements contained material errors, the errors should be corrected by restating the figures retrospectively.

For example, in its 2006 financial statements, Nokia recognised prior-period errors with respect to warranty and other provisions and the effect that these had on deferred tax. This correction had the effect of increasing prior-year deferred tax assets and retained earnings by €154 million, representing a 1.2% increase in net assets.

Discontinued Activities

IFRS 5 *Non-current Assets Held for Sale and Discontinued Operations* deals with the distinction between continuing and discontinued operations.

> **Think!**
>
> Why might it be useful to distinguish between continuing and discontinued operations when reporting profits or losses?

The first reason for highlighting the effects of discontinued operations is that users will have a better appreciation of the performance of the ongoing elements of the business. That should provide a more relevant basis for predicting future profitability.

Shareholders might also wish to have some explanation for the closure of a part of their business. It would be reassuring to know that it was closed for a sound business reason, such as the fact that it had been making losses or that it was sold for an attractive price.

Finally, the closure of a part of a business is likely to involve significant costs associated with making employees redundant and the costs of managing the process of closure, such as legal and consulting fees and gains and losses on the disposal of assets.

IFRS 5 defines a discontinued operation as a component of an entity that either has been disposed of or is classified as held for sale. This means that, if the operation has not been disposed of yet, then management must anticipate selling it in the near future. That would normally mean that its disposal is regarded as 'highly probable' and that the whole process of seeking a buyer is under way and is likely to lead to a closure within a year.

The definition also defines a discontinued operation as a separate major line of business or geographical area of operations. There are other aspects of this definition, but we need not go into those for the purpose of this chapter. To qualify as a 'component of the entity', the part of the business must be capable of being clearly distinguished from the rest of the entity, both in terms of operations and cash flows.

Once the discontinued operations have been identified, the next step is to disclose the results in the statement of comprehensive income. These should be stated as a single amount in the statement of comprehensive income comprising the total of:

- the post-tax profit or loss of discontinued operations;
- the post-tax gain or loss recognised on the measurement to fair value less costs to sell or on the disposal of the assets constituting the discontinued operation.

This total should be analysed to show:

- the revenue, expenses, and pre-tax profit or loss of discontinued operations;
- the related income tax expense;
- the gain or loss recognised on the measurement to fair value less costs to sell or on the disposal of the assets constituting the discontinued operation;
- the related income tax expense.

For example, CSM is a Netherlands-based multinational company engaged in manufacturing cakes and other goods. According to the company's 2007 annual report, the company made a profit of €56.1 million from continuing operations. During the year, the company discontinued the operations of CSM Sugar. This part of the business generated a profit after tax of €3.9 million during the year before the final closure, and the disposal itself generated a profit after tax of €142.8 million. A note to the financial statements shows the sales and various costs incurred in this operation, combining to leave an operating profit of €5.3 million, less tax of €1.4 million to leave the €3.9 million operating profit.

This information is presented in the following manner (note, this is a simplified version of CSM's financial statements):

	€m
Continuing operations	
Revenues	2485.6
Cost of sales	(2061.8)
Gross profit	423.8
Operating expenses	(364.0)
Operating profit	59.8
Financial income	12.1
Financial charges	(31.7)
Profit before tax from continuing operations	40.2
Tax[3]	15.9
Profit after tax from continuing operations	56.1
Discontinued operations	
Result after taxes CSM Sugar (note 1)	3.9
Gain on disposal after taxes	142.8
Result after tax from discontinued operations	146.7
Profit after tax	202.8

Note 1 – Discontinued operation
Discontinued operations for 2007 comprise the result of CSM Sugar up to and including April 2007 and the result from the sale of CSM Sugar as at 24 April 2007.

	(4 months) €m
Revenues	58.2
Cost of sales	(46.8)
Gross profit	11.4
Operating expenses	(6.1)
Operating profit	5.3
Tax	(1.4)
Result after tax CSM Sugar	3.9
Gross gain on disposal	142.8
Tax on gain	—
Gain on disposal after tax	142.8

[3] CSM was in the happy position of having a credit on its taxes rather than a charge.

IAS 33 *Earnings per Share* requires that EPS should be calculated both before and after allowing for the effects of discontinued operations. CSM's EPS based on continuing operations only is €0.82, and including discontinued operations it is €3.06. Thus, shareholders not only have a clear understanding of the impact of the disposal on the company's performance for the year but also have an indication of the likely ongoing returns that can be offered from continuing operations.

Segmental Reporting

Once you have come to terms with the terminology in real sets of financial statements, the biggest source of frustration that you are likely to encounter is the fact that most large businesses are quite complicated, with interests in more than one business and, frequently, overseas operations.

For example, Björn Borg AB is listed on the OMX Nordic Exchange. The company has operations in five product areas: clothing, footwear, bags, eyewear, and fragrances. These products are sold in 14 markets, the largest of which are the Netherlands and Sweden.

It is perfectly possible to take an overview of the business from its financial statements. For example, the company had a profit before tax and interest of SEK (Swedish kronor) 149 478 000 for the year ended 31 December 2007 and capital employed of SEK 424 065 000, which equates to a very healthy return on capital employed of 35%. This compares with a return of SEK 84 166 000 and capital employed of SEK 250 660 000, or a return on capital employed of 34% in the previous year.

These figures raise a number of questions. The company has expanded rapidly during the year, but where has that expansion occurred? Which of the product areas is expanding and which, if any, are in decline? Where has the growth occurred in terms of the geographical spread of the company? The other issue is in terms of comparing the company with competitors. It is highly unlikely that any other company sells precisely the same mix of products and operates in exactly the same countries. Thus, any comparison between our company and similar businesses could prove highly misleading.

The solution is to be found in the segmental information provided in the notes to the financial statements. IFRS 8 *Operating Segments* requires the analysis of some of the key figures in the financial statements to enable users to evaluate the nature and financial effects of its business activities and the economic environments in which it operates.

This standard raises a number of problems that highlight one of the major dilemmas facing accounting standard-setters.

> **Think!**
>
> Why might company directors be reluctant to provide a detailed and meaningful analysis of the company's operations?

One of the biggest problems with this standard is that analysing results by geographical or business segment can provide competitors with extremely useful information. Revealing that one particular product line or market is extremely profitable simply invites greater competition in the very area that the company wishes to protect.

> **Think!**
>
> Why would the shareholders wish their company to publish information that could be used to undermine its business interests?

Shareholders would not wish to attract competitors or to make it more difficult for their company to earn profits. At the same time, the shareholders also need to know how the business operates in order to monitor management's stewardship of their investment. They also need to have sufficient understanding of the company's performance in order to make informed decisions about the risks that they are taking.

The IFRS reduces the threat somewhat by restricting itself to companies whose securities are traded on the open market or who are in the process of seeking a listing that would permit them to trade. That does not reduce the threat to those companies that are required to publish segmental information, but it does have the effect of protecting small companies whose securities are not listed in any way and also those whose securities are not traded and who are, by implication, held by a restricted group of shareholders who can probably obtain information without relying on the annual report.

IFRS 8 came into effect for accounting periods beginning on or after 1 January 2009, so it is a relatively new standard. It brings IFRS requirements into line with the US standards that have been in force for some time, so it is possible to get some indication of its effects.

Ford's 2007 annual report devotes two notes to segmental information. The first is headed 'segment information' and analyses both revenue and profit before tax, broken down into the following main categories:

- Ford North America;
- Ford South America;
- Ford Europe;
- (Ford) Premier Automotive Group – dealing with certain 'prestigious' brands;
- Financial services.

This analysis is supplemented by a second note headed 'geographic information', which shows both sales revenue and property, plant, and equipment analysed between:

- North America, split between
  - United States
  - Canada
  - Mexico;
- Europe, split between
  - United Kingdom
  - Germany
  - Sweden
  - other Europe;
- All other.

This segmental information is fairly typical of the analysis published by most companies. Ford is a major multinational company with a range of interests and a turnover in excess of $170 billion. In spite of this, the only breakdown by industrial segment is between automotive and financial services. There is no breakdown of the automotive segment to show how much came from cars as opposed to commercial vehicles. This should not be viewed as a particular criticism of Ford, but is merely an observation about the typical limitations of the segmental information published by companies in general.

In an ideal world, companies would publish a matrix showing their results broken down both by industry and by geographical area:

	Industry A	Industry B	Total
Area 1			
Area 2			
Total			

That would give readers a much clearer understanding of the risks that the company faced and would provide a much stronger basis for comparing different businesses.

Identifying Segments

The most difficult aspect of regulating segmental reporting is the definition of segments in such a way that companies disclose useful information regardless of the reluctance of the directors to assist their competitors. There is a story, which is probably apocryphal, of a company that analysed its performance between revenues and profits earned in the Eastern and Western hemispheres (which is arguably the least useful basis for analysis – look at a map).

The IFRS defines segments in both qualitative and quantitative terms. This makes it far more difficult to comply with the formal letter of the rules without also meeting the spirit.

In qualitative terms, an operating segment is engaged in business activities from which revenues are earned and expenses incurred and for which discrete financial information is available. The crucial factor is that an operating segment's operating results are regularly reviewed by the entity's senior management to make decisions about how resources are to be allocated to the segment and also to assess its performance.

Returning to our example of Björn Borg AB, if senior management require information about the revenues and expenses associated with trading in the Netherlands, then that is probably a segment in its own right.

The qualitative aspect of the definition is complemented by a quantitative criterion. Companies must report separately information about any operating segment that meets *any* of the following quantitative thresholds (*source: IFRS 8*):

(a) Its reported revenue, including both sales to external customers and intersegment sales or transfers, is 10 per cent or more of the combined revenue, internal and external, of all operating segments.
(b) The absolute amount of its reported profit or loss is 10 per cent or more of the greater, in absolute amount, of (i) the combined reported profit of all operating segments that did not report a loss and (ii) the combined reported loss of all operating segments that reported a loss.
(c) Its assets are 10 per cent or more of the combined assets of all operating segments.

Clearly, this could require the publication of extremely detailed reports. It is quite possible that senior management reviews some very detailed analyses. IFRS 8 permits the aggregation of operating segments, provided the segments have similar economic characteristics. The IFRS lists attributes that must be considered, such as the nature of the products and the manner in which they are manufactured.

Segmental Disclosures

Firstly, IFRS 8 requires disclosure of the factors that were used to identify the entity's reportable segments. For example, the analysis could be by line of industry or by geographical areas. The company should also state the type of products and services from which each reportable segment derives its revenues.

A measure of profit or loss and total assets should be reported for each segment, and a measure of liabilities if that information is normally provided for managers. These totals should be reconciled to the totals according to the statement of comprehensive income and the statement of financial position, as appropriate. In addition, a variety of detailed disclosures should be made for each segment, including:

- revenues from external customers;
- revenues from transactions with other operating segments of the same entity;
- interest expense;
- interest revenue;
- depreciation and amortisation;
- any material items of income or expense disclosed separately in response to IAS, as discussed above;
- income tax expense or income;
- material non-cash items other than depreciation and amortisation.

Summary

There are several requirements in place to ensure that readers of financial statements are adequately informed about factors that should enable them to appreciate and understand the company's performance. These are largely about ensuring that factors that might distort the results are adequately disclosed. There is also a requirement to break the ongoing results down into individual segments.

The background to these requirements is a belief that the manner in which information is reported can have an effect on the reader's reaction to it. Thus, a distortion of the earnings per share figure might be motivated by the belief that overstating EPS will enhance the share price, even though the distortion may be very obvious and visible.

The rules are not just designed to prevent distortion. The IASB also wishes companies to provide readers with useful information so that they can fully understand the risks and returns associated with the business. This creates a dilemma for preparers because there are commercial costs to publishing a suitably detailed analysis.

Tutorial Questions

Question 1

Bring a set of financial statements to class. Analyse the notes and be prepared to discuss the usefulness of the segmental information in the notes to the accounts. Is there sufficient information to make a meaningful comparison of the company's performance with that of its closest competitors?

Question 2

Discuss the proposition that it should not matter if the financial statements are distorted in a manner that is disclosed clearly in the notes to the accounts so that it can be corrected by readers.

Question 3

Transglobe Retail and Leisure plc are planning the implementation of IFRS 8 *Operating Segments*. The company operates chains of stores, including a major chain of clothing shops and a major chain of music shops. Some of the company's retail interests are wholly UK based, but others operate in several countries and the company also has a small number of chains in Germany and Scandinavia. Furthermore, the company owns two separate hotel chains, one of which offers low-cost accommodation through 70 hotels in the United Kingdom, Ireland, and France, and the other of which offers high-class tourist accommodation in many popular tourist resorts.

The directors are concerned that providing segmental information to the shareholders will provide competitors with too much information. The production director has suggested that the board should stop using detailed analyses of performance across the different business sectors so that the company could reduce the information that had to be released in this way.

(a) Discuss the conflict between informing shareholders and withholding information from competitors, and explain which consideration ought to have priority.
(b) Discuss the options open to Transglobe plc with regard to the publication of segmental information.
(c) Explain why IFRS 8 has related the identification of reportable segments to the information used by management.

Question 4

D plc has been involved in two lines of business: the operation of a chain of retail pharmacies and the manufacture and sale of medicines. The following summarised trial balance has been extracted from the books of D plc:

D plc: trial balance at 31 March 20X1

	£000	£000
Retail sales		12 000
Cost of retail sales	4 930	
Medicine sales		1 600
Cost of medicine sales	880	
Administration expenses	1 900	
Distribution costs	1 600	
Closure costs	920	
Taxation	100	
Dividends	1 700	
Property, plant, and equipment – cost	7 700	
Property, plant, and equipment – depreciation		1 600
Inventory at 31 March 20X1	411	
Trade receivables	240	
Bank	27	
Trade payables		310
Deferred tax		600
Share capital		4 000
Retained profits		298
	20 408	20 408

 (i) The company closed down its medicine factory during the year. This involved expenses totalling £920 000. The costs of administration and distribution relate to retail sales.
 (ii) The balance on the taxation account comprises the amount left after the final settlement of the corporation tax liability for the year ended 31 March 20X0.
(iii) The company expects to receive tax relief of £240 000 on the costs incurred in closing the medicine factory. Corporation tax on the operating profits for the year has been estimated at £1 020 000, split 80:20 between continuing and discontinued operations.
(iv) The provision for deferred taxation is to be increased by £90 000.

Prepare a statement of comprehensive income and statement of financial position for D plc. These should be in a form suitable for publication (in so far as is possible given the information provided).

Further Work

The answers to these end-of-chapter questions can be found at the back of the book.

Question 1

Remake plc manufactures spare parts for popular makes of motor cars. During the year, it closed down a chain of service centres that had carried out basic repairs and servicing for retail customers. Remake plc's year-end trial balance is as follows:

Trial balance at 31 December 20X7

	£000	£000
Service centre sales		9 000
Cost of service centre sales	3 000	
Spare part sales		14 300
Cost of spare part sales	7 500	
Administration expenses – service centre	900	
Administration expenses – spare parts	2 000	
Distribution costs – service centre	600	
Distribution costs – spare parts	2 200	
Redundancies and reorganisation costs	2 700	
Tax		300
Dividends paid during year	3 000	
Property, plant, and equipment – cost	15 000	
Property, plant, and equipment – depreciation		4 200
Inventory at 31 December 20X7	800	
Trade receivables	900	
Bank	42	
Trade payables		310
Deferred tax		1 400
Share capital		5 000
Revaluation reserve		3 000
Retained profits		1 132
	38 642	38 642

- The redundancies and reorganisation costs can be split between the service centres and spare parts manufacturing as follows:
  - redundancies and costs directly attributable to closing service centres = £2 million, before allowing for £600 000 of tax relief;
  - redundancies and other costs associated with scaling back production of spare parts = £0.7 million.
- The balance on the taxation account comprises the amount left after the final settlement of the corporation tax liability for the year ended 31 December 20X6. The directors have estimated the tax charge on this year's trading profits at £2.4 million, split £1.6 million to the spare parts business and £0.8 million to the service centres.
- The provision for deferred taxation is to be increased to £1.6 million.
- The figures for property, plant, and equipment include some land and buildings that were valued at £7 million in 20X4 and have since been depreciated by £450 000.
- The directors had this property revalued at 31 December 20X7, and the independent valuer who conducted this exercise valued the property at £9 million. No adjustments have been made in respect of this, but the directors wish the revaluation to be reflected in the financial statements.

Prepare a statement of comprehensive income, a statement of changes in equity, and a statement of financial position. These should be in a form suitable for publication and should be accompanied with notes (in so far as is possible given the information provided).

Hint:
- Watch out for the total tax liability.

Question 2

C plc is a large manufacturing company. The company's latest trial balance at 31 December 20X3 is as follows:

C plc
Trial balance at 31 December 20X3

	£m	£m
Administrative expenses	20	
Bank	6	
Cost of sales	120	
Creditors		11
Debtors	36	

Deferred tax		12
Distribution costs	20	
Dividend paid	50	
Finance charges on leases	4	
Finance leases		25
Interest	21	
Loans (repayable 20X9)		230
Property, plant, and equipment	822	
Retained earnings		26
Sales		434
Share capital (£1 shares – fully paid)		217
Share premium		162
Stock as at 31 December 20X3	15	
Tax	3	
	1 117	1 117

(i) All of C plc's production activities take place in the United Kingdom. Its sales are, however, worldwide. Sales and profits can be analysed as follows:

United Kingdom	45%
Republic of Arteria	35%
Southland	12%
Rest of the world	8%

C plc is subject to the disclosure requirements of IFRS 8.

(ii) The deferred tax balance consists entirely of the differences arising between the book value and tax written down value of tangible fixed assets. The tax written down value of C plc's property, plant, and equipment was £762 million at 31 December 20X3. The closing balance on deferred tax should be adjusted to take account of this, assuming that tax will be paid at a rate of 30% when the difference reverses. The balance on the taxation account represents the balance remaining after settling the tax charge for the year ended 31 December 20X2. The directors have estimated the tax charge for the year ended 31 December 20X3 at £32 million.

Prepare C plc's statement of comprehensive income for the year ended 31 December 20X3 and its statement of financial position as at that date.

References

Francis, J., *et al.* (2005), The market pricing of accruals quality. *Journal of Accounting and Economics*, **39**, 295–327.

Muiño, F. and Trombetta, M. (2009), Does graph disclosure bias reduce the cost of equity capital? *Accounting and Business Research*, **39**(2), 83–102.

Property, Plant, and Equipment

Contents

Learning Objectives

After studying this chapter you should be able to:

- explain how property, plant, and equipment should be recognised;
- explain the depreciation of property, plant, and equipment;
- discuss the impairment of property, plant, and equipment;
- explain the accounting treatment of investment properties.

Introduction

This chapter deals with property, plant, and equipment. You might be forgiven for thinking that this is a straightforward topic that should be familiar from the earliest stages of your studies. To an extent that is true, although there have been substantial problems concerning tangible assets to be overcome in arriving at the present set of regulations. This has led to some rather complicated rules.

Again, the rules have been heavily influenced by history. Almost every gap in earlier rules has been exploited in order to enhance the figures.

The Nature of Tangibles

Property, plant, and equipment are tangible assets that have a physical presence. That suggests that they are likely to have a limited useful life (even buildings will deteriorate to the point where they have to be demolished). The recognition requirements associated with tangible assets means that almost all businesses will have some in their statements of financial position. This has been a complicated and heavily contested area of accounting over the years.

> **Think!**
>
> What might be the problems associated with accounting for property, plant, and equipment?

For example, consider a business that has just moved into a new corporate headquarters. In theory, that should be a simple addition to non-current assets, but the following problems have cropped up in the past:

Construction work finished last year, but the building was not occupied until the start of this year.	When should the cost of the building have been recognised in the financial statements? *When the building work was completed? When it was first occupied? When the first (or last) payment was made to the contractor?*

The business has financed the construction of the building by means of a bank loan, most of which was drawn five years ago in order to pay the contractor's costs. The loan will continue for a further fifteen years before it is due to be paid off.	How should the interest associated with the building be treated? *Should any or all of the cost be capitalised as part of the cost of the building?*
The building uses an innovative new construction system and has been constructed around the wiring and infrastructure of the company's IT system.	What depreciation policy should be adopted? *Should the building be depreciated at all (buildings tend to appreciate in value)? Should we estimate the physical life expectancy of the building? What about the risk of obsolescence?*
The value of property tends to rise over time.	What about future years? *Should the building be valued at cost less depreciation for the remainder of its life or should it be revalued from time to time?*

We will deal with these issues over the rest of this chapter. The primary source of regulation that we will look at is IAS 16 *Property, Plant, and Equipment*.

Recognition

IAS 16 defines 'property, plant, and equipment' (a phrase that might be used interchangeably with tangible non-current assets) as:

tangible items that:

(a) are held for use in the production or supply of goods or services, for rental to others, or for administrative purposes; and
(b) are expected to be used during more than one period.

Before an item can be recognised as an asset at all, it must be controlled by the entity and it must be expected to yield future economic benefits.

The definition in IAS 16 indicates that a tangible non-current asset is one that will be used in the business and is expected to be used for more than one accounting period. This might be contrasted with a current asset, which is likely to be either cash or converted into cash in the normal course of business.

Additions to property, plant, and equipment are recorded, at least initially, at their cost. Cost is recognised as an asset if and only if:

- it is probable that future economic benefits associated with the item will flow to the entity; and
- the cost of the item can be measured reliably.

Even that can be complicated. For example, an airline might purchase spare engines at the same time as buying a new aircraft. The aircraft itself is undoubtedly a non-current asset, but the treatment of the spare engines is less clear cut. There are valid arguments for either capitalising them and depreciating their cost over their expected useful lives (which might differ from that of the aircraft itself) or for treating them as an inventory of spare parts and bringing their cost into the income statement as and when they are fitted to the aircraft.

IAS 16 and Initial Recognition

IAS 16 indicates that the cost of an item of property, plant, and equipment might include more than the basic purchase price. *Major* spare parts and stand-by equipment qualify as part of the cost of the asset when the entity expects to use them during more than one period. That would cover the cost of the spare aero engines in our example.

The economic benefit criterion can be applied to items acquired for safety or environmental reasons. Even though the construction of, say, a waste filtration system might not generate any additional revenue on its own, the company can capitalise the expenditure on the grounds that it might not be possible to use other non-current assets without protecting the environment in this way.

The initial recognition should be at cost, where cost comprises:

- the purchase price of the asset, including any taxes and after deducting any trade discounts and rebates;
- any costs directly attributable to bringing the asset to the location and condition necessary for it to be capable of operating in the manner intended by management (e.g. any installation costs);
- the initial estimate of the costs associated with any obligation to dismantle and remove the item and restore the site on which it is located. These costs are accounted for in IAS 37 *Provisions, Contingent Liabilities, and Contingent Assets*, which is discussed in Chapter 11.

The need to deal with the removal of assets can create some significant balances. For example, the 2008 annual report of Lukoil, Russia's largest oil company, had a liability totalling $728 million in respect of the costs of dismantling and removing assets. The following analysis was provided to show how that balance had moved during the year:

	$m
Asset retirement obligations as of January 1	821
Accretion expense	78
New obligations	54
Changes in estimates of existing obligations	(88)
Spending on existing obligations	(8)
Property dispositions	(3)
Foreign currency translation and other adjustments	(126)
Asset retirement obligations as of December 31	728

Borrowing Costs

The accounting treatment of borrowing costs associated with the acquisition of non-current assets, particularly buildings, has been such a contentious matter that there is an IAS dedicated to the topic.

Arguably, there are three possible treatments of the cost of interest associated with buying a property:

- write off all of the interest as an expense as and when it is incurred;
- capitalise all of the interest incurred on financing the acquisition of the property; or
- capitalise interest during the early stages of acquisition, perhaps during the construction phase, but write off all subsequent borrowing costs as they are incurred.

Think!

Think about the merits of each of the above treatments, paying particular attention to the recognition criteria for property, plant, and equipment.

Arguably, the entity must anticipate future economic benefits from acquiring the property, and the fact that it is paying interest over and above the basic cost of the asset is evidence that it is confident of doing so. Furthermore, the interest paid on a loan associated with acquiring a property should be relatively easy to calculate objectively. On that basis, it would be reasonable to capitalise interest as part of the cost of the property.

The argument against capitalising all interest is that doing so will lead to inconsistencies in the treatment of the costs of financing property. The cash required to purchase a property might be drawn from the company's cash reserves, and so it might not be possible to link the financing costs to a particular financial instrument.[1] The opposite possibility also arises that a company will take out a loan specifically secured against a building but in order to finance a completely unrelated transaction. It is, therefore, difficult to determine the costs associated with financing a specific asset.

A compromise might enable a realistic assessment of the total cost of the property. Capitalising some finance costs, but not all, offers a partial remedy to this dilemma.

IAS 23 *Borrowing Costs* offers a compromise treatment of the cost of financing the acquisition of property.

The core principle is that 'borrowing costs that are directly attributable to the acquisition, construction, or production of a *qualifying asset* form part of the cost of that asset. Other borrowing costs are recognised as an expense'.

IAS 23 defines a qualifying asset as 'an asset that necessarily takes a substantial period of time to get ready for its intended use or sale'. In principle, this could include assets other than property, plant, and equipment.

Capitalisation of finance costs commences when all three of the following criteria are satisfied:

- expenditures for the asset are being incurred;
- borrowing costs are being incurred; and
- activities that are necessary to prepare the asset for its intended use or sale are in progress.

Capitalisation is suspended for any extended periods during which the asset is not being actively developed.

Capitalisation ceases when the asset itself is complete or ready for sale. To reduce the risk of obvious loopholes in this rule, if any minor tasks are left

---

[1] Remember that assets = capital + liabilities. When you come to study finance, you will see that measuring the cost of equity is a complicated calculation that requires a number of assumptions.

outstanding so that the asset is substantially complete, then the capitalisation of finance charges would stop.

If the nature of the asset means that parts can be used while the remainder is complete (the IAS gives the example of a business park that is being constructed in phases), then capitalisation of finance charges ceases on those parts for which work is completed.

The calculation of finance charges depends on how the acquisition was financed. If a loan was taken out in order to finance this purchase, then the actual borrowing costs incurred should be used. If there is no direct loan between the property and the finance, then the weighted average of the entity's borrowing costs should be used to estimate the cost of the funding used.

The financial statements have to disclose both the amount of the borrowing costs that have been capitalised and the capitalisation rate.

IAS 16 and Subsequent Costs

The accounting treatment of subsequent costs is a complicated area in practice, not least because management's preferred treatment might be motivated by a desire to make the results look better.

Think!

How could the accounting treatment of cash spent on an asset affect the reported figures?

If expenditure is capitalised as part of the cost of an asset, then reported profit will be higher in the short term and the book value of property, plant, and equipment will be increased. Depreciation will be increased in subsequent years because the cost will have to be written off over its useful life. If the cost is written off as an expense, then there will be an immediate charge to the income statement.

If material amounts have been spent, then management might be tempted to bias their choice of accounting treatment towards that which gives their preferred effect on the statements. If the profit is likely to be disappointing, then costs will be capitalised and reported profit will be greater for the present year. If the profit is likely to be high, then additions to assets might be written off as repairs or renewals. That will push the present year's profit down to a level that is easier to maintain in future years, and long-term depreciation will also be reduced.

IAS 16 requires that the cost of day-to-day servicing should be written off as an expense. Larger items require a little more consideration.

The cost of larger items can be capitalised if it meets the same recognition criteria of future economic benefits and reliable measurement. The standard does not provide a clear-cut distinction between costs that must be written off as routine servicing and maintenance and those that might be capitalised. There is an implication that they should be fairly substantial and should not be incurred on a very frequent basis. For example, a furnace might have to be taken out of service every few years and the brick lining dismantled and rebuilt with new bricks. The cost of this could, potentially, be treated as a separate cost. Indeed, the entity might even have a separate carrying value for the lining and treat any remaining book value of the old bricks as a disposal before adding the cost of the replacement lining to property, plant, and equipment.

Depreciation

You should remember the accounting treatment of depreciation from your earlier studies. This section will discuss the rules in a little more detail.

Some Ancient History

The accounting treatment of depreciation is a very good example of an important accounting issue where companies have adopted potentially confusing accounting policies. The most significant area of concern has been the depreciation of buildings:

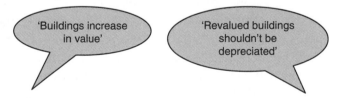

It has been difficult to set accounting standards that ensure that all buildings are depreciated. There have been arguments to the effect that the market values of buildings tend to rise, which counters the need to depreciate them. This led to a specific requirement that all non-current assets that have a finite useful life (effectively everything except land) must be depreciated.

Companies were able to find loopholes even once the rules had been clarified. One notable case created a whole new concept – 'split depreciation'. In the 1980s a major UK retailer split its depreciation charge. The company had a large property portfolio that had been revalued many times. The company split its depreciation charge into two parts as follows:

- Depreciation charged on the original cost of the property was treated as an expense in the income statement, as normal.
- Depreciation charged on the value arising from the revaluation was charged against the revaluation reserve, with no charge to the income statement.

Split depreciation had the effect of increasing reported profit and earnings per share. This one event led to the revision of the accounting standard in force in the UK in order to ensure that all depreciation was charged to the income statement.

What is Depreciation?

IAS 16 defines depreciation clearly and succinctly as 'the systematic allocation of the depreciable amount of an asset over its useful life'. Depreciable amount is the cost of an asset, or other amount substituted for cost, less its residual value.

> **Think!**
>
> How does the definition of depreciation deal with the argument that property values tend to rise over time?

According to the definition provided above, depreciation is not intended to revise the book values of property, plant, and equipment to any particular approximation of 'value'. The depreciation adjustment is intended to show a charge in the income statement to reflect the fact that part of the life of each non-current asset has been consumed in the course of the period. This is consistent with the definition of expenses as 'decreases in economic benefits during the accounting period in the form of outflows or depletions of assets . . . '.[2]

Thus, by definition, depreciation is intended to reflect the passing of the useful lives of non-current assets in the income statement. If the charge has the effect of leaving book values in the balance sheet that are of little interest for decision-making purposes, then there are remedies that we will discuss later in this chapter (although note that revalued amounts have to be depreciated in exactly the same manner as costs).

---

[2] Framework for the Preparation and Presentation of Financial Statements, paragraph 70.

Charging Depreciation

IAS 16 requires that non-current assets, whether valued at cost or revalued, should be depreciated. If an asset's cost can be broken down into separate components, then it might be necessary to depreciate each separately. For example, if a new furnace is built that has an expected useful life of twenty years but has a brick lining that will have to be replaced every five years, then the cost of the lining could be written off over the shorter timeframe.

All depreciation should be charged to the income statement (so IAS 16 specifically forbids split depreciation).[3]

The depreciable amount of an asset shall be allocated on a systematic basis over its useful life.

Think!

How would you go about deciding the useful life of an asset? What problems have to be overcome in the process?

In many cases, estimating useful life is a technological matter. Past experience, engineering assessments, advice from suppliers, and so on, might suggest that an asset is likely to last for a particular length of time. The resulting period is only an estimate, and there is every chance that the actual life will be longer or shorter, but it is often possible to arrive at a realistic estimate.

New technologies can create problems, as can highly specialised assets. For example, changes in the design of assets can complicate the process of estimating their physical lives. Manufacturers' claims that a new generation of equipment will last longer might be difficult to assess.

Another major problem is that the physical life expectancy is only part of the process. Useful lives can be affected by technological and commercial considerations. Personal computers (PCs) are an obvious example. Most individuals who own a PC can recall disposing of a perfectly functional machine that is no longer powerful enough to run the latest software.

Useful lives can be shortened by factors other than just technological obsolescence. For example, an oil production platform might never reach

---

[3] There is a very minor exception, where depreciation is incurred in the acquisition of another non-current asset. Thus, a construction company that has built its own head-quarters can capitalise the depreciation on the equipment used on the project as part of the cost of the new building.

the end of its physical life if the price of oil falls to a level where it is uneconomic to run the platform. If there is no expectation of a price increase, then it might become cheaper to scrap the platform than to operate it. Similarly, the life expectancy of an airliner might be shortened if more economical aircraft are developed in the future, forcing replacement in order to remain competitive, or if the environmentalist movement's concerns about air travel dissuade passengers from flying.

Most companies deal with the problem by having a series of very broad categories of assets and charging depreciation based on an estimated life for each category.

IAS 16 requires companies to review the estimates of residual value and life expectancy on an annual basis.

This process can be seen in action by looking at the accounting policy notes of real companies; for example, the depreciation policies in the 2009 annual report of Emirates, a major international airline based in the United Arab Emirates:

Land is not depreciated. Depreciation is calculated on other items of property, plant, and equipment so as to write off its cost, less estimated residual values, on a straight-line basis over the estimated useful lives of the assets concerned. The estimated useful lives and residual values are:

- Passenger aircraft – new 15 years (residual value 10%)
- Passenger aircraft – used 8 years (residual value 10%)
- Aircraft engines and parts 5–15 years (residual value 0–10%)
- Buildings 5–20 years
- Other property, plant, and equipment 3–15 years or over the lease term, if shorter

Major overhaul expenditure is depreciated over the shorter of the period to the next major overhaul or lease term or useful life of the asset concerned.

The assets' residual values and useful lives are reviewed, and adjusted if appropriate, at each balance sheet date.

Not only does this give an indication of the approach taken by Emirates, but it also enables readers to draw some comparisons between the policies adopted by similar businesses. For example, the Australian airline Qantas states in its 2008 annual report that aircraft are depreciated over estimated useful lives of 2.5–20 years, with an estimated residual value of 0–20%. Clearly, it would not be possible to restate either company's depreciation charge on a comparable basis with the other's, but at least there is a warning that the figures might not be directly comparable.

Depreciation Methods

You should remember the straight-line method and reducing balance method from your earlier studies. These charge depreciation over time. In fact, these are almost certainly the only methods that you are ever likely to encounter.

IAS 16 requires that the depreciation method used shall reflect the pattern in which the asset's future economic benefits are expected to be consumed by the entity.

Think!

Compare and contrast the straight-line and reducing balance methods in terms of reflecting patterns of consumption.

Can you think of any alternative approaches that would not focus on the passage of time?

The straight-line basis writes off the carrying value in equal instalments. It might be argued that this is a realistic treatment if the asset is consumed in equal amounts year by year.

The reducing balance method writes off the asset more rapidly in the earlier years of its life, with the charge declining in later years. This might be regarded as very slightly more realistic because assets decline in value more rapidly when they are newer and more slowly when the assets get closer to the ends of their lives. Furthermore, the reducing balance approach means that more will be written off in the early years, so that any reduction in the estimated expected useful lives or residual values will have less of an effect when that is corrected.

For example, an asset that has an estimated useful life of ten years and very little residual value can either be written off at 10% of cost per annum (straight line) or 25% of carrying value (reducing balance). If the asset cost $100 000, then the following figures would appear in the financial statements for the first three years:

	Straight line		Reducing balance	
Year	Depreciation charge	Balance sheet value	Depreciation charge	Balance sheet value
1	$10 000	$90 000	$25 000	$75 000
2	$10 000	$80 000	$18 750	$56 250
3	$10 000	$70 000	$14 062	$42 188

Neither set of figures is more 'correct' than the other. Both sets of book values would be reduced to zero (or very close to it[4]) by the end of year 10, and both approaches would have charged a total of $100 000 to the income statement over that whole period.

Examination questions always give very explicit instructions about the calculation of depreciation, so there is no real need to worry about anything other than being ready to explain the resulting figures if the question asks you to do so.

The fact that almost all questions and almost all companies use either straight line or reducing balance or both does not mean that there are no alternatives. It might, in fact, be more relevant to calculate depreciation in terms of wear and tear rather than the passage of time. For example, a delivery van might be regarded as having a useful life of 50 000 miles rather than, say, three years. If the van cost $30 000, then it might be depreciated at $0.60 per mile (i.e. $30 000/50 000). If it covered 12 000 miles in year 2, then that year's depreciation charge would be 12 000 × $0.60 = $7200.

There are other ways in which wear and tear might be measured. For example, aircraft go through a cycle of expansion and contraction every time they climb to altitude and come back down again. This is perfectly safe throughout the lifetime of each aircraft, but eventually the metal in the airframe is weakened and the aircraft must be taken out of service. An airline could determine the safe maximum number of flights for each type of aircraft and divide that into the cost of the airframe in order to derive a cost per flight.

It could be argued that methods that link depreciation to usage are more realistic, but that ignores two facts:

• Linking depreciation to usage might prove very complicated and expensive in practice. A company's computerised bookkeeping system can calculate straight-line or reducing balance depreciation very easily without any further input. A method that is linked to wear and tear would require usage data to be both collected and input. The cost of the additional clerical effort might far outweigh the benefits of any additional accuracy.
• If assets are used steadily throughout their lives, then calculating depreciation in terms of usage might not affect the resulting depreciation charge. If an aircraft is expected to fly safely for twenty years and make exactly 600 flights per annum during that time, then both methods of depreciation will prove identical (unless the pattern of usage actually alters significantly during the period).

---

[4] There is always a very small residual figure with reducing balance, and there would also be a rounding error in this example.

Revaluing Assets

Valuing property, plant, and equipment at cost less depreciation will almost inevitably lead to reporting balance sheet values that are increasingly remote from their 'real' economic value. IAS 16 deals with this problem by offering companies a choice. Subject to a variety of conditions, assets can be shown at their fair value instead of cost less depreciation, where fair value is defined by IAS 16 as 'the amount for which an asset could be exchanged between knowledgeable, willing parties in an arm's length transaction'.

Thus, companies have to choose between valuing assets at cost less depreciation or at their market values.

There are several conditions that have to be met before a company revalues any of its assets:

- It must be possible to measure fair values reliably.
- Once an asset has been shown at valuation, it must be revalued regularly (at least often enough for the balance sheet value not to differ materially from market value).
- The fair value of land and buildings should *normally* be undertaken by professionally qualified valuers using market-based evidence.
- If an item of property, plant, and equipment in a particular category is shown at valuation, then every other item in that category must be shown at valuation too (otherwise companies might be tempted to 'cherry-pick' the assets that had increased in value for valuation and leave those that had fallen in value at cost less depreciation).

> **Think!**
>
> Can you think of any advantages or disadvantages associated with revaluing assets? Is market value the best way to value a non-current asset?

The easiest and cheapest way to value assets is to show them at cost less depreciation. That will simplify the preparation of the financial statements. It will also reduce the subjectivity associated with the figures (although we have seen that there is quite a lot of subjectivity in deciding the cost and calculating depreciation).

Some assets will be very difficult to value because there are no observable markets. For example, large city-centre office blocks are not bought and sold sufficiently often to be able to tell day by day (or even year by year) exactly what a particular block would sell for. Even experts cannot say for certain how much an asset might sell for.

In theory, valuing the assets ought to give better information to the shareholders. Costs can become out of date, and cost less depreciation will not necessarily indicate how much an asset is worth to the business or how much a prospective buyer would pay for it.

Valuing assets at their market value can be useful for certain decisions, but not all:

- Knowing what an asset would sell for gives shareholders an idea of the alternatives – knowing that the non-current assets could be sold for $100 million might be of some interest if the company is not doing well. If the directors have been entrusted with assets that could be sold for that amount, then they should be generating a return that justifies that investment.
- The market value of the assets gives lenders a clear idea of the security that the company can offer as collateral against a loan. That information is useful to the shareholders, who need to know the borrowing capacity of their business.

   But . . .

- The market value does not necessarily reflect the cash flows that it will generate for the business under its present use. For example, a major Scottish shopping centre is called 'The Forge' because it was previously the site of a heavy engineering factory that forged massive rollers for use in the steel industry. The company that owned the factory sold it to a retail developer because its directors realised that the factory's market value as a piece of land for development far outweighed its potential to generate income as a factory.
- For some decisions (e.g. insurance or pricing) it is more important to know how much it would cost to replace the asset. The cost of a replacement is not necessarily the same as its selling price on an open market. For example, there might be very few potential buyers for a specialised asset, and so its market value might be low or even zero. That same asset could be vital to its owner and might be very expensive to replace.

Accounting for Gains and Losses

There is a lack of symmetry in the treatment of gains and losses on revaluation:

- Gains on revaluation are normally credited to the revaluation reserve, which appears in the equity section of the statement of financial position.

• Losses on revaluation are normally charged to the income statement as an expense.

This treatment may appear to be inconsistent, but it does ensure that all revaluation losses are brought to the shareholders' attention. If the directors feel that there is a misleading impact on the income statement, then this can be explained in the annual report.

Taking gains to a separate equity account avoids the risk of confusion between operating profits and other gains. We have already seen that they will be highlighted separately as 'other comprehensive income' in the statement of comprehensive income.

There are minor exceptions to the above rules:

• If a gain on revaluation arises on an asset that has previously been revalued at a loss, then the gain should be taken to the income statement, but only to the extent that it reverses a previously recognised loss – any additional increase goes to the revaluation reserve.
• Conversely, a loss on the revaluation of an asset that has previously been revalued at a gain should be charged to the revaluation reserve; again, this is restricted to the amount of the previously recognised gain, and any remaining amount is taken to the income statement.

The mechanics of revaluation are quite simple. Normally, the depreciation on the asset is reduced to zero and the figure for cost is restated to the revalued amount. The net movement on the asset's value is taken to the income statement and/or the revaluation reserve, as appropriate.

The adjustments are made for each separate asset. Thus, it is never appropriate to offset gains on some assets against losses on others.

After revaluation, the new carrying amount is depreciated over the remaining expected useful life of the asset.

One Problem with Values

The following case is one of the most extreme examples of things going wrong with professional valuations. It is not intended that you should treat such valuations with outright suspicion, but do always bear in mind that there is a great deal of subjective judgement underlying almost every valuation. An expert might give advice as to a realistic valuation for an asset, but that is only ever an estimate, and the asset can only be sold for that amount if a buyer is willing to pay it. Valuations can only be regarded as objective when there is a transparent and active market for virtually identical items.

If you own a popular make and model of car, then you can look at the prices offered by a variety of garages for similar cars of its age and tell how much you could sell it for. If you own a house, then market prices can change quickly from month to month, so knowing how much a similar house nearby sold for last year tells you relatively little. Location is important too, so knowing how much similar houses sell for in a nearby town may not tell you a great deal either.

This problem was highlighted in the Queens Moat Houses case in 1992. The company had been expected to report a profit of approximately £80 million, but actually reported a loss of £1040.5 million. The large loss was partly attributable to an £803.9 million reduction in property values.

The property write-off was considered shocking because the company's properties, mainly hotels, had been professionally valued at £2 billion for the 1991 accounts. The same valuers were asked to value the same properties at the end of 1992 and attached a much lower value. A different firm of valuers was appointed, and they valued the same properties as at the end of 1992 at only £861 million.

These adjustments were not the only source of concern about the company's financial statements, although the valuation of property had, by far, the greatest impact on the 1992 figures that led to the controversy. The company's board was replaced. The case attracted a great deal of debate and discussion, including the following comments from *Accountancy*, the professional journal of the Institute of Chartered Accountants of England and Wales:

> On the face of it, there is little in the Queens Moat Houses affair to encourage the user of accounts to place reliance on current values. The group's properties were professionally valued at the end of 1991. They were valued again, by a different firm, at the end of 1992, and the result was to reduce their stated value in the accounts from £2,079.1m to £737.6m.
>
> This remarkable fall in value is accompanied by an even more remarkable statement from QMH's new board: 'The current directors consider that they do not have a sufficient understanding of the 1991 property valuation to enable them to provide a full explanation for the decline in property values from 31 December 1991 to 31 December 1992 of £1,341.5m.'
>
> Equally strange and equally unfortunate in its own way is the information that the 1991 valuers at one time put forward a draft valuation for the 1992 year end almost £500m higher than the one the new valuers produced.
>
> The QMH affair underlines three important points about valuations in accounts. First, their usefulness varies from business to business. A property valuation in the hotels business is less useful than a property valuation in most

other businesses. This is because when you value a hotel you may well be valuing the business itself rather than the property. In other words, what purports to be a 'property' valuation actually contains a large element of goodwill.

Second, valuations are unreliable. (The polite way of putting this is to say that they are subjective.) Different valuers are liable to come up with materially different valuations.

Third, values are volatile. And if balance sheet values feed into the [income statement], then volatility in the balance sheet will increase volatility in the [income statement].

Impairment

So far, we have presented the decision to show assets at either cost less depreciation or at valuation as an accounting choice. There is one situation in which management cannot choose between the two approaches, and that is when an asset is *impaired*.

IAS 36 *Impairment of Assets* states that assets should not be carried in the balance sheet at more than their recoverable amount:

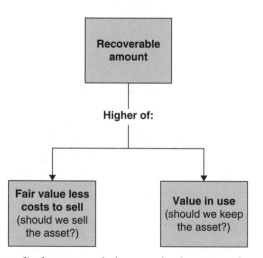

An asset is 'impaired' if it is worth less to the business than its carrying value according to the books. We make this comparison on the basis of a rational decision by the business as to the most sensible way to treat the asset.

For example, an item of equipment is valued in the books at cost less depreciation of $500 000. This equipment could be sold for $100 000 after allowing for selling costs. The equipment is expected to generate cash flows worth $350 000.

Is the equipment impaired?	Yes, the best that can happen is that the business will keep the equipment and use it to generate cash flows worth $350 000.
What value should be placed on the equipment?	The equipment is worth $350 000 to the business because the rational decision would be to retain the asset and generate cash flows worth that amount.

IAS 36 applies to both tangible and intangible non-current assets. Effectively, it means that companies cannot deliberately value their assets at cost less depreciation in order to avoid recognising a loss on revaluation. Where assets are worth less than their book values, they must be written down.

Impairment losses are treated in a very similar manner to losses on revaluation. Generally, they are shown in the income statement, but can go directly to the revaluation reserve whenever the assets in question were previously revalued at a gain (subject to the usual upper limit of the gain that has been recognised on those assets).

Companies are required to consider the possibility of impairment whenever they prepare a set of financial statements, although a detailed impairment review would normally be carried out only if there were some indication of impairment (e.g. assets that are obsolete or damaged). Annual impairment reviews are mandatory only in respect of intangible assets that have indefinite useful lives or purchased goodwill.

Ideally, the impairment review should be conducted for each individual asset, but that is not always possible, and so the review must sometimes be conducted for collections of assets that IAS 36 describes as 'cash-generating units', which are defined as 'the smallest identifiable group of assets that generates cash inflows that are largely independent of the cash inflows from other assets or groups of assets'.

For example, the safety equipment in a factory might have no value in and of itself, but could be required by law, so the factory would have no value without it. In that case, the factory (including the equipment) should be regarded as a cash-generating unit.

Investment Properties

The accounting treatment of investment properties might be regarded as an example of the power of lobbying in the standard-setting process. Property companies have managed to argue successfully that it is unnecessary to depreciate buildings under certain circumstances *even where it is possible that the companies will own the properties for the whole of their useful lives.*

IAS 40 *Investment Property* defines investment property as:

property . . . held (by the owner or by the lessee under a finance lease) to earn rentals or for capital appreciation or both, rather than for:

(a) use in the production or supply of goods or services or for administrative purposes; or

(b) sale in the ordinary course of business.

Investment properties have to pass the normal criteria for recognition as non-current assets. Initially, they should be recognised at cost. Thereafter, companies have a choice:

- *Fair value model* – the property must be shown at its fair value as at each balance sheet date, with gains and losses on changes in fair value going to the income statement.
- *Cost model* – if it is impossible reliably to determine the fair value of a property (e.g. if it is of a nature for which there is no active market), or, *if the company so chooses*, an investment property can be valued at cost less depreciation under the same basis that would be applied under IAS 16.

Thus, there will be no depreciation on investment properties shown at fair value. This means that any company that owns a property that it does not occupy may be able to classify it as an investment property. If it adopts the fair value model, then it need not depreciate the property, although all fluctuations in fair value will appear in the income statement.

Disclosure Requirements

IAS 16 lays down some detailed disclosure requirements. These are necessary because of the scope for subjective judgement in accounting for property, plant, and equipment.

Companies are required to disclose their accounting policies:

- measurement bases;
- depreciation methods;
- useful lives or depreciation rates.

The opening and closing balances on cost/valuation and accumulated depreciation should be disclosed, along with a reconciliation of the movements during the year, including:

- additions;
- increases or decreases resulting from revaluations;
- impairment losses;
- depreciation charge;
- other changes (e.g. disposals).

Companies should also disclose information that might be necessary for an understanding of the company's rights and obligations, such as restrictions on title or pledges against property, plant, and equipment.

Details should also be given of the revaluation of property, plant, and equipment:

- date of revaluation;
- whether an independent valuer was involved;
- the methods and significant assumptions applied in arriving at fair values;
- the extent to which the items' fair values were determined directly by reference to observable prices in an active market;
- for each revalued class of property, plant, and equipment, the carrying amount that would have been recognised had the assets been carried under the cost model;
- revaluation surplus, indicating the change for the period.

Summary

Accounting for property, plant, and equipment has attracted a great deal of attention from standard-setters over the years. This is partly because of the very real complexities that have arisen in practice. It is also the result of the adoption of some rather dubious accounting treatments that have had the effect of making financial statements appear more attractive to readers.

Most of the rules relating to accounting for non-current assets can be found in IAS 16. This offers companies the choice between valuing assets at cost less depreciation and fair value. This choice has to be made category by category for all assets. In other words, all vehicles, say, have to be valued at cost less depreciation or at fair value. IAS 16 also requires every item of property, plant, and equipment that has a finite useful life to be depreciated.

IAS 36 requires assets that are impaired to be written down to their recoverable amount. This requirement effectively stipulates that individual assets that have suffered a decline in value be shown at valuation rather than cost less depreciation.

IAS 40 effectively permits companies to choose not to depreciate investment properties. This is a slightly specialised area of business, but it does illustrate the power of lobbying in terms of accounting regulation. The requirement to depreciate all buildings was so unpopular with the property industry that the rules were changed in response.

Tutorial Questions

Question 1

Never has always valued its land and buildings and other non-current assets at cost less depreciation. The directors are debating the merits of showing their property, plant, and equipment at valuation. They are concerned that IAS 16 *Property, Plant, and Equipment* has an 'all or nothing' approach that would impose a duty on them to maintain up-to-date valuations in the balance sheet for all categories of revalued assets into the indefinite future.

(a) Explain why IAS 16 requires those companies who revalue fixed assets to revalue all of the assets in the relevant classes, and why these valuations must be kept up to date.
(b) Explain whether it is logical for IAS 16 to offer companies a choice between showing all assets in a category at either cost less depreciation or at valuation.

Question 2

Wight's finance director has asked a factory manager to conduct a review to identify any assets that might be impaired. The manager has walked through the factory and also reviewed the plant register, and has prepared the following schedule:

	Net book value $000	Market value $000	Cash flows $000
Grinding machine 5	250	210	218
Diesel forklift	2	3	8
Safety monitors	500	10	?

The safety monitors have very little resale value because they were made specifically for Wight's factory. The cash flows that they will generate are difficult to separate from those of the factory itself. If the monitors were removed, then the factory would have to close down until they were repaired or replaced. The factory as a whole is highly profitable and is expected to continue to trade at a profit.

(a) Explain which, if any, of the above assets are impaired.
(b) Discuss the difficulties in identifying impaired assets.

Question 3

A nervous company director has suggested that the profit figure according to the draft income statement is too low. He has suggested that the company should double the estimated useful lives of all tangible non-current assets in order to reduce the depreciation charge. He argues that the figure is, after all, an estimate, and he feels that careful maintenance could easily double the lives anyway.

Discuss the logic of this proposal.

Question 4

IAS 40 *Investment Property* would not apply to an office block that was being used by its owner as a corporate headquarters, even if the owner could show board minutes where it had been agreed that the office had been purchased because of its investment potential and that the directors were committed to selling the office at a huge capital gain in five to ten years.

Discuss the logic of excluding this property from the scope of IAS 40.

Question 5

T plc is a quoted company that owns a large number of hotels. The company's latest trial balance is as follows:

T plc
Trial balance as at 31 December 20X7

	£000	£000
Administrative expenses	3 000	
Bank	300	
Creditors		1 700
Distribution costs	4 000	
Food purchases	2 100	
Heating and lighting	3 000	
Hotel buildings – cost	490 000	

Hotel buildings – depreciation to date		46 200
Hotel fixtures and fittings – cost	18 000	
Hotel fixtures and fittings – depreciation to date		9 400
Interest	5 950	
Inventory as at 31 December 20X6	450	
Loans (repayable 20Y0)		110 000
Retained profit		86 000
Sales of accommodation and food		68 500
Share capital (£1 shares, fully paid)		220 000
Wages – administrative staff	6 000	
Wages – housekeeping and restaurant staff	9 000	
	541 800	541 800

During the year, the company spent a total of £12.0 million on a new hotel and purchased new fixtures for £7.0 million. These acquisitions have been included in the relevant trial balance totals.

Hotels are to be depreciated by 2% of cost, and fixtures and fittings by 25% of the reducing balance, with a full year's depreciation to be charged in the year of acquisition.

Closing stocks of foodstuffs and other consumables were valued at £470 000 on 31 December 20X7.

The directors are considering the implications of revaluing the company's hotels. They have commissioned the following report:

	Original cost	Depreciation to 31.12.20X7	Market value at 31.12.20X7	Estimated useful life from 31.12.20X7
	£000	£000	£000	Years
Hotel A	800	180	1 300	50
Hotel B	700	120	850	30
Hotel C	1 000	140	650	40

Required:
(a) Calculate the effects of the revaluation of the three hotels on the depreciation charge for the year ended 31 December 2007, assuming that a full year's depreciation is charged on the revalued amounts, and

calculate the balance that would appear on the revaluation reserve in respect of the revalued hotels.

(b) Prepare T plc's statement of comprehensive income for the year ended 31 December 20X7 and its statement of financial position as at that date.

(c) During the year ended 31 December 20X8, the directors are planning to start a major programme of repairs and refurbishment on the company's hotels. Over a five-year period the buildings will be checked to ensure that they are structurally sound, and they will be repaired wherever necessary. Preliminary investigations suggest that some of the hotels will not achieve their expected useful lives if the company does not invest in this preventive maintenance. The company will also redecorate the hotels and replace most of the furniture in the bedrooms and restaurants. The redecoration will create a new corporate image for all of T plc's hotels, and that will improve the company's marketing and promotion.

Describe the factors that will have to be considered in deciding whether these costs should be capitalised.

Further Work

The answers to these end-of-chapter questions can be found at the back of the book.

Question 1

Welloil owns a production platform in the Arabian Gulf. The following costs have been identified:

- building costs charged by Scott Fabrication for the initial construction of the platform;
- professional fees paid to Cromarty Marine Engineering, the engineering company that Wattoil paid to oversee the construction and manage the commissioning of the rig;
- legal fees paid to Snoop, a law firm that specialises in international contract law for the oil industry, for the provision of legal services associated with purchasing the rig;
- fees paid to Biglift barges for the cost of transporting the rig from its construction site on the North East coast of Scotland to its present location;

- annual cost of repainting the rig with an anticorrosion coating;
- the cost of a major refit in years 5 and 10 of the platform's life – these refits involve taking the rig off-line for several weeks and are necessary if the rig is to reach its estimated lifespan;
- the anticipated costs of removing the rig from its site and disposing of it in an environmentally responsible manner;
- borrowing costs associated with the rig started when the company took out a twenty-year loan at the start of construction work, which lasted for five years, and continued for the term of the loan.

Classify the list of costs as capital or revenue.

Question 2

KL shipping owns four ships. These are specialist vessels that are presently shown at cost less depreciation. The company's policy is to depreciate ships at 5% of cost each year.

KL had each of the four ships revalued on 1 January 20X7. The following table shows the result of that exercise:

Ship	Original cost	Cumulative depreciation as at 1 January 20X7	Valuation at 1 January 20X7	Estimated useful life from 1 January 20X7
A	$20m	$7.0m	$15.0m	10 years
B	$30m	$3.0m	$29.0m	20 years
C	$18m	$9.9m	$6.0m	4 years
D	$25m	$5.0m	$19.0m	18 years

Required:
(a) Calculate the book value of ships as at 31 December 20X7 and the depreciation charge for ships for the year then ended using the following bases:
  - historical cost less depreciation;
  - revaluation.
(b) Identify the problems in arriving at a valuation for such assets.

Question 3

Host plc manufactures electronic equipment for the aerospace industry. It has several factories. The company's most recent year-end trial balance is as follows:

Host plc
Trial balance at 31 December 20X8

	£000	£000
Administration costs	7 200	
Bank	450	
Deferred tax		8 000
Distribution costs	6 400	
Dividends	7 000	
Inventory at start of year	2 500	
Loan interest	1 200	
Long-term loans		15 000
Manufacturing costs	9 400	
Property, plant, and equipment – cost or valuation	75 000	
Property, plant, and equipment – depreciation		14 000
Purchases of materials and parts	26 000	
Retained earnings		23 450
Revaluation reserve		6 000
Revenue		92 000
Share capital		10 000
Tax	600	
Trade payables		2 300
Trade receivables	4 000	
Wages – administration	6 000	
Wages – manufacturing	16 000	
Wages – distribution	9 000	
	170 750	170 750

(i) Inventory was counted at the end of the year and was valued at £3.2 million.

(ii) The balance on the tax account comprises the amount left after the final settlement of the corporation tax liability for the year ended 31 December 20X7.

(iii) The directors have estimated the tax charge on this year's profits at £4.2 million.

(iv) The provision for deferred taxation is to be increased by £800 000.

(v) The figures for property, plant, and equipment include two production lines that the directors have reviewed for impairment. The following information has been obtained:

Asset	Net book value (cost less depreciation) £000	Net present value £000	Net realisable value £000
Flux line	1 200	1 300	1 000
Coating line	7 800	5 000	2 000

(vi) The company owns three factory buildings that have been shown at valuation less depreciation. The factories were revalued at the end of the year:

- The Perth factory was purchased for £13 million. It was revalued four years ago at £15 million and has since been depreciated by £500 000. The revaluation reserve includes £2.2 million in respect of this factory. The factory's current value has been set at £17 million.
- The Glenrothes factory was purchased for £16 million. It was revalued three years ago at £17 million and has since been depreciated by £200 000. The revaluation reserve includes £800 000 in respect of this factory. The factory's current value has been set at £16.5 million.
- The Drymen factory was purchased for £12 million. It was revalued five years ago at £13 million and has since been depreciated by £300 000. The revaluation reserve includes £200 000 in respect of this factory. The factory's current value has been set at £8 million.

The current values indicated above are to be incorporated into the financial statements for the year ended 31 December 20X8.

Required:

(a) Prepare a statement of comprehensive income, a statement of changes in equity, and a statement of financial position for Host plc. These should be in a form suitable for publication and should be accompanied with notes (in so far as is possible given the information provided).

(b) Explain your treatment of the assets that were subject to an impairment review in (v) above.

INTANGIBLE NON-CURRENT ASSETS: MEASUREMENT AND DISCLOSURE

Contents

Learning Objectives

After studying this chapter you should be able to:

- discuss the nature of different types of intangible asset;
- explain whether intangible assets meet the criteria for recognition in the financial statements;
- explain how research and development expenditure should be accounted for under IAS 38;

- discuss the problems of accounting for intangible assets;
- be aware of the practical difficulties that can arise in accounting for intangible assets.

Introduction

This has been a difficult and contentious area over the years. Intangible assets are frequently the most important asset that the business owns, and yet they are often excluded from the financial statements because they are so difficult to value with any accuracy.

One asset in particular, the cost of developing new products, has been a heavily contested area of accounting. The treatment laid down by IAS 38 is a rather grudging acceptance that costs can be carried as assets under a very narrowly defined set of circumstances. That is a concession granted by the standard-setters to companies who claimed that writing off all research and development would render such activities uneconomic.

The Nature of Intangibles

The accounting treatment of intangible assets is dealt with in IAS 38 *Intangible Assets*. This standard deals with the vast majority of intangible assets. We shall look at some of the exceptions in later chapters; otherwise you should apply the rules summarised here.

The distinction between tangible and intangible assets is simply one of the dictionary definitions of the two words. Tangible assets have a physical presence. Intangible assets do not have a physical presence. The only difference is that one type can be seen and touched and the other cannot. In theory, intangible assets should create the same accounting problems as tangible assets. Where an intangible asset meets the recognition criteria laid down for tangible assets and has a measurable useful life, then the accounting treatment is virtually identical to that of a tangible asset.

The biggest problems associated with intangible assets are related to measurement. Intangibles are often extremely valuable, but their value can be difficult to measure, and their expected useful lives can also be difficult to estimate.

> **Think!**
>
> When might it be difficult to value an intangible asset?

The easiest way to identify the problems is to consider the accounting treatment of tangible assets and think about how intangibles might differ.

Initial recognition	Some intangibles are purchased from a third party, and so their cost can be determined with relative ease.
	Many intangibles are created through the operation of normal business activities, and so the cost is virtually impossible to determine.
Useful lives	Some intangibles have a clearly delineated life laid down by law or in a contract.
	Many intangibles have the potential to retain their value for decades, well into the indefinite future.
Valuation	A very few intangible assets can be bought and sold in a free and visible market.
	Most intangible assets are almost impossible to value in an objective manner.

The simplest possible case would be an intangible that is purchased from a third party, such as the right to manufacture a product that is protected by patent. The cost of this will be relatively easy to establish. If the contract specifies a time limit, then the maximum useful life is specified from the outset, although it is possible that the rights could be rendered worthless in a shorter timeframe if demand for the product declines before the end of the contracted period.

There are far more complicated problems when dealing with internally generated intangibles. For example, a company's marketing managers might develop a brand name. The value of that brand name can be developed by a combination of advertising and other promotional activities. If it is successful, then that asset could prove enormously valuable, but the cost of creating it will be very difficult to determine. The salaries paid to the staff will be almost impossible to allocate to specific outcomes, such as particular brand names. The advertising and other promotional efforts will have helped to build up brand awareness, but even that will be an indirect effect. Certainly, spending $1 million on an advertising campaign does not mean that it would be appropriate to capitalise that amount as part of the cost of the brand.

The useful life of an intangible can also be extremely difficult to determine. Business history is full of cases where intangible assets have been rendered worthless for all sorts of reasons. This can be through accident or simply the nature of the legal rights. One unfortunate case of business accident happened in the United Kingdom when the chief executive of a national jewellery retail chain was making a point about pricing and claimed that one particular product was cheap because it was 'total crap'.[1] Perhaps this was a slow news day, but the press reported this as front-page news, implying that the gentleman in question had described the company's entire product range in those terms. Sales slumped immediately and the company was forced to close many of its stores and also change its name. The chief executive himself had to resign for the sake of the company.

There need not be any mismanagement or poor judgement for an intangible to decline in value. For example, for many years Glaxo Wellcome's best-selling drug was an anti-ulcer treatment called Zantac. Patent protection on pharmaceutical products lapses after approximately 20 years in most countries, and other manufacturers were able to make and sell their own versions of this product from July 1997 onwards, albeit under a different name. Glaxo Wellcome lost 60% of the market for its product by October 1997, in spite of retaining the Zantac trademark and having had total domination of this market for almost 20 years.

The accounting treatment of non-current assets is complicated at the best of times, but the problems are magnified when dealing with intangible assets:

• Intangible assets are sometimes acquired in a straightforward transaction, and there can be a clearly observable cost, but that is often not the case. For example, the most valuable asset owned by many businesses is that of customer loyalty. It would be impossible to separate the cost of generating a loyal customer base from

---

[1] The actual quote was far more specific and reads as if the speaker was trying to make a humorous point rather than sabotage the company: 'We also do cut-glass sherry decanters complete with six glasses on a silver-plated tray that your butler can serve you drinks on, all for £4.95. People say, 'How can you sell this for such a low price?', I say, 'because it's total crap'.

the other running costs of the business. There is clearly a cost to acquiring a good reputation (e.g. by spending more on quality management or motivating employees), but that cost can be difficult to isolate.

- Non-current assets must be depreciated[2] over their estimated useful lives. That is a difficult matter for a tangible asset, but there are – at least – physical observations and measurements that might help. Some intangible assets can be even easier. For example, a patent might have five years left to run. That does not necessarily mean that it will have any value for the whole of the five years – if there is no market for the product, then the sole right to sell it is not worth anything. It does, however, provide a clean upper limit to the right's useful life. Other intangible assets are rather more complicated. Some brand names have been popular for many decades and continue to be well received. It is, perhaps, possible that Coca-Cola or Pepsi will become unpopular, but it is highly unlikely that they ever will.

- Most tangible assets have some kind of observable market. Land and buildings are bought and sold, as are vehicles and some types of equipment. Generally, intangible assets either cannot be sold separately (e.g. customer loyalty, which can only be sold as part of the business) or are rarely sold on their own (e.g. brand names, which could – theoretically – be sold, but that would leave the business without a product). The fact that there is no market means that there is no independent way to check in the statement of financial position after valuations.

Recognition Criteria

The recognition criteria that we encountered for property, plant, and equipment apply equally to intangibles:

- It is probable that any future economic benefit associated with the item will flow to or from the entity.
- The item has a cost or value that can be measured with reliability.

> **Think!**
>
> Which of these criteria is likely to be the more problematic with respect to intangible non-current assets?

---

[2] The concept of depreciation applies to intangible assets, but it is referred to as 'amortisation'.

An asset should not appear in the statement of financial position unless it is likely to yield a future economic benefit. This is unlikely to pose a problem in relation to intangible assets. The word 'probable' does not necessarily lend itself to quantification, although 'more likely than not' or 'better than 50:50' are probably realistic clarifications. There will be very few potential assets, whether tangible or intangible, for which this will be a potential problem.

The bigger problem is in measuring the cost or value of many intangible assets. Those that have been purchased outright have a clearly observable cost, but those that are created internally will not. Very few intangible assets will have measurable values. Many intangible non-current assets will not be recognised because their cost and value are difficult to measure reliably.

Regulation is necessary because the recognition of intangible assets will inevitably reduce the gearing ratio and so make the statement of financial position appear more healthy, at least if the figures are taken at face value.

In the 1980s it briefly became fashionable to attach values to internally generated brand names and capitalise those as intangible assets. The Framework had not been finalised at that stage; however, it might not have prevented such behaviour.

Think!

How could a company justify capitalising the value of an internally generated brand name when it has to meet the criteria of future economic benefit and reliable measurement?

It is almost self-evident that a recognised brand name will generate future economic benefits. The very fact that companies invest great deals of money in promoting brand names through sponsorship, public relations, and advertising indicates that brands are a resource worth protecting. For example, the James Bond film 'Die Another Day' was dubbed 'Buy Another Day' by some critics when it was revealed that twenty companies had paid between them a total of $70 million for the privilege of seeing their products on the big screen.

The biggest problem with accounting for brands is arriving at a reliable measurement of value. This can, however, be overcome in practice. One approach, which was used extensively when brand accounting was in vogue, is to engage a marketing consultant who claims expertise in brand management. Various consulting firms have models that, they claim, can generate defensible figures for brand valuations. While the resulting numbers cannot be regarded as objective, they have some basis in logic and economics and so might be regarded as reliable.

IAS 38

IAS 38 deals with most intangible assets, except for financial assets[3] and assets that are broadly associated with exploration and extraction of oil, gas, and other natural minerals.[4]

IAS 38 defines an intangible asset as 'an *identifiable* non-monetary asset without physical substance' (emphasis added). The word 'identifiable' distinguishes intangible assets from the broader concept of goodwill. The concept of goodwill is discussed in Chapters 11 and 12 in the context of buying whole businesses. Goodwill is essentially the value that arises over and above the value of the separately identifiable assets, whether tangible, intangible, or financial.

An asset is identifiable if it can be separated or divided from the business and somehow sold or realised by transferring, licensing, renting, or exchanging it. In addition, it is identifiable if it arises from a contractual or legal right, regardless of whether it can be transferred or sold.

For example, a brand name can be sold to another business, and so that would make it identifiable. If the purchaser of a brand had to agree that the brand could never be resold to a third party, then it would not be separable or divisible from the business but it would be identifiable because it arose from a legal right arising from the contract with the vendor.

Assets such as customer loyalty could not be separated from the business and could only be transferred by selling the business as a whole, and so they could not be treated as intangibles under IAS 38.

In 2003, the notion of separability was highlighted when one of the airlines operating out of Heathrow airport sold two pairs of slots for almost £20 million to the Australian airline Qantas. A slot is essentially the right to land or take off from a given airport. Slots can become valuable commodities because demand for the use of some busy airports far outstrips the capacity of the airport. Buying another airline's slots makes it possible to add new routes or flight times. Even before this sale, slots at Heathrow changed hands from time to time at a price in the region of £5–6 million for a pair of slots.

An intangible asset shall be measured initially at cost.

---

[3] These are dealt with by IAS 39 *Financial Instruments: Recognition and Measurement.*
[4] These are dealt with by IFRS 6 *Exploration for and Evaluation of Mineral Resources.*

Intangibles that have been Separately Acquired

IAS 38 indicates that intangibles that are acquired as a separate transaction are the simplest possible case in terms of recognition and measurement:

* Logically, they must be expected to yield future economic benefits or the buyer would not make the investment.
* The fact that there is a transaction means that the cost can normally be ascertained reliably and without too much difficulty.

The cost of a separately acquired intangible asset comprises:

* its purchase price, including import duties and non-refundable purchase taxes, after deducting trade discounts and rebates; and
* any directly attributable cost of preparing the asset for its intended use.

'Directly attributable costs' include both employee costs and professional fees associated with bringing the asset to its working condition.

Intangibles Acquired by Way of Government Grant

Some assets are granted by the government at either a zero charge or for a nominal consideration. IAS 38 defers to IAS 20 *Accounting for Government Grants and Disclosure of Government Assistance* by offering a choice:

* show the asset at its nominal cost plus any additional costs required to bring the asset into use; or
* capitalise the fair value of the asset.

Internally Generated Goodwill

Internally generated goodwill cannot be treated as an asset because it does not meet the criteria of being separable or arising from contractual or other legal rights.

The goodwill might be the most valuable resource contributing to the value of the business, but it cannot be an asset for financial reporting purposes.

Internally Generated Intangible Assets

These can, sometimes, be capitalised at cost. We will return to the whole issue of accounting for such assets when we discuss development and other internally generated intangibles.

Goodwill and Intangibles Acquired as Part of a Business Combination

This topic will be discussed in Chapters 11 and 12.

The fact that there is a transaction can mean that goodwill and other intangibles can be treated as an asset in the group accounts under certain circumstances.

Development and Other Internally Generated Intangibles

The accounting treatment of research and development costs has been a major source of controversy in the past, leading to a great deal of debate about the role of accounting regulation.

There are two issues associated with accounting for research and development:

• Can the costs involved be capitalised, and, if so, which?
• What disclosures should be made?

Issues Associated with Capitalising Research and Development

Many companies spend a large percentage of their revenue on research and development. This may be for a range of activities ranging from 'blue sky' research, where the research is motivated by a desire to gather knowledge that might not be exploited for commercial purposes for many years, to the final development work on a product that is about to be brought to the market.

There is a general tendency for company directors to wish to capitalise costs rather than write them off. Capitalising any cost will always boost profit in the short term. The directors will also be concerned that the shareholders could misinterpret the expensing of research costs as an indication that their money has been wasted on fruitless projects. IAS 38 has had to lay down some very detailed rules to ensure that there is consistency in the treatment of research and development.

As an example, Sony's 2009 annual report showed research and development costs of approximately ¥497 billion. That is equivalent to 6.4% of sales revenue for the year. The company reported a net loss before tax of ¥175 billion, so the company could have restated a pre-tax loss as a profit if it had capitalised the cost of research and development for the year.

Returning to the issue at the centre of this section, the danger with regulating the capitalisation of R&D expenditure is that company directors can argue that forcing them to write off all costs immediately they are incurred gives them no incentive to invest in this area. That argument is not particularly logical, alth there was evidence of a reduced expenditure in the United States when rule first introduced forcing all costs to be expensed. Presumably, the directors' that the shareholders will have less confidence in the decision to invest product development if costs are treated as expenses, which could be read as implying that no further benefit will be derived from that outlay. If that is true, then the directors will be deterred from investing in development.

We will see below that IAS 38 permits the capitalisation of development costs provided a very strict set of criteria is met. The ability to capitalise some costs has been attributed to the effects of lobbying by specific industry groups, most notably the aerospace industry, which claimed that the massive costs associated with developing new aircraft would have rendered it uneconomic to do so if all costs were written off in the year in which they were incurred. This case was discussed in the UK context by Hope and Gray (1982).

Disclosure Issues

The preparers of financial statements have a further dilemma when it comes to disclosing their research and development activities. The more open and transparent they are, the more confident the users will be that the company is working and investing in order to remain competitive. Unfortunately, every piece of information that is released into the public domain will also inform and assist competitors. For obvious reasons, many companies are unwilling to provide too much information about research and development activities because competitors might take advantage.

In the absence of regulation, there would be relatively little consistency about the disclosures concerning research and development activities. For example, Microsoft has a reputation for providing considerable amounts of information about its plans for new operating systems and major software upgrades. That both keeps the shareholders informed and enables business contacts to make their own plans accordingly. The opposite is true with respect to the motor industry. If a new model is likely to be introduced in the near future, then consumers are reluctant to buy existing inventory. Information about styling and specifications can be used by competitors. It is quite common for prototypes of new cars to be road tested with competitors' name badges on their boot lids and dummy body panels attached to disguise the shape and even the size of the car underneath.

Yet another example occurred in 2006, when Amazon, the Internet retailer, denied claims that it was on the brink of launching an innovative new video-download service. The rumours that prompted this denial had been sparked by Wall Street analysts speculating on the company's increased expenditure on research and development.

Research versus Development

IAS 38 applies the same accounting logic to all internally generated intangibles, regardless of whether they are research and development or have arisen in some other way. In practice, it is difficult to imagine many intangibles that might be internally generated that would meet the recognition criteria.

The IAS states that the generation of an intangible has two phases:

(a) a research phase; and
(b) a development phase.

The distinction is that, during the research phase of an internal project, it is impossible to demonstrate that an intangible asset exists that will generate probable future economic benefits. For example, a project aimed at obtaining new knowledge or even some fairly specific investigation of possible improvements to existing products or processes are both in the research phase because it is impossible to demonstrate that this work will generate future economic benefits.

All expenditure incurred on research[5] or the research phase of a project should be written off as incurred, even though there may be some expectation that the outlay will ultimately benefit the business. For example, a pharmaceutical company might fund academic research into the properties of the common cold virus in the hope that it might one day make it possible to develop a cure that would be commercially viable. There is a good chance that this expenditure will be a waste of money, but, if the company funds many such projects, then some will succeed and, over the range of studies, the funding could be a commercial success.

IAS 38 has rather more stringent criteria for determining the development phase of a project. In order to qualify as such, the project has to meet each of the following criteria:[6]

• The completion of the intangible asset must be technically feasible so that it will be available for use or sale.
• The company must intend to complete the intangible asset and use or sell it.
• The company must intend to use or sell the intangible asset.
• There must be a clear expectation that the intangible asset will generate probable future economic benefits. For example, is there a market for the output

---

[5] IAS 38 defines research as: 'original and planned investigation undertaken with the prospect of gaining new scientific or technical knowledge and understanding'. That is a more specific definition than the broader concept of the research phase of a project, but the fact that an asset with future economic benefits cannot be identified is implicit in it.

[6] There should not be any reason to memorise these criteria by rote learning. Essentially, the project must be likely to generate a viable product. If there are any technical or commercial barriers that still have to be overcome, then at least one of the criteria has not been satisfied.

of the intangible asset or for the intangible asset itself? If it is to be used internally, will the intangible asset be useful?

- The company must have available adequate technical, financial, and other resources to complete the development and to use or sell the intangible asset.
- The company must be able to measure reliably the expenditure attributable to the intangible asset during its development.

The costs incurred on an intangible asset from the time that the project first meets these criteria must be capitalised as an asset. In practice, it will be difficult to meet these criteria, and so only a very few projects are likely to be eligible for capitalisation. If, for some reason, the directors wish to write off the costs of those few projects as soon as they are incurred, then all they need do is decide that they do not intend to complete the project or use the results, or take a pessimistic view of any one of the other criteria. Such a decision need not prevent them from actually making commercial use of the resulting product, process, or other output.

For example, if our pharmaceutical company has got to the stage of testing an effective cure for the common cold that will almost certainly sell well and is almost certainly safe for human consumption, then it could capitalise any further costs incurred during the development phase. This might include the cost of any final tweaks and tests to deal with questions such as the precise dosage to put in each tablet or the reaction of consumers to particular shapes and colours of pill. The costs incurred during the research phase should not be reinstated in any way. They have already been written off against profit and they should be left there as part of the retained earnings figure.

One specific requirement of IAS 38 is that internally generated brands, mastheads, publishing titles, customer lists, and items similar in substance cannot be recognised as intangible assets. This is because expenditure on such items cannot be distinguished from the cost of developing the business as a whole. Therefore, such items are not recognised as intangible assets. For example, one of the most famous advertising campaigns in the UK involved paying Jamie Oliver, a famous television chef, to advertise the Sainsbury's supermarket chain. This launched in 2000 and was still running in 2006. This campaign is credited with generating billions of pounds in additional turnover for the company and hundreds of millions of pounds in additional profit. Indeed, the company's 2006 annual report devoted two pages to a full colour photograph of an advert being filmed and made further mention of the ongoing success of the adverts in the body of the report. Nevertheless, it would not be appropriate to capitalise the costs of this campaign as an intangible asset because the effects of this advertising cannot really be distinguished from internally generated goodwill. This is evidenced by referring to the intangible non-current asset disclosures in Sainsbury's 2006 annual report. The company's intangibles comprise purchased goodwill from company acquisitions, pharmaceutical licences (which give the company the right to sell certain products from its stores), and computer software. There is no mention of the very valuable internally generated goodwill from the Jamie Oliver campaign.

Capitalising Costs

If a project has been capitalised as development, then the costs that can be capitalised are those that are directly attributable to creating, producing, and preparing the asset to be capable of operating in the manner intended by management. These include all materials and labour expended on the project from the date that it met the development criteria, the costs associated with registering a legal right, and so on.

Costs previously recognised as an expense (e.g. when the project was in the research phase) cannot be reinstated.

It is not possible to capitalise selling, administrative, and other general overhead expenditure unless this expenditure can be directly attributed to preparing the asset for use. Initial costs incurred in the process of bringing the asset to its planned performance and training costs to enable staff to operate the asset cannot be capitalised either.

Recognition of an Expense

By now you might be forming the opinion that IAS 38 is written so as to make it as difficult as possible to capitalise intangibles. It is difficult to classify purchased intangibles as non-current assets, and the criteria for internally created intangibles are even more stringent. Just to make sure, IAS 38 adds some further exclusions.

In 2006, PwC, a major international accounting firm, set up a new operation in Japan. We do not need to go into the background of this, but the setting up costs provide an interesting set of questions in terms of accounting for intangibles.[7]

> **Think!**
>
> Assuming that there were no rules to the contrary, what arguments could you put forward for capitalising the initial setting up costs of a new business (e.g. the cost of recruiting staff, staff costs incurred during the setting up period, etc.)?
>
> What arguments could you put up against capitalising?

---

[7] PwC is an accountancy firm and does not have to prepare financial statements in the same manner as its clients. That does not prevent us from using the case as an example.

In the first instance, the firm will have to establish an office and recruit staff. At first there will be relatively little for the staff to do because even a firm with PwC's status will take some time to establish a client base. Staff recruited locally may have to be trained in PwC's approach to work, and expatriates recruited from other PwC offices will have to learn about Japanese business and accounting practices. Throughout this period, the firm will be paying rent and salaries and will have little or no fee income to offset against these.

In terms of satisfying the recognition criteria, we have a clearly defined and measurable set of costs. The firm is unlikely to have gone into the country without having a very clear idea of the size of the market and the ability to generate fee income (i.e. economic resources). There could be an argument for treating the initial costs as an intangible asset.

The counterargument is that the resulting investment is not in a specific asset that might be separable from the business itself. It is very similar to (but not quite the same as) an investment in internally generated goodwill. This is not a convincing argument on its own, but it does suggest that we are incapable of ensuring consistency of accounting practice without some further guidance.

IAS 38 states that expenditure on an intangible item shall be recognised as an expense when it is incurred unless it meets the recognition criteria that we have already discussed or should be classified as goodwill because of the effects of the business combination process that we have also discussed previously.

To deal with at least some of the potential disagreements that might arise, IAS 38 specifically forbids the capitalisation of expenditure on:

- start-up activities, such as those discussed above, unless the expenditure results in the acquisition of a tangible asset;
- training activities;
- advertising and promotional activities;
- relocating or reorganising part or all of an entity.

Furthermore, once a cost has been written off, it cannot be reinstated as an intangible asset at a later date.

Measurement after Recognition

So far we have dealt with accounting for intangibles at cost. It is acceptable to value intangible non-current assets at cost less amortisation and impairment losses. We will deal with the issue of amortising intangibles later in this chapter. We dealt with impairment in Chapter 8.

There is an alternative approach, which is to show intangibles at a revalued amount. If an entity chooses to revalue an asset in a particular class (e.g. trade licences or software), then all of the assets in that class must be revalued too. This is to prevent a company from going through the list of intangibles on its balance sheet and 'cherry-picking' those that are worth more than their book value and leaving the rest as they are.

Revaluation is only possible if there is an active market in similar assets. This means that:

• the items traded in the market are homogeneous;
• willing buyers and sellers can normally be found at any time; and
• prices are available to the public.

For example, we have already mentioned in passing that airport landing slots are freely bought and sold on an open market and so it would be legitimate for an airline that owned slots at a major airport to show them at their valuation. Other possible assets that would be suitable for revaluation include freely transferable taxi licences, fishing licences, or production quotas.[8] However, an active market cannot exist for brands, newspaper mastheads, music and film publishing rights, patents, or trademarks because each such asset is unique and transactions are relatively infrequent.

Revalued assets are subject to amortisation and impairment reviews, but the revaluation exercise has to be repeated with sufficient frequency for the carrying amount of the assets not to differ materially from their fair value.

If subsequent revaluations are no longer possible because there is no suitable active market, then the carrying amount of the asset shall be its revalued amount at the date of the last revaluation less any subsequent accumulated amortisation and any subsequent accumulated impairment losses.

If an intangible asset in a class of revalued intangible assets cannot be revalued because there is no active market for this asset, the asset shall be carried at its cost less any accumulated amortisation and impairment losses.

Amortisation of Intangibles

Amortisation is just another word for depreciation, but applied to intangibles rather than tangible non-current assets.

---

[8] These are available for sale and purchase in some countries, but not necessarily all. If there is no market, then there can be no revaluation.

The first issue is to determine the estimated useful lives of the assets. In some cases these will have a clear upper limit. For example, a patent might have five years left to run, or a licensing agreement might give the right to build ten helicopters of a particular type. Such a restriction will normally form the upper bound to the estimated useful life for accounting purposes, although the company might extend this if there is a strong likelihood that any legal agreement will be extended without any great difficulty.

There is no guarantee, though, that the asset will continue to generate economic benefits for the whole of that life. For example, the company might cease sales of the patented product within three years, or the air force might only wish to buy eight of the helicopters. The company should draw on any and all information that is available that might give an indication of how long the asset is likely to last.

Estimating the useful life of intangibles can be extremely difficult. For example, the 'millennium bug' scare at the end of 1999 arose because many commercial software packages were written using legacy Cobol code that had been programmed in the fairly distant past, when computer storage was so expensive that dates were written with only two digits for years (e.g. 1987 was written as 87). Much to the surprise of everyone, including the original programmers, much of this software was still in use in 1999, and there were serious concerns that the roll-over from 99 to 00 would have catastrophic consequences.

In the case of the millennium bug, the estimated useful life of the intangible had been massively underestimated, but it is just as easy to overestimate useful lives. For example, in the United Kingdom it was briefly popular for major corporations to change their corporate identities, usually at very great cost in terms of replacing stationery, replacing signage on buildings and vehicles, and so on.[9] For example, Royal Mail rebranded itself as 'Consignia'. In many cases, the new names and identities lasted for only a few months before public opinion led to the re-instatement of the old identities.

Once an estimate of the useful life has been arrived at, the next step is to spread the depreciable amount of each asset on a systematic basis over its useful life. As with the depreciation of tangible assets, there are several acceptable bases for doing so. The straight-line method is probably simplest and most realistic, although it would be acceptable to use reducing balance, units of production, or any other basis that gave a more realistic allocation.

Entities are required to review their amortisation method and period every year.

---

[9] Such costs could not be capitalised under IAS 38, but that does not affect the point of the example. It is difficult to tell how long an investment in this type of resource will continue to generate value.

In principle, an intangible asset could have an indefinite useful life. For example, Imperial Tobacco's 2008 annual report states that purchased trademarks include the Davidoff cigarette trademark and some premium cigar trademarks that are considered to have indefinite lives because they are 'established international brands with global potential'. Other trademarks, whose longevity is less assured, are amortised over periods of up to 30 years.

Intangibles with infinite useful lives should not be amortised, although the assumption that the useful life is infinite should be reviewed each accounting period.

Disclosure

IAS 38 provides detailed provisions concerning intangibles. There are so many areas requiring estimates and assumptions that entities have to give detailed insights into the effects that intangibles have had on their figures. That makes it easier to compare different companies' financial statements.

The following should be stated for each class of intangible assets (e.g. computer software or production quotas), distinguishing between internally generated and other intangible assets:

- amortisation rates or estimated useful lives and methods of amortisation (if an infinite life is assumed, then that should be stated);
- the gross carrying amount and any accumulated amortisation at the beginning and end of the period;
- the line item(s) of the income statement in which any amortisation of intangible assets is included (arguably, the amortisation figure is so heavily affected by estimates that almost any figure could be justified);
- a reconciliation of the carrying amount at the beginning and end of the period, showing details of additions, disposals, amortisation, and other adjustments.

If intangible assets are accounted for at revalued amounts, then an entity shall disclose the following for each class of intangible assets:

- the effective date of the revaluation;
- the carrying amount of revalued intangible assets; and
- the carrying amount that would have been recognised had the revalued class of intangible assets been measured at cost less amortisation.

An entity shall disclose the aggregate amount of research and development expenditure recognised as an expense during the period. This need not be analysed between research and development or show details of particular projects.

Summary

This chapter deals with a complicated area. The complexity arises in part because of the history of accounting practice in this area. Before the introduction of rules to prevent such behaviour, companies used to recognise all sorts of intangible assets in their balance sheets. They did this, in part, to remind readers of the financial statements that they owned valuable brand names, goodwill, patent rights, and the rest. They were also motivated by a desire to reduce gearing ratios.

IAS 38 deals with the accounting treatment of intangibles, although a recurring theme of this chapter has been that it is difficult to capitalise a cost as an intangible and even more difficult to introduce a revalued amount for an asset once it has been purchased. It could be argued that IAS 38 is almost as much about excluding intangibles from the balance sheet as it is about accounting for those assets that are recognised.

Tutorial Questions

Question 1

The 2005 annual report of the Scottish Media Group plc states that the principal activities of the group are 'the production and broadcasting of television programmes, local and national radio production and broadcasting, the sale of advertising airtime and space in these media and in outdoor, cinema and Internet services'.

Turning to the group's statement of financial position, the only asset listed is goodwill on consolidation (i.e. the accounting adjustment arising on the acquisition of a subsidiary company).

Required:
- List other intangibles that the Scottish Media Group is likely to own and state the arguments for and against capitalising each in the published balance sheet.
- Explain whether it 'matters' that the statement of financial position excludes some assets that could have been shown as assets.

Question 2

Assume that Flyaway Airlines has decided to enter into the London to Singapore market and has purchased a pair of slots from BA for £8 million. Assume that the following costs were also incurred:

- Legal fees of £0.5 million.
- Managing director's time involved in negotiation and planning the purchase. The MD estimates that at least a working month has been spent on this acquisition over the past two years. The MD's employment costs are £240 000 per year.
- Cost of rental of airport facilities before the flights actually started to operate: £0.8 million.
- Cost of running the flights at a loss for the first few months until the route became popular and it regularly passed its breakeven point: £2.5 million.

Required:
Discuss the following:

(a) How difficult would it be to decide whether the cost of the pair of slots had met the recognition criteria? List the criteria that would have to be taken into account.
(b) Assuming that the cost is to be capitalised, what is the total cost that should be taken to the statement of financial position?

Question 3

The accounting policies note for intangibles in the 2006 annual report of Emirates (an international airline based in the United Arab Emirates) reads as follows:

Intangible assets
Intangible assets are capitalised at cost only when future economic benefits are probable. Cost includes purchase price together with any directly attributable expenditure.

When the carrying amount of an intangible asset is greater than its estimated recoverable amount, it is written down immediately to its estimated recoverable amount.

Intangible assets are amortised on a straight-line basis over the estimated useful lives which are:

- Service rights 15 years
- Computer software 5 years

A note to the financial statements shows details of the major movements on the cost and cumulative amortisation of those assets.

Explain how the company's accounting policies with respect to intangibles appear to comply fully with IAS 38.

Question 4

Discuss the extent to which accounting for research and development is a political issue.

Question 5

Explain why some football players are capitalised as assets on the statement of financial position of their clubs and others are not.

Further Work

The answers to these end-of-chapter questions can be found at the back of the book.

Question 1

H is a major electronics company. It spends a substantial amount on research and development.

The company's latest annual report included a page of voluntary disclosures about the effectiveness of the company's research programme. This indicated that the company's prosperity depended on the development of new products, and that this could be a very long process. In order to maintain its technical lead, the company often funded academic research studies into theoretical areas, some of which led to breakthroughs that H was able to patent and develop into new product ideas. The company claimed that the money spent in this way was a good investment because for every twenty fruitless projects there was usually at least one valuable discovery that generated enough profit to cover the whole cost of the research activities. Unfortunately, it was impossible to tell in advance which projects would succeed in this way.

A shareholder expressed dismay at H's policy of writing off research costs in this manner. He felt that this was unduly pessimistic given that the company earned a good return from its research activities. He felt that the company should depart from the requirements of IAS 38 in order to achieve a fair presentation.

Required:

(a) Explain why it might be justifiable for H plc to capitalise its research costs.

(b) Explain why IAS 38 imposes a rigid set of rules that prevent the capitalisation of research expenditure and make it difficult to capitalise development expenditure.

(c) Explain whether the requirements of IAS 38 are likely to discourage companies such as H from indulging in research activities.

(d) Describe the advantages and disadvantages of offering companies the option of departing from the detailed requirements of standards in order to achieve a fair presentation.

(e) H's 20X6 year-end trial balance includes the following costs incurred on new projects started during the year. Explain whether each of these projects should be capitalised.

• *Project A – new music player*. Expected to cost a total of £800 000 to develop. Expected total revenues £2 000 000 once work is completed – probably late 20X7. Costs incurred to date = £280 000.

• *Project B – new mobile telephone*. Expected to cost a total of £3 000 000 to complete. Future revenues are likely to exceed £5 000 000. The completion date is uncertain because external funding will have to be obtained before research work can be completed. Costs incurred to date = £150 000.

• *Project C – investigation of a new microprocessor recently developed in the aerospace industry*. If this proves effective, then the company may well generate significant savings by using it in place of existing microprocessors. Costs incurred to date = £110 000. The company has successfully applied for a patent for the use of this microprocessor in conjunction with other fabrication techniques.

Question 2

Wave manufactures echo sounding equipment for naval ships and fishing boats. The company's latest trial balance as at 31 December 20X8 is as follows:

	£000	£000
Administration costs	800	
Bank overdraft		700
Factory – cost	17 200	
Factory – depreciation		1 800
Factory running costs	1 200	
Loan interest	1 680	
Long-term loans		12 000
Machinery – cost	13 000	

Machinery – depreciation		8 000
Manufacturing wages	1 300	
Opening inventory	1 300	
Purchases – parts and materials	2 300	
Research and development	5 300	
Retained profits		380
Sales		10 000
Sales salaries	600	
Share capital		15 000
Trade fair	1 000	
Trade payables		600
Trade receivables	2 800	
	48 480	48 480

(i) Inventory was counted at 31 December 20X8 and valued at £1 230 000.

(ii) No depreciation has been charged for the year ended 31 December 20X8. The company depreciates the factory at 2% of cost per annum and all machinery at 25% per annum on the reducing balance basis.

(iii) The balance on the research and development account is made up as follows:

Opening balance (development costs brought forward)	£2 100 000
Calibrating equipment purchased for laboratory	600 000
Long-range sonar project	900 000
Diminishing echo project	1 700 000
	£5 300 000

The opening balance comprises expenditure on new products that have just been introduced to the market. The company has decided that these costs should be written off over ten years, starting with the year ended 31 December 20X8.

The new calibrating equipment is used in the company's research laboratory. It is used to ensure that the measurement devices used during experiments are properly adjusted. (*Note: take care with this item, it is a bit of a trick question!*)

The long-range sonar project is intended to adapt existing military sonar equipment to enable fishing boats to detect shoals of fish from a much greater distance. The company has built a successful prototype and has had strong expressions of interest from a number of potential customers. It is almost certain that the company will start to sell this product early in the year 20Y0, and that it will make a profit.

The diminishing echo project is an attempt to apply some theoretical concepts to create a new sonar system for use in tracking submarines. Initial experiments have been promising, but there is little immediate prospect of a saleable product because the transmitter is far too large and heavy to install in a naval ship.

(iv) During the year, the company spent £1 000 000 in order to exhibit its product range at a major trade fair. This was the first time that Wave had attended such an event. No orders have been received as a direct result of this fair, although the sales director has argued that contacts were made that will generate sales over the next few years.

Required:

(a) Prepare Wave's statement of comprehensive income for the year ended 31 December 20X8 and its statement of financial position as at that date.

(b) Explain how each of the following items should be treated in Wave's financial statements:

Research and development

(i) new calibrating equipment purchased for laboratory;

(ii) long-range sonar project;

(iii) diminishing echo project.

(c) Explain how the costs associated with the trade fair should be treated in Wave's financial statements.

Reference

Hope, T. and Gray, R. (1982), Power and policy making: the development of an R&D standard. *Journal of Business Finance and Accounting*, **9**(4), 531–558.

ACCOUNTING FOR INVENTORY AND CONSTRUCTION CONTRACTS

10

Contents

Learning Objectives

After studying this chapter you should be able to:

- describe the problems associated with accounting for inventory;
- apply the accounting treatments laid down for inventory by IAS 2;
- account for construction contracts.

Introduction

This chapter deals with two quite separate issues. The first is accounting for inventory, a topic that will affect virtually every business that sells a physical product. This is an important area of accounting because any distortions in the profit figure will distort reported profit by that same amount. The second topic is construction contracts. Perhaps very few companies will have such contracts, but the amounts involved can be staggering, and they do require a great deal of care in the recognition of revenues, costs, and balance sheet figures.

The Problems with Inventory

Inventory comprises assets that are held for trade. They are either finished goods held for resale or materials and partly completed goods that will be converted into finished goods in the normal course of business.

The basic mechanics of bookkeeping mean that the value attributed to inventory can have a significant impact on the reported profit. You should remember that the opening inventory figure is added to the other components of cost of sales and the closing inventory figure is deducted.

When a company's directors are drafting their financial statements, they will be aware that increasing inventory by any given sum will reduce the cost of sales by exactly that figure and thereby increase reported profit by the same amount. Reducing closing inventory will reduce reported profit in exactly the same way. If the directors wish to smooth out any trends in their profit from year to year, then finding excuses to increase or decrease closing inventory may be the easiest way to do so.

The temptation to misstate profit in this way may be increased because any overstatement of closing inventory will automatically overstate the following period's opening inventory and so the distortion will be cancelled the following year. That is a far more flexible means of adjusting or distorting the figures than some of the alternative approaches to 'creative accounting'. For example, capitalising revenue expenses as non-current assets will leave the company with assets in the statement of financial position that will have to be depreciated for the remainder of their notional lives.

A related issue is the fact that valuing inventory is actually quite difficult in practice. There are a number of estimates and assumptions that will be open to challenge at the best of times. Regardless of the honesty and integrity of the preparers of the financial statements, the inventory figure is always open to challenge. That means that a dishonest board of directors will be able to claim that they misstated the figures accidentally because of a forecasting error or inaccurate accounting assumption.

The Three Basic Problems

The three basic issues that have to be established in dealing with accounting for inventories are:

- establishing the quantity of inventory at the year end;
- establishing the cost of that inventory;
- valuing the inventory at the lower of cost and net realisable value.

Establishing quantities often involves a physical inventory count. Electronic inventory control systems can keep detailed records of the items recorded as received and issued, but they are by no means foolproof. For example, a supermarket's electronic point-of-sale system can update the inventory records for every item scanned through the tills, but there is no way to keep an accurate record of the goods that have been stolen by customers and staff or of any goods that were spoiled because of careless storage that were not written off because the staff responsible did not wish to be blamed.

The physical inventory count is essentially an accounting exercise, but it tends to be discussed in auditing texts rather than financial accounting texts such as this. It has been mentioned in passing because it is worth noting that accountants do have to go out into the factory or the store and get their hands dirty from time to time.

A manufacturing business will normally have at least three categories of inventory: raw materials, work in progress, and finished goods. One of the details that will have to be recorded in the course of the inventory count is the stage of completion of the work in progress so that the associated costs can be determined.

Establishing the cost and net realisable value of a given unit of inventory requires a number of decisions to be made, and these will be discussed separately below.

IAS 2

The main source of regulation in this area can be found in IAS 2 *Inventories*. The IAS deals with virtually all inventories apart from the following specialised types:

- Work in progress arising under construction contracts is dealt with by IAS 11 and is discussed separately later in this chapter
- Financial instruments that are held for trading purposes by financial institutions are dealt with by IAS 32 and IAS 39 and are beyond the scope of this text.
- Biological assets related to agricultural activities are dealt with by IAS 41 and are also beyond the scope of this text.

The basic requirement in IAS 2 is deceptively simple. Inventories are to be valued at the lower of cost and net realisable value.

Cost

Cost includes any and all costs that have been incurred in bringing the inventories to their present location and condition.

C & C Group plc, the Irish manufacturing company, highlights some of the factors that must be considered when deciding the accounting policy for arriving at cost in its accounting policies note on inventory:

> Inventories are stated at the lower of cost and net realisable value. Cost includes all expenditure incurred in acquiring the inventories and bringing them to their present location and condition and is based on the first-in first-out principle.
>
> In the case of finished goods and work in progress, cost includes direct production costs and the appropriate share of production overheads plus excise duties where appropriate. Net realisable value is the estimated selling price in the ordinary course of business, less estimated costs of completion and estimated costs necessary to complete the sale.
>
> Provision is made for slow-moving or obsolete stock where appropriate.

Unless the entity has a very simple business model, the cost of goods will often include several additions to the basic purchase price. Even trading companies that buy and sell goods manufactured by third parties may have to keep track of delivery charges and any duties or taxes other than sales taxes that can be reclaimed by the entity.

Some entities can track each unit of inventory separately and determine the costs associated with each unit held at the year end. For example, a vehicle dealer will be able to keep track of each vehicle separately using its chassis number or some other identifying mark. It may have purchased and sold many cars during the year, but it will be able to determine the purchase price of each vehicle in inventory as at the end of the year simply by looking up the appropriate invoices from the manufacturer. IAS 2 requires that such items are valued individually.

It becomes more difficult when dealing with items that cannot be identified in this way. For example, a food retailer may be unable to tell whether a case of canned fruit was part of a consignment that cost 50 cents per can to purchase or one that cost 55 cents. IAS 2 deals with this by offering the choice between two accounting assumptions:

- first-in, first-out (FIFO), which assumes that the oldest units are used first;
- weighted average, which recalculates the average cost per unit whenever inventory is acquired and values all despatches on the basis of that average cost.

These are by no means the only assumptions that can be made, and management accountants can and do argue that others may be more useful or appropriate for decision-making purposes. The methods permitted by IAS 2 have the advantage that they are generally acceptable to tax authorities and so they avoid having to restate the closing inventory for tax purposes.

In a simple example, suppose that a supermarket started to purchase a new product during the year. It acquired 10 000 units for 50 cents per can on 1 October and a further 20 000 units for 55 cents per can on 15 November. It had 8000 units left at the year end of 31 December.

The company purchased a total of 30 000 units costing a total of (10 000 × €0.50) + (20 000 × €0.55) = €16 000. It sold a total of 30 000 − 8000 = 12 000 units during the year. We need to decide how much the units that were sold cost the company, and how much the remaining units cost.

Under FIFO, the assumption is that the company sold the 10 000 units that were purchased for 50 cents and 2 000 of the units that cost 55 cents. The cost of sales was (10 000 × €0.50) + (2000 × €0.55) = €6100, and closing inventory was €16 000 − 6100 = €9900.

Under weighted average, the assumption is that each unit purchased cost €16 000/30 000 = 53.33 cents. The units sold cost 12 000 × €0.5333 = €6399.60, and closing inventory cost €16 000 − 6399.60 = €9600.40.

In our simple example, the choice of assumption would affect closing inventory and the reported profit to the tune of almost €300 (€9900 − 9600.40 = €299.60). And yet the same physical items would have been consumed in either case, and the cash flows would have been identical.

There are two important points worth noting:

- Firstly, the choice of assumptions is an accounting matter and need not reflect the underlying physical management of the inventory. There is no need to use the oldest inventory first in order to apply FIFO, or to mix different consignments evenly in order to use weighted average.
- Secondly, when prices are increasing, the FIFO assumption will tend to provide the lower cost of sales and so the higher profit figure. Historically, prices tend to increase over time, and so FIFO will tend to yield the higher reported profit. That explains why the tax authorities are so interested in the assumptions that might be used to determine the cost of closing inventory.[1]

IAS 2 offers the choice between FIFO and weighted average without indicating a preference for one over the other. The only condition is that companies must be

---

[1] The lowest profit, and hence the lowest tax, would arise if companies made the last in, first out assumption (LIFO). LIFO is generally not permitted by the tax authorities, nor by the IASB, even though it could be argued that it charges the most recent process to the income statement.

consistent in their choice, unless inventories have a different nature or use that would justify using FIFO for some and weighted average for others.

There are two possible alternatives to FIFO and weighted average, but they are only permissible where the results would be close to the figures that would be determined using these figures.

Many businesses, particularly those involved in manufacturing, use standard costs for internal reporting and accounting. Standard costing is essentially a management accounting technique. Typically, it involves specifying the inputs to a product (material, labour, and overheads) both in terms of quantity and unit cost. These standard cost specifications are meant to be a realistic estimate of the costs that should be incurred in manufacturing each unit. So, each unit could require two kilos of material with a standard cost of €1.50 per kilo, one hour of labour with a standard cost of €10.00, and overheads of €5.00. That means that the standard cost per unit would be $(2 \times €1.50) + (1 \times €10.00) + €5.00 = €18.00$.

IAS 2 permits the valuation of closing inventory at this standard cost provided the actual costs are not significantly different from standards. It is not difficult to ensure that this is the case in practice because one of the main reasons for using standard costing is to compare actual and standard costs and to analyse variances between the two on a regular basis so that reasons can be investigated and understood.

A second approximation is the so-called retail method. That can be used in a business that has a policy of adding a fixed mark-up to cost in order to arrive at selling price. A small retailer that sets selling prices at cost plus one-third could conduct a physical inventory count and record the selling prices of each line of inventory. If the retailer has goods that it is offering for sale at €40 000, then the cost of those goods is approximately €30 000.

Standard cost and the retail method are not really alternatives to FIFO and weighted average. They are permitted in situations where they would produce reasonable approximations to the main methods and might be adopted because they are likely to save time and effort. The ongoing sophistication of electronic inventory control systems may mean that even small businesses will have very little need of such short cuts.

Manufacturing Companies

The calculation of cost becomes more complicated when an entity manufactures goods because there is a wider range of expenses that may or may not be included.

IAS 2 clarifies the treatment of expenses with the following guidance on conversion costs:[2]

---

[2] That is, the cost of converting raw materials into finished goods.

- All costs of conversion should be included, including the cost of direct labour.
- All production overheads should be included, with any allocations made in a systematic manner.
- The allocation of fixed overheads should be based on normal activity levels if actual activity is significantly out of line with normal activity.

The reason for allocating fixed overheads using normal activity levels is the distortions that would arise if actual levels were used in years when output was unusually low. For example, suppose that total fixed production overheads are €2 million per year and normal output is 500 000 units per year. That would mean that the fixed overhead per unit would be €2 million/500 000 = €4.00 per unit. Suppose that the company had a really poor year, with output cut back to 200 000 units. If total fixed production overheads remain at €2 million, then the closing inventory would include €2 million/200 000 = €10.00 per unit for fixed production overheads. It might be argued that the use of an actual output level that is artificially low would have the effect of carrying forward an excessive cost to the following year, thereby understating cost of sales and overstating profits in poor years. Thus, the fixed production overhead will be approximately €4.00 per unit regardless of production levels.

Other Costs

Other costs are to be considered in terms of the basic criterion of whether they contributed to bringing goods to their present location and condition.
 IAS 2 offers some examples:

- If goods are designed or commissioned, then there may be times when certain costs that are not associated with production should be included; for example, design costs associated with creating goods for specific customers.
- Abnormal amounts of wasted materials, labour, or whatever should not normally be included. This may require some thought. It would certainly be acceptable to treat normal levels of wastage as part of cost.
- Storage costs are not normally to be included unless storage is regarded as part of the production process. For example, partly completed items might be set to one side to cure and harden before they move on to the next process. Any costs associated with this holding period would be regarded as part of the cost.
- Administrative costs that do not bring the goods to their present location and condition should be excluded, as should any selling costs.

Net Realisable Value

IAS 2 requires that each line of inventory be valued at the lower of cost and net realisable value.

> **Think!**
>
> Why should inventory be valued at the lower of cost and net realisable value?

Introducing net realisable value into the valuation process has the effect of recognising gains on inventory only when the inventory is sold, but losses are recognised as soon as they are foreseen. In a sense this means that the costs associated with inventory losses are recorded during the period in which they occur rather than waiting until the item is sold at a loss.

Net realisable value is defined as the expected selling price, assuming that the inventory is being sold under normal trading conditions, less any costs to complete the goods and any costs necessary to make the sale.

The comparison of cost and net realisable value should normally be done on a line-by-line basis. In practice, it is relatively easy to identify lines of inventory that are at risk of being written down. The physical count is an opportunity to look for inventory that is damaged or seems to have been in stock for a very long time. Computerised inventory systems can also identify lines that are old and whose value should be considered.

Disclosure

IAS 2 requires a number of disclosures:

- the entity's accounting policies for valuing inventory;
- the total value of inventory, broken down into suitable classifications such as raw materials, work in progress, and finished goods;
- the value attached to any inventory that is carried at net realisable value;
- the amount of inventories recognised as an expense during the period;
- the amount recognised as an expense due to inventory being written down in value and also the amount of any reversal in write-downs recognised with a statement of the circumstances that led to the reversal;
- the value of any inventories pledged as security for a liability.

It may seem unlikely that any inventory that has been written down to net realisable value will subsequently increase in value, but the detailed disclosure requirements will reduce the temptation to write down inventory in good years with the intention of recognising a much larger profit when it is sold in a later period. There is no accounting justification for doing so, but it would be a useful means of smoothing out temporary upswings in profits.

In spite of the importance of inventory in terms of its impact on reported profit, the disclosures provided are rarely particularly extensive. For example, the 2008 annual report of Volkswagen, a German vehicle manufacturer, ran to almost 300 pages, and yet the inventory note took up less than half a page:

- A table breaking the total inventory of almost €18 billion down between five categories:
  - raw materials, consumables, and supplies;
  - work in progress;
  - finished goods and purchased merchandise;
  - current leased assets;[3]
  - payments on account.
- A brief narrative note states that the total includes inventories of approximately €2.5 billion at net realisable value, and that inventories of roughly €91 billion were recognised in cost of sales for the year.

Construction Contracts

Construction contracts frequently span two or more accounting periods. From the point of view of the contractor who is responsible for the work, this means that there are complicated issues associated with deciding how much profit was earned in any given year.

> **Think!**
>
> Is it realistic to recognise profit on a partly completed construction contract before it is completed? Is it inconsistent to recognise gains on such work in progress when retailers and manufacturers have to wait until their inventory has been sold before any profit is recognised?

Construction contracts are almost certainly the subject of considerable care and attention before they are signed. The contractor is unlikely to agree to build a bridge or a stretch of motorway without making sure that the work can be done to the required standard at a profit. The client will also have to provide various assurances of solvency. It is common practice for work to be paid for in instalments when the contract reaches agreed stages of completion.

---

[3] We will deal with leased assets in Chapter 11.

The most typical arrangement would be for both parties to appoint an independent expert to review progress on a regular basis and to certify that the various milestones had been reached. Then the client would pay the agreed value of that work, less a 'retention'. The purpose of the retention is to give the contractor an incentive to complete the project to a satisfactory standard because an agreed proportion of the fee will be held back until such time as the work is finished and has been examined and tested to the client's satisfaction.

The contractor will almost certainly be expert in estimating the costs associated with any given contract. The contract itself may be for a fixed sum, or there may be some flexibility built in to renegotiate for any unforeseen contingencies. Sometimes there is a clause that adjusts for the effects of changing prices, so that the contractor need not worry if, say, concrete prices rise by 7% because the cost of the increase can be invoiced to the client.

When a retailer buys inventory with a view to selling it at a profit, there is always a slight risk that the inventory will remain unsold or will have to be sold at a loss. It is therefore quite realistic to wait until the goods have been sold at a profit before recognising any gain. When a contractor enters into a five-year construction project, there is a clearly identified customer who has not only signed a contract but will almost certainly have provided further evidence that the funding is in place to pay for the work. It may be impossible to predict the financial outcome of the project with absolute certainty, but the contractor will undoubtedly have access to expert opinion on the likely profit. On that basis, it is not merely reasonable to recognise profit as and when it is earned during the course of the project, it is necessary to do so. The income statement would be extremely misleading if the whole profit were recognised at the conclusion of the project when the contractor's management was keeping a very close watch over progress.

IAS 11

The accounting treatment of construction contracts is set out in IAS 11 *Construction Contracts*. The basic requirement of the IAS is that profits should be recognised throughout the contract, although there is a great deal of discretion as to how the profits should be determined from period to period.

IAS 11 requires the contract to be treated as if it has been 'sold' in instalments throughout the course of its completion:

- Turnover is ascertained in an appropriate manner.
- Profit should be recognised as the difference between reported turnover and related costs on a contract-by-contract basis.
- Losses should be recognised as soon as they are foreseen.

Ideally, profit should be recognised in a manner that reflects the period's activity.

Every year the contractor will consider the likely outcome on each contract that is in progress. The total revenue may be fixed at an agreed sum, or it may be open to adjustment or negotiation. For example, some government contracts are on a 'cost-plus' basis under which the contractor has to submit detailed accounts of the costs incurred and the fee is equal to that figure plus a percentage for profit.

The actual costs incurred to date are often very easy to track. Most expenses will be incurred for specific projects, and so there will be very little need to allocate costs. For example, a civil engineering company may have six contracts under way. Each contract will have its own accounts in the bookkeeping records. If an invoice is received for, say, materials or subcontracted labour, then the site to which the materials were delivered or where the work was undertaken will be indicated on the invoice, and so it will be very straightforward to establish where the costs were incurred.

Predicting the costs that are still to be incurred will be more difficult, although civil engineers often say that 'the three most important things in managing a contract are cost, cost, and cost'. Businesses that engage in this type of work will normally have their own experts in project management and cost control.

Provided the outcome of the project can be predicted with reasonable reliability, IAS 11 requires that the profit earned to date be accounted for. There is no specific guidance provided by the standard, but the following would be acceptable bases:

- proportion of value completed to date × expected profit;
- proportion of estimated total costs incurred × expected profit;
- proportion of estimated total labour costs incurred × expected profit;
- physical stage of completion.

A Simple Example

A contractor has agreed to build a road from Eastown to Westown for €3.0 million.

The contractor estimated that the work would cost €2.0 million and would take three years.

The contractor recognises profit on the basis of the percentage of total cost incurred to date.

The contract proceeded as follows:

Year 1	
Costs incurred to date	€1.0m
Estimated costs to completion	€1.1m
Estimated profit	€0.9m
Profit earned to date	€0.9m × 1.0/2.1 = €0.43m

By the end of the first year, it appears that the estimated total cost of the project is €1.0 + 1.1 = €2.1 million. The selling price is fixed at €3.0 million, so the expected profit is €0.9 million.

The contractor has completed €1.0/2.1 = 47.6% of the contract, so €0.9 million × 47.6% = €0.43 million has been earned to date.

All of the work to date was undertaken this year, so all of the profit earned to date was earned this year too.

Year 2	
Costs incurred to date	€1.8m
Estimated costs to completion	€0.4m
Estimated profit	€0.8m
Profit earned to date	€0.8m × 1.8/2.2 = €0.65m
Profit earned in year 2	€0.65 − 0.43 = €0.22m

At the end of year 2 we have revised the estimated total cost to €1.8 + 0.4 = €2.2 million. The selling price remains fixed at €3.0 million, so the anticipated profit is now €0.8 million.

The contract is now €1.8/2.2 = 81.8% completed, so €0.8 million × 81.8% = €0.65 million has been earned to date.

We have already recognised €0.43 million prior to this year, so the profit earned in year 2 = €0.65 − 0.43 = €0.22 million.

Year 3	
Costs incurred to date	€2.3m
Estimated costs to completion	Zero

Profit earned to date	€0.7m
Profit earned in year 3	€0.7 − 0.65 = €0.05m

By the end of year 3, the contract is 100% complete. A total of €2.3 million has been spent on a contract worth €3.0 million, so the final profit is €3.0 − 2.3 = €0.7 million.

A total of €0.65 million was recognised in earlier years, so the profit earned in year 3 = €0.7 − 0.65 = €0.05 million.

Turnover

IAS 11 does not give any specific guidance on the recognition of turnover. The basis used will normally be the same as that for the recognition of profit.

If we apply that logic to our simple example above, we get the following figures:

Year 1	
Turnover	€3.0m × 1.0/2.1 = €1.43m
Profit	€0.43
Cost of sales	€1.0m

The total turnover for the contract will be €3.0 million using the same arguments as for profit, and we have earned a total of €1.43 million by the end of year 1.

If turnover is €1.43 million and profit is €0.43 million, then cost of sales must be the difference = €1.43 − 0.43 = €1.0 million.

Year 2	
Turnover (cumulative)	€3.0m × 1.8/2.2 = €2.45m
Turnover (year 2 only)	€2.45m − 1.43m = €1.02m
Profit	€0.22m
Cost of sales	€1.02m − 0.22m = €0.8m

The cumulative turnover earned to date by the end of year 2 is €2.45 million, which includes €1.02 million earned in year 2.

Profit for year 2 was calculated above at €0.22 million, so cost of sales for the year is €0.8 million.

Year 3	
Turnover (cumulative)	€3.0m
Turnover (year 3 only)	€3.0m − 2.45m = €0.55m
Profit	€0.05
Cost of sales	€0.55m − 0.05m = €0.5m

The same logic shows that turnover for year 3 was €0.55 million, profit had already been worked out at €0.05 million, and so cost of sales was €0.5 million.

Foreseeable Losses

When a loss is foreseen, the whole of the loss is recognised immediately. The basic mechanics are exactly the same as before, except that there is no need to worry about the proportion complete.

For example, suppose that the first year of the road-building project described above had gone as before, but that the contractor uncovered some problems that would increase the costs of completing the contract to €2.7 million.

Our calculations at the end of year 1 would be as follows:

Year 1	
Costs incurred to date	€1.0m
Estimated costs to completion	€2.7m
Estimated loss	(€0.7m)

The contract will cost €3.7 million to complete and the selling price is only €3.0 million, so the loss will be €0.7 million.

The contract is €1.0/3.7 = 27.0% complete. Turnover for the year is €3.0 million × 27.0% = €0.81 million.

The whole of the loss is recognised immediately, so cost of sales is €1.51 million to give a recognised loss of €0.7 million on a turnover of €0.81 million.

Statement of Financial Position

The most complicated balance is effectively just a balancing figure.
  Gross amount due from (or to) customers is calculated as:

- total costs incurred to date;
- plus attributable profits (or minus foreseeable losses);
- minus progress billings to the customer.

The resulting figure will normally be positive because it is effectively the value of the unbilled work done to date for the customer. If it is positive, then it should be shown as a current asset: 'Gross amounts due from customers'.

In the event that the figure is negative (because of accrued losses or because of billings in advance), then it will appear as a current liability: 'Gross amounts due to customers'.

The other balance that might arise is any unpaid amount that has been billed to the customer. These balances might be settled within a short period if the customer intends to pay the amount in full in the immediate short term, or they could be retentions that might not be collectable for several months or even years.

A Comprehensive Example

Blend has agreed to build a bridge on a government contract. The company has no other contracts in progress and no other sources of income.

The bridge will take three years to complete. The contract price is €14.0 million. Blend recognises profit and turnover on the basis of the proportion of work certified by an independent architect.

At the end of the first year of the contract, the company's trial balance is as follows:

	€m	€m
Revenue		5.0
Retention	1.0	
Material and labour costs	4.0	
Bank	5.1	
Trade payables		0.8
Share capital		3.0
Retained earnings		1.3
	10.1	10.1

The architect inspected the work done to date just before the year end and certified that work to the value of €5.0 million had been completed. This was invoiced to the customer, and, in accordance with the contract, 80% of the invoiced amount was paid immediately, with the remainder being held back as a retention.

The directors estimate that it will cost a further €5.3 million to complete this contract.

No other adjustments have been made in respect of this contract.

Solution to the Comprehensive Example

In order to prepare the financial statements from this information, the first step is to determine whether the contract will prove profitable. In this case, it will cost an estimated total of €4.0 + 5.3 = €9.3 million and will be sold for €14.0 million. Thus, there is an anticipated profit of €4.7 million.

The stage of completion is based on architect's certificates. (This is an important point – the question must always specify the manner in which turnover and profit are recognised.) On that basis, turnover to date is the total value certified, which is €5.0 million. The proportion of the work completed is €5.0/14.0 = 35.7% of the contract as a whole. Thus, profit of €4.7 million × 35.7% = €1.7 million has been earned to date.

If turnover is €5.0 million and profit is €1.7 million, then cost of sales must be €5.0 − 1.7 = €3.3 million.

The figure for gross amounts due to or from customers is €4.0 + 1.7 − 5.0 = €0.7 million.

So, the income statement for the year will be as follows:

Income statement	
	€m
Revenue	5.0
Cost of sales	3.3
Profit	1.7
Statement of financial position	
	€m
Current assets	
Trade receivables	1.0
Gross amount due from customers	0.7
Bank	5.1
	6.8

Equity	
Share capital	3.0
Retained earnings (1.3 + 1.7)	3.0
	6.0
Current liabilities	
Trade payables	0.8
	6.8

Disclosure

IAS 11 requires that companies disclose the amount of contract revenue recognised in the period. The notes should also make it clear how contract revenue and the stage of completion of contracts are determined.

The aggregate amount of costs incurred and recognised profits (less recognised losses) to date have to be disclosed, along with the amounts of advances received and retentions.

The notes must also state the gross amount due from or to customers for contract work as an asset or as a liability, whichever is appropriate.

Summary

This short chapter is designed to give you the confidence to read through a real set of financial statements. You will find it helpful to read some annual reports because it will help you to become familiar with the presentation requirements. It will also help you to appreciate the fact that accounting is a practical discipline and that the accounts are read by shareholders and others with a view to making decisions.

Many companies make their financial statements available electronically, and others will supply printed copies on request. It is possible to acquire several sets without going to any great trouble.

Tutorial Questions

Question 1

Foy manufactures briefcases. The variable costs of making a single briefcase have been established as follows:

Per unit	£
Raw materials	10.00
Import duties on above	2.50
Direct labour	30.00

In addition, the following costs are also incurred every month:	£
Factory power	8 000
Supervisors' salaries	12 000
Depreciation of plant	7 000
Sales department costs	18 000
Administration costs	22 000
	20 000

The normal activity level is 5000 units produced per month. The selling price is £120 per briefcase.

The directors are arguing about the valuation of stocks produced during August. The competing views are as follows:

1. As the company manufactures only one product, all of the costs incurred by the company should be shared equally by each unit.

2. As, during August, only 4000 units were produced, the overheads should be shared out between those units.

3. It would be imprudent to include any overheads in the valuation of inventories.

You are required to discuss the views expressed by the directors and to recommend a valuation of the units produced during August.

Question 2

S Ltd is a manufacturing company. It held its annual stock count on 31 March 20X2, the company's year end. The accounts department is currently working its way through the stock sheets, placing a value on the physical stocks. The company has had a difficult year, and profits are likely to be lower than in the previous year.

• *Raw materials*. Stocks of raw materials are valued at cost. The finance director has suggested that the cost has been understated in previous years because the company has not taken the costs of delivery or insurance into account. These can be substantial in the case of imported goods. It has been proposed that these costs be taken into account in the valuation of closing stocks of raw materials.

• *Work in progress*. The cost of work in progress includes an element of overheads. The following table of figures has been prepared in order to assist in the calculation of the overhead absorption:

	£
Fixed costs:	
Factory rent, rates and insurance	150 000
Administration expenses	240 000
Factory security	110 000
Variable costs:	
Factory heat, light and power	300 000
Sales commissions and selling costs	120 000
Depreciation of machinery	200 000
Depreciation of delivery vehicles	70 000

Overheads are usually absorbed on the basis of labour hours. The stock sheets suggest that 500 labour hours have been included in work in progress. A total of 70 000 hours has been worked by production staff during the year. This figure is, however, much lower than the normal figure of 95 000 hours.

• *Finished goods*. Finished goods have already been valued at £400 000. This figure includes some obsolete stocks that cost £70 000 to produce but that are likely to be sold at a scrap value of £500. There are also several batches of a new product that will be launched early in the new financial year. These cost £90 000 to manufacture. Independent market research suggests that it is very likely that the new product will be sold for considerably more than this. If, however, the launch is unsuccessful, the new product will have to be sold as scrap for £1000. The finance director has said that the aggregate net realisable value of all closing stocks of finished goods is at least £500 000, and so there is no need to worry about the obsolete and new stock products.

Required:
(a) (i) Explain whether the costs of delivery and insurance should be included in the valuation of raw materials.
   (ii) Assuming that the change is made, state how the change should be accounted for.
(b) (i) Explain how IAS 2 requires overheads to be treated in the valuation of closing stocks.

(ii) Calculate the value of overheads to be absorbed to S Ltd's closing stock of work in progress.

(c) (i) Explain whether the valuation of closing stocks at the lower of cost and net realisable value should be done on an item-by-item basis or on the basis of the aggregate cost of all items as compared with their aggregate net realisable value.

(ii) State how you would value the obsolete items and the new product line, giving reasons for your valuation in each case.

Question 3

K plc designs and installs computer systems for large companies and government organisations. Most of the company's sales involve several months of activity, and some contracts can take up to two years to complete.

The company's trial balance at 30 September 20X0 was as follows:

	£000	£000
Contract A – Costs incurred to date	1 200	
Contract B – Costs incurred to date	3 100	
Contract A – Invoiced to client		2 000
Contract B – Invoiced to client		3 000
Contract A – Amount due from client	200	
Contract B – Amount due from client	300	
Administration expenses	2 200	
Bank	40	
Cost of sales	7 700	
Distribution costs	1 400	
Dividends	1 200	
Dividends received		480
Fixed asset investments	2 500	
Inventory at 30 September 20X0	560	
Property, plant, and equipment–cost	7 500	
Property, plant, and equipment–depreciation		1 300
Retained profits		2 300
Sales		14 000
Share capital		5 500
Taxation		100
Trade payables		380
Trade receivables	1 160	
	29 060	29 060

(i) The figures for sales and cost of sales relate to work done during the year ended 30 September 20X0, excluding all transactions relating to contracts A and B.

(ii) K plc recognises turnover and profit on long-term contracts on the basis of the proportion of total contract price invoiced to customers. All anticipated losses are recognised as soon as they are foreseen. The company's standard contract usually permits customers to withhold 10 per cent of the invoiced value of work done until the system has been installed and agreed to be satisfactory.

(iii) Contract A commenced during the year ended 30 September 20X0. The contract has a total value of £5 million. K plc anticipates that it will spend a further £1.5 million in order to complete this contract.

(iv) Contract B also commenced during the year ended 30 September 20X0. The contract has an agreed total value of £4 million. There have been some problems with this project that were not anticipated when the contract was drafted. K plc expects to spend a further £1.2 million in order to complete the contract. This includes £800 000 of additional costs that relate to the unforeseen problems. K plc's lawyers are currently attempting to negotiate a revised contract price of £4.8 million, although the customer is insistent that the system be completed for the original price. K plc's lawyers are 'reasonably confident' that they can make the customer pay for the additional costs. There is no possibility of these negotiations being completed before the financial statements have to be finalised.

(v) Closing stocks at 30 September 20X0 included a batch of computer workstations intended for resale. These had cost K plc £250 000, but they were sold for only £120 000 in October 20X0. A new product was brought on to the market on 1 October 20X0, which reduced the market value of the workstations.

(vi) The directors have estimated the tax charge for the year at £800 000.

K plc's finance director has made the following points to the board:

• The company should account for contract B on the assumption that its eventual selling price will be £4 million and not the £4.8 million that the company is seeking from the customer, even though there is a strong possibility that the higher amount will be obtained.

• The loss on the stock sold during October 20X0 should be taken into account in the calculation of profit for the year ended 30 September 20X0, even though the information available at the year end suggested that the stock would be sold at a profit.

Required:

(a) It has been suggested that there can be considerable inconsistency between companies in the manner in which they recognise profits on partly completed long-term contracts. Explain why this might be, and explain why IAS 11 permits the anticipation of such profits, in spite of the accounting problems that this may cause.

(b) Explain why, for accounting purposes, K plc should assume that contract B will be sold for £4 million.

(c) Explain why the loss on the workstations should be anticipated, even though it was not realised until after the year end.

(d) Prepare K plc's income statement for the year ended 30 September 20X0 and its statement of financial position as at that date. These should be in a form suitable for publication.

Question 4

Bild is a civil engineering company. It is currently working on two projects:

	Bridge $000	Jetty $000
Contract price (fixed)	3 000	5 000
Date work commenced	1 October 20X0	1 October 20X1
Proportion of work completed during year ended 30 September 20X1	30%	Nil
Invoiced to customer during year ended 30 September 20X1	900	Nil
Cash received from customer during year ended 30 September 20X1	800	Nil
Costs incurred during year ended 30 September 20X1	650	Nil
Estimated cost to complete at 30 September 20X1	1 300	
Proportion of work completed during year ended 30 September 20X2	25%	45%
Invoiced to customer during year ended 30 September 20X2	750	2 250
Cash received from customer during year ended 30 September 20X2	700	2 250

Costs incurred during year ended 30 September 20X2	580	1 900
Estimated cost to complete at 30 September 20X2	790	3 400

Bild recognises revenue and profit on long-term contracts in relation to the proportion of work completed.

Calculate the figures that will appear in Bild's income statement for the year ended 30 September 20X2 and its statement of financial position as at that date in respect of long-term contracts.

Further Work

The answers to these end-of-chapter questions can be found at the back of the book.

Question 1

Joy manufactures scarves, which it sells to a large chain of retailers. Joy has a contract to supply 500 000 scarves every year for the retailer. The retailer has granted Joy a contract to be its exclusive manufacturer for scarves on condition that Joy does not manufacture scarves for any other customer.

Joy is given a detailed product specification for each year's scarf collection. It buys the retailer's choice of fabric and manufactures scarves steadily throughout the year, building up inventories so that it can meet the demands for inventory during the autumn and winter seasons.

The retailer has suffered declining sales and has warned Joy that this year's order will be for 400 000 scarves only. Joy has had to cut back its production capacity in response to this reduced order.

The reduced order took effect during Joy's year ended 30 September 20X1. At that date the company had 40 000 scarves in inventory. It also had 5000 partly completed scarves that were 100% complete in terms of fabric and 50% complete in terms of labour and overheads. Raw materials inventories comprised $10 000 of fabric. Joy's total output for the year ended 30 September 20X1 was 430 000 scarves.

Each scarf contains fabric costing $1.00.

Joy's accountant has prepared the following summary of costs for the year ended 30 September 20X1:

	Fixed overheads $	Variable overheads $	Labour $
Manufacturing	20 000	40 000	400 000
Administrative	15 000	10 000	50 000
Distribution	8 000	6 000	12 000
	43 000	56 000	462 000

(a) Calculate the cost of Joy's closing inventories.
(b) Discuss the problems of determining the net realisable value of Joy's inventories.

Question 2

Cobb is a civil engineering company. It started work on two long-term projects during the year ended 30 September 20X7. The following figures relate to these projects as at the balance sheet date:

	Motorway lights	Pedestrian footbridge
	$000	$000
Contract price	9 000	8 000
Costs incurred to date	1 400	2 900
Estimated costs to completion	5 600	5 200
Value of work certified to date	2 800	3 000
Value of work invoiced to date	2 800	3 000
Cash received from contractee	2 600	3 400

The costs to completion for the pedestrian footbridge include the costs of dealing with an underground stream that has complicated the foundations. Cobb's lawyers are reasonably confident that they can pass these extra costs on to the client. If negotiations are successful, then the contract price will increase to £10 million.

Cobb plc recognises turnover and profits on long contracts on the basis of work certified to date.

Required:
(a) Explain whether the contract price for the footbridge should be taken as $8 million or $10 million.
(b) Calculate the figures that would appear in Cobb's financial statements in respect of each of the projects.

ACCOUNTING FOR LIABILITIES

11

Contents

Learning Objectives

After studying this chapter you should be able to:

- describe the problems associated with defining liabilities and preventing off-balance-sheet financing;
- apply the formal definition of a liability in the context of leases;
- account for provisions and contingent liabilities.

Introduction

This chapter deals with a number of issues that might not seem to present any obvious problems at first glance. However history suggests that there have been problems in tying down the precise nature of liabilities, and that has led to finance being excluded from the statement of financial position. Companies have also recorded liabilities that have relatively little real substance in order to smooth out undesirable fluctuations in trends in reported profits from one year to the next. In the past it has been possible to take a pessimistic view of the future when times have been good so that some of the profit earned in good years can be carried forward to be released into the income statement in poorer years.

Liabilities

Most introductory accounting courses start with the balance sheet equation: assets = capital + liabilities.[1] That is presented as the easiest way to understand that users of financial statements need to be told both what their businesses have (assets) and how they were paid for (capital and liabilities). The equation is also used as the starting point for explaining how double-entry bookkeeping works.

Surprisingly, the concepts of assets and liabilities are presented as simple and straightforward to first-year students, and yet they have proved difficult and elusive concepts to define and regulate in the real world.

For example, picture a car dealership that specialises in new vehicles. Car manufacturers are very selective about who is permitted to sell their products, both in terms of the quality of the service that they will provide and also the potential to maximise sales. One of the terms associated with most contracts is that manufacturers will send a regular allocation of cars to the dealership 'on consignment'. The precise manner in which this works varies between manufacturers, but, in essence, the system is as follows:

- The manufacturer delivers new vehicles to the dealer but retains legal ownership of the cars.
- Ownership passes to the dealer when the vehicle is sold to a customer, so that the dealer can make a legally binding sale.
- Once a vehicle has been with the dealer for a specified period, perhaps six months, ownership passes and the vehicles must be paid for.
- The dealership cannot return the vehicles to the manufacturer without agreeing to pay a penalty, and the dealer cannot request the return of a vehicle without offering some incentive.

---

[1] Maybe the first lecture is devoted to users of accounts, as was stated in Chapter 5, but the balance sheet equation comes a close second.

This is one of those cases where the legal interpretation of a relationship would lead to misleading accounting figures. Legally, the consignment inventory belongs to a third party, and so the dealership neither owns the vehicles nor owes any money to the manufacturer. Accounting for the vehicles in this way would be extremely misleading.

The reality is that custom and practice in the motor trade mean that manufacturers provide a period of extended credit when they supply cars. They can allow for the cost of that credit when setting the selling prices charged to dealerships. Retaining legal ownership gives the manufacturer a degree of protection in case the dealership goes out of business.

A rational reading of the economic reality of the consignment arrangement is that the dealer has effectively purchased the vehicles on credit as soon as they have been delivered. The dealer bears all of the risks that a model will prove unpopular and difficult to sell and will have to pay for the vehicle after the consignment period has expired. On the other hand, the dealer enjoys all of the rewards of ownership. The dealer can sell the car and make a profit. If a particular model becomes popular, then the manufacturer cannot simply take it back or transfer it to another dealership.

The economic argument wins in this case. Provided it is clear that the dealer holding the inventory enjoys the rewards of ownership and bears the risks, it is accepted that there is an asset. By the same token (and harking back to our balance sheet equation), increasing the asset of inventory will typically involve increasing trade payables by the same amount. Recognising a liability is also appropriate because the dealer is committed to making a payment to the manufacturer at some point in the future.

This principle can be seen in the 2008 annual report of Pendragon plc, a UK-based company that owns a large number of new car dealerships in the United Kingdom and United States. The company shows consignment inventory of £96.2 million as a current asset and a trade payable of the same amount as a current liability, in spite of the fact that it is not, technically, the legal owner of the vehicles.

Off-Balance-Sheet Financing

Off-balance-sheet financing has been defined in a technical release issued by the Institute of Chartered Accountants in England and Wales in 1985 as 'the funding or refinancing of a company's operations in such a way that, under legal requirements and existing accounting conventions, some or all of the finance may not be shown on its balance sheet'.

The point of off-balance-sheet financing has been mentioned already in previous chapters. Excluding borrowings from the statement of financial position will reduce the gearing ratio and thereby make the company seem less risky. It will also reduce capital employed and so make the company appear more profitable in terms of the return on capital employed ratio. Unfortunately, off-balance-sheet financing can only alter the appearance of risk and return. The funding still exists, and so the commitments must still be met regardless of whether they appear in the statement of financial position.

Off-balance-sheet financing has been a difficult problem to deal with, and it is unlikely that it will ever be totally eliminated. There are two broad approaches, the first being to deal with specific techniques for excluding liabilities and introducing detailed rules that force a different treatment and disclosure for each. One such example is to be found in the following discussion about leasing. The advantage of this approach is that it should deal with the specific problems in a very effective way because each will now be the subject of a specific rule. The disadvantage is that the approach is necessarily reactive. There are commercial banks and other organisations that specialise in designing such schemes and then offering them to their customers in return for a fee.

The other approach to resolving off-balance-sheet financing is to lay down general rules for prohibiting the practice and hope that these give external audit firms sufficient basis for refusing to accept particular treatments proposed by their clients. That has the advantage of dealing with newly devised schemes, although there may well be problems of definition and interpretation.[2]

> **Think!**
> _____
>
> Is off-balance-sheet financing always wrong?

---

[2] The possibility that standards can be open to interpretation has even led to a practice called 'opinion shopping', whereby companies will interview potential replacements for their present auditors by asking whether they would tolerate their preferred reading of a particular regulation. This is, of course, potentially detrimental to the independence of the existing firm. Some studies indicate that opinion shopping is a serious problem (for example, Lennox (2003)). Other papers do not find evidence that opinion shopping is harmful (for example, Lu (2006)).

Company directors who indulge in off-balance-sheet financing may be motivated by fear or by a desire to cut costs and protect the company. They could be afraid that shareholders or lenders will be reluctant to provide further finance in order to enable expansion. Or they might demand high rates of return, making some projects uneconomic. The directors might not benefit personally from off-balance-sheet financing, but it could assist the company to grow.

Even if directors are correct in their concern that the readers are overcautious and might overreact to an accurate statement of the business' funding, it is still dishonest to mislead them. It would be far better to report honestly and to communicate the reasons for optimism in evaluating the effects of these borrowings. For example, the directors might be able to reassure readers that the company is very stable and that it will have no difficulty in servicing its debts.

Dealing with Off-Balance-Sheet Financing

The IASB's basic approach to dealing with off-balance-sheet financing boils down to defining the elements of the financial statements in such a way that schemes are difficult to design without being picked up in the general requirement to report a true and fair view or present fairly.

Assets are defined in the Framework as 'rights or other access to future economic benefits controlled by an entity as a result of past transactions or events'.

Liabilities are defined as 'obligations to transfer economic benefits as a result of past transactions or events'.

Even though these are brief definitions, their wording has had quite profound impacts. In the past, the question of ownership has figured prominently in the identification of assets, but now the emphasis is entirely on control. It was relatively easy to claim that a particular item was owned by a third party and so it could not be regarded as an asset. The question of whether or not an asset is controlled is relatively non-controversial, and so it is far more difficult to design a scheme that would permit assets and their associated funding to be excluded from the statement of financial position.

The same logic applies to the definition of a liability. It is not necessary to 'owe' something in a legal sense for there to be a liability. If a past event means that it is likely that a future transfer will be made, then there is a liability.

Sale and repurchase is one of the off-balance-sheet schemes that has effectively been eliminated by these definitions. This was particularly popular in the whisky industry because distillers have to hold stocks for many years so that they can mature and be sold as 'twenty-year-old Scotch'. Distillers often entered into complex agreements with banks, who would buy the maturing inventory from the distiller. The bank would also receive an option to sell the whisky back before it finally matured and at a price that was more or less the same as the original selling price plus the interest that would have been charged if the distiller had taken out a loan of that amount and duration. The whisky would remain exactly where it was on the distiller's premises. There was never any doubt that the bank would exercise the option to sell the inventory back.

In the past, sale and repurchase schemes (and the consignment inventory scheme discussed above) were classic forms of off-balance-sheet financing. The distiller's financial statements reflected the literal interpretation of the agreement, showing the sale when the cash was received from the bank and then nothing until the purchase of the inventory when the bank exercised its option. Any challenge would have been met with a puzzled expression and a photocopy of the bank's agreement to purchase the inventory. Technically, the bank had to exercise its option before there was a legal obligation to buy the inventory back, and so it could be argued that nothing was owed prior to that date.

Since the publication of the Framework, it would be unacceptable to treat these balances in such a manner. The need to reflect substance over form means that devices such as options granted to third parties have to be read in a realistic manner. If the circumstances mean that an option will almost certainly be exercised, then the financial statements should be prepared on the basis that the payment or other transfer has already been agreed. That would certainly be the case with the sale and repurchase arrangement, if only because there is no commercial logic to a bank wishing to retain ownership of industrial quantities of inventory.

There is, however, a need for specific guidance on particular figures. Lease agreements create enormous problems of classification.

Leases

Leasing was one of the earliest and most popular forms of off-balance-sheet financing. Indeed, the author's recollection of finance textbooks studied in the late 1970s and early 1980s described the advantages of indulging in off-balance-sheet financing to companies.[3]

The basic nature of a lease is that the lessor, the owner of the asset, permits the lessee to use it in return for a payment. In some cases, the lessor will buy an asset at the lessee's request under an agreement that commits the lessee to leasing the asset for the whole of its expected useful life.

---

[3] Sadly, those textbooks (and study materials provided for professional training) have been lost during the 30 years or so since they were first acquired. The fact that off-balance-sheet financing was being promoted in such positive terms suggests that the world was a different place back then.

> **Think!**
>
> What is the economic substance of a long-term lease such as the one described in the previous paragraph?

Provided both parties are behaving rationally, the economic substance of this arrangement is that the lessor has made a loan to the lessee that is equal to the capital value of the leased asset. The lessee's lease payments will be equivalent to the loan repayments on that loan plus the interest that would have been charged.

> **Think!**
>
> Are all rental agreements likely to be equivalent to loans?

Long-term leases are effectively a financial instrument that can be used as an alternative to a more traditional loan. One of the attractions in the past was that such leases could be excluded from the statement of financial position, but they have other benefits. For example, the lessor always owns the asset, and so there is a degree of security built into this arrangement.

The problem is that leases can be short term and are not even remotely equivalent to a loan. The obvious case would be where a company leases a van for a month to give some additional delivery capacity at a busy time of year. It would be most unrealistic in that case to treat the contract as a financial instrument that was used to finance the purchase of the asset. Rather, it is what the legal form of the agreement says. A short-term lease is a payment for the convenience of being able to use an asset for a brief period and then return it to the lessor.

The problem is in drawing the line between the two categories of lease:

Easy to distinguish – this is a financial instrument	Difficult to distinguish	Easy to distinguish – this is not a financial instrument
The lease payments are £1000 per month for five years. If the company had	The lease payments are £1000 per month for three years. If the	The lease payments are £1200 for the use of the asset for 28 days. The asset will

borrowed the capital value of the asset it would cost £1000 per month for five years to service the loan.	company had borrowed the capital value of the asset it would cost £1000 per month for five years to service the loan.	be returned at the end of that period.
The lease agreement is for five years. The asset's useful life is estimated at five years.	The lease agreement is for three years. The asset's useful life is estimated at five years.	The lease agreement is for 28 days. The asset's useful life is estimated at five years.

Using the general principle of substance over form, there are many leases that are clearly financial instruments that should be treated as borrowing by the lessee and many that are not. These examples could be pushed quite a long way from the extremes before getting into the grey area where the distinction is unclear. For example, leasing the asset for two months would not be a financing arrangement, nor would leasing it for six months, but three years is a more difficult call. It is difficult to say.

UK accounting standards used to have a '90% rule' that could be used to distinguish the two types of lease. If the net present value of the lease payments was 90% or more of the fair value of the asset, then it was treated as a financial instrument. If it was less than 90%, then it was not.[4]

> **Think!**
>
> What is the obvious limitation of the 90% rule?

The 90% cut-off created clarity. Unfortunately, it also created an opportunity for avoiding the disclosure requirements. It was difficult, but not impossible, for leasing companies to structure deals so that the lessee had the asset for its entire useful life even though the lease payments were worth very slightly less than 90%

---

[4] SSAP 21 *Accounting for Leases and Hire Purchase Contracts*, 1984.

of the asset's value. For example, a leasing company that specialised in commercial vehicles could combine orders from many lessees and obtain a massive discount from a supplier. That might make it possible to design the lease so that it fell outside the limits imposed by the standard while making a profit.[5]

IAS 17

IAS 17 *Leases* defines two forms of lease. A finance lease is 'a lease that transfers substantially all the risks and rewards incidental to ownership of an asset'. Finance leases are the ones that should be recognised as borrowing in the statement of financial position. An operating lease is 'a lease other than a finance lease'. Operating leases are not treated as financial instruments. The lease payments on operating leases are shown as expenses in the income statement.

IAS 17 takes care not to provide more specific guidance as to the distinction between finance leases and operating leases. That is very much a strength of the standard because it makes it difficult for a lessor to structure a lease so that it narrowly misses the definition of a finance lease and becomes classified as an operating lease by default.

The standard lists a number of factors that would indicate that the lease is a finance lease. These include:

- The lease term covers most of the asset's estimated useful life.
- When the lease commences, the net present value of the minimum lease payments is at least close to the fair value of the asset.
- The asset is specialised in nature and would probably require some modification before it could be used by anybody else.

Rather than memorise these points (or any others) as a checklist, the easiest way to deal with this risk and reward criterion is to imagine the thoughts of the lessor when arranging the lease. If the lessor is likely to regard this arrangement as a risky venture, then the lessor probably retains the risks associated with ownership. A commercially minded lessor would be unlikely to pass the rewards associated with ownership on to the lessee unless the lessee was bearing the risks too.

---

[5] For example, buying vehicles with a fair value of £10 million for £8 million and leasing them out to lessees for their entire useful lives for payments with a net present value of £8 999 999. It might not be necessary to obtain such a large discount. The leasing company might be entitled to claim government grants or tax reliefs that would make it possible to accept a lease payment that was worth much less than the fair value of the assets.

> **Think!**
>
> Is the distinction between finance leases and operating leases now clear and unambiguous?

The IAS 27 definition of a finance lease is unlikely to provide a clear distinction in every single case. That might create some problems in the real world. From an examination perspective, questions are likely to offer marks for explaining the reasoning behind classifying a lease as either finance or operating. As a broad rule of thumb, if there is serious doubt as to the classification, then the lease must transfer enough of the risks and rewards to make it likely that it is a finance lease even if that is only a likelihood rather than a certainty.

Anti-Avoidance

IAS 27 takes care to reduce the scope for introducing artificial provisions into leases so that they can be excluded from the definition of finance leases.

The definition of the lease term includes 'any further terms for which the lessee has the option to continue to lease the asset . . . when at the inception of the lease it is reasonably certain that the lessee will exercise the option'. That deals with the possibility that the lessor agrees to a series of short-term leases, none of which would be classified as an operating lease in itself. For example, a lessee might enter into a two-year lease on a vital piece of equipment that has an estimated life of ten years. At the outset of this arrangement, both parties are aware that the lease will be renewed at the end of the initial term, and so it might be classified as a finance lease on that basis.

Similarly, the definition of minimum lease payments includes any amounts guaranteed by the lessee. That could include any guaranteed residual value agreed at the start of the lease. For example, both parties agree that, if the asset is worth less than £10 000 at the end of the lease term, then the lessee will make up the difference. It could also include the cost of exercising the right to buy the asset at an agreed price after the lease term has concluded if the lessee is likely to take up that option.

Accounting for Leased Assets

In essence, the lessee must treat a finance lease as if it has taken out a loan and purchased the asset. Thereafter, the lease liability will be accounted for as if it was a traditional loan and the asset will be accounted for in almost the same way as if it did belong to the company.

Once a lease has been analysed and classified as a finance lease, the first thing that is required is to determine the interest rate implicit in the lease. To all intents and purposes, the interest rate implicit in the lease is the rate that equates the net present value of the minimum lease payments to the fair value of the asset.[6] Effectively, this gives the interest rate that the lessor is charging the lessee on the finance that is being provided.

Determining the interest rate implicit in the lease requires some understanding of the concept of discounted cash flow.[7] If the cash flows are very simple, then it is sometimes possible to work out the interest rate using discounting tables. Otherwise, there is no mathematical solution and the process requires either trial and error or access to a spreadsheet's internal rate of return (IRR) function. In a sense, the difficulty associated with establishing the interest rate can actually make exam questions easier because the examiner must normally state the interest rate in the question.

A Simple Example

For example, on 1 January 20X0, Lessee entered into a five-year lease on a computer system that has a five-year estimated useful life. Most dealers are charging £6000 for this system. The lease payments are £1500 per year, with the first payment made on 31 December 20X0. The lease is not cancellable.

The fact that this asset is being leased for the whole of its expected useful life suggests that Lessee will obtain all of the rewards of ownership. The lease cannot be cancelled, so Lessee bears all of the risks of the system becoming obsolete during the term of the lease. That means that the lease is a finance lease.

The interest rate implicit in the lease is the rate at which five annual payments of £1500 have a net present value of £6000. Dividing £6000 by £1500 gives 4.000. Looking along the five-year row of an annuity table for a factor of 4.000 gives a rate of approximately 8%.[8] Putting these cash flows into a spreadsheet and using a

---

[6] Strictly speaking, the interest rate should take account of cash flows associated with initial direct costs borne by the lessor and any unguaranteed residual value that the asset might have. These adjustments will not be discussed in this text.

[7] Discounted cash flow (or net present value) calculations adjust cash flows for the effects of interest rates on the value of payments and receipts that will occur in the future. For example, a receipt of £1020 in one year at a time when interest rates are 2% per annum is worth only £1000 today. The reason for that is that £1000 could be invested for a year to give £1020.

[8] At 8%, the discount factor for a five-year annuity is 3.993. At 7%, the discount factor is 4.100. That means that the interest rate implicit in the lease is somewhere between 7% and 8% and closer to 8%.

formula to determine the internal rate of return gives a rate of 7.93% (accurate to two decimal places).

The lease liability account for the five-year term of the lease will be as follows:

Lease liability					
31/12/X0	Bank	1500	1/1/X0	Equipment	6000
31/12/X0	Bal c/d	4976	31/12/X0	Interest	476
		6476			6476
31/12/X1	Bank	1500	1/1/X1	Bal c/d	4976
31/12/X1	Bal c/d	3871	31/12/X1	Interest	395
		5371			5371
31/12/X2	Bank	1500	1/1/X2	Bal c/d	3871
31/12/X2	Bal c/d	2678	31/12/X2	Interest	307
		4178			4178
31/12/X3	Bank	1500	1/1/X3	Bal c/d	2678
31/12/X3	Bal c/d	1391	31/12/X3	Interest	213
		2891			2891
31/12/X4	Bank	1500	1/1/X4	Bal c/d	1391
			31/12/X4	Interest	109
		1500			1500

At the start of this lease, Lessee effectively borrowed £6000 from the lessor. At the end of the first year the interest charged was 7.93% of the £6000 that was outstanding throughout the year. That gave a charge for the year of £6000 × 7.93% = £476 (rounded to the nearest £). That is added to the lessor's balance, and the £1500 paid at the end of the year is deducted to give a closing balance of £4976.

In the statement of financial position as at 31 December 20X0, the £4976 total will have to be broken down between current and non-current liabilities. The trick is to look at the payments that will be made in the next financial year. During the year ended 31 December 20X1, the payment will be £1500, of which £395 will be interest.

The balance of £4976 at 31 December 20X0 includes £1500 − 395 = £1105, which will be repaid in the next twelve months, and £4976 − 1105 = £3871, which will be repaid after twelve months.

Thus, there is a current liability of £1105 and a non-current liability of £3871.

The asset will be capitalised as an addition worth £6000 and accounted for as if it were owned by the company. It will be depreciated over its expected useful life, as estimated by Lessee. The fact that the asset will be returned after five years means that the estimated life cannot be any longer, but it could be shorter if Lessee believes that the system might reach the end of its useful life before the end of the lease.

Disclosure Requirements

The net book value of leased assets must be stated for each class of non-current assets.

Think!

Why do assets held under operating leases have to be highlighted separately if lessees enjoy all the risks and rewards of ownership?

Leased assets are controlled by the entity and can be used to generate economic benefits, but they differ from owned assets in one crucial respect. Leased assets cannot be pledged as security for liabilities. The company's lenders should be made aware of the assets that will be available in the event of the company's failure.

The company is also required to reconcile the total future minimum lease payments and their net present value, broken down to show the amounts due within one year, between one year and five years, and after five years.

The reconciliation for the simple example above, assuming that this was the company's only finance lease, would be:

	Minimum lease payments £	Present value of minimum lease payments £
Within one year	1500	1105
Greater than one year but less than five years	4500	3871
Total minimum lease payments	6000	4976

The minimum lease payments are simply the cash amounts that will be paid. There is one instalment due of £1500 within one year and three remaining in the remainder of the lease after next year, all due within five years.

The present value of the minimum lease payments is the cash amount minus the interest that will be paid in the period. So, we anticipate paying interest of

£307 + 213 + 109 = £629 during the period after one year but within five years, and so the present value is £4500 − 629 = £3871.

Operating Leases

Generally, the costs associated with operating leases require little or no effort to calculate. The amount paid during the year will normally go straight to the income statement as an expense.

The only complication that might arise would be where the lease ran for more than one year. In that case the cost of the lease is recognised on a straight-line basis, unless another systematic basis is more representative of the user's benefit.

For example, a lessee might have a three-year operating lease on a building that it requires as a temporary base. The lessor charged £14 000 in the first year and £20 000 in each of the other two years. The lessee would have an annual expense of (£14 000 + 20 000 + 20 000)/3 = £18 000.

Operating leases do not normally appear in the statement of financial position, unless there are accruals or prepayments arising from the need to recognise charges on a straight-line basis. In the above example, at the end of year 1 there will have been an expense of £18 000 and a cash payment of only £14 000, so there will be an accrual of £4000 under current liabilities.

The notes to the accounts will disclose the minimum lease payments due under operating leases in force at the year end, broken down between amounts due within one year, after one year but within five years, and after five years. These amounts will not be reflected in the statement of financial position, but they will give readers an indication of any commitments arising under leases that were not classified as finance leases.

Provisions and Contingent Liabilities

Leases are by no means the only forms of liability that can prove complicated. Provisions and contingent liabilities have been implicated in some very serious accounting scandals in the past. They are areas that often require considerable judgement.

IAS 37 *Provisions, Contingent Liabilities, and Contingent Assets* deals with these areas.

Provisions

IAS 37 defines a provision as 'a liability of uncertain timing or amount'. Companies frequently have to estimate liabilities and recognise them in their financial statements. Where there is more than a minimal amount of uncertainty about the prospective payments, the balances can be classified as provisions to warn readers about the potential for error.

IAS 37 lays down three conditions that must be met before a provision can be recognised:

* There must be a present obligation arising from a past event.
* It must be probable that a payment (or other outflow of resources) will have to be made.
* It must be possible to estimate the obligation reliably.

If these criteria are not met, then the provision cannot be recognised in the financial statements.

Think!

Why might company directors wish to recognise unnecessary provisions?

Before IAS 37 was published, it was relatively common for company directors to use provisions to smooth out trends in reported profit. If the company was going to report good profits, then some provisions for spurious costs might be introduced, such as a rather excessive provision for repairs under customer warranties. That would be set so that the reported profit was high enough to impress shareholders without setting an impossible target for growth in future years.

When profits started to decline, those excessive provisions could be 'corrected' so that the general trend could be maintained.

Sometimes this practice was taken to extremes when the company was likely to report terrible profits. Then directors were inclined to indulge in a practice known as 'big bath accounting'. This would be used where it was clear that a large loss would be reported regardless of any accounting adjustments or accounting choices. In that case, the directors often decided that the shareholders would be dis-appointed and angry no matter what happened, so they might as well make matters seem even worse on the grounds that they had nothing further to lose.

The 'big bath' involved making substantial provisions that increased the loss even further. The purpose of that was that the directors could reverse those provisions in future years, assuming they survived the shareholders' reaction to the initial bad results. Reversing the excessive provisions had the effect of boosting profits and so making it easier for the company to appear to be recovering and returning to profit.

IAS 37 effectively forbids the use of provisions to manipulate profits by overstating provisions one year in order to recognise higher profits in the future.

Obligations can be either legally binding or constructive. A constructive obligation arises when a valid expectation has been created in the minds of a third party. For example, an announcement that a company will contribute to a charity would create a constructive obligation. Sometimes patterns of behaviour can create a constructive obligation. For example, if a company has always given employees a bonus after ten years' service, then there could be a constructive obligation to those who are likely to reach this milestone even if they have no contractual rights.

It is sometimes unclear whether there is an obligation. In that case, the entity should consider whether a future payment is more likely than not. If so, there should be a provision. If not, then no provision should be made. 'More likely than not' implies a probability of more than 50%, although that can be a very difficult criterion to apply.

Provisions arise from past events, and so future plans cannot create recognisable liabilities. For example, if the directors have decided to close down a factory but no announcement has been made, then there is neither a legal nor a constructive obligation to implement that plan, and so it would be inappropriate to make a provision for, say, redundancy payments to the employees who will lose their jobs. That prevents the directors from making provisions on the basis of proposals that may not be implemented so that the provisions are reversed.

It is only permissible to make provisions arising from changes in the law if the legislation has been enacted or there is reasonable certainty as to the legal obligations that will be in force. Thus, draft legislation cannot create a legal obligation for the purposes of IAS 37 unless it is virtually certain that the law will be drawn up in accordance with the draft. If the company announced that it would implement a particular proposal regardless of any legal compulsion, then that might be sufficient to create a constructive obligation.

Provisions should be valued at the best possible estimate of the cost of resolving the matter. That might equate to the most likely outcome. If the settlement is likely to be in the future, then it is possible to state the net present value of the future transfers. The amounts of provisions should be reviewed and adjusted from year to year if the circumstances that led to them are continuing and better estimates become available.

To sum up, the requirements of IAS 37 are intended to ensure that provisions are recognised when a business is likely to make a payment (or other transfer) in the future, but it must be probable that the payment will actually be made. This is to prevent the recognition of spurious provisions that are intended to smooth out fluctuations in profit.

Contingent Liabilities

Contingent liabilities are not recognised in the financial statements themselves, but they are disclosed in the notes to the accounts.

Contingent liabilities can arise in three main ways:

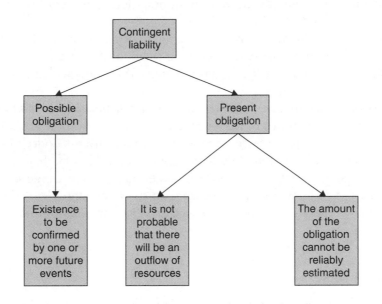

The classic example would be a legal claim pending against the business. In the initial stages there would be a possible obligation unless there is near certainty as to the eventual resolution of the claim. In that case there would be a possible obligation whose existence would only be resolved once the case had been heard in court.

As the case progressed, it might become clearer that the company will lose, which would create a present obligation. However, there can be uncertainty as to whether any costs or damages will be paid (perhaps because of a legal technicality) or the likely costs may be impossible to estimate.

The distinction between provisions and contingent liabilities boils down to the degree of uncertainty involved. Provisions are when future transfers are 'probable' rather than 'possible'. Provisions can be estimated with reasonable reliability and contingent liabilities cannot. Thus, a legal claim for a specific amount in circumstances where the courts would be very likely to find against the company would have to be provided for rather than being treated as a contingent liability.

Contingent liabilities are disclosed in the notes to the financial statements rather than appearing in the actual statements themselves. The notes will indicate the estimated financial impact of the contingency, the uncertainties surrounding the timing or amount, and the possibility of any reimbursement for each contingent liability.

IAS 37 permits the disclosures to be restricted in cases where full disclosure would seriously undermine the company's position. That could happen in the case of a legal claim where both sides are attempting to negotiate a settlement and the other side might gain an advantage from information in the contingent liability note.

Disclosure is not required in the case of contingent liabilities where the likelihood of a future settlement is regarded as 'remote'; for example, if a claim is lodged that the company's legal advisors believe the courts will almost certainly reject.

The possibility that there are contingent liabilities means that readers have to pay close attention to the notes to the financial statements. In some cases it will be impossible fully to appreciate the financial position without understanding the contingent liabilities that could result in significant outflows, perhaps in the near future. One possible problem that can arise is that there are electronic services that carry extracts from annual reports, focusing on the main statements themselves. Readers who rely on such services could easily miss all mention of contingent liabilities.

Contingent Assets

Assets are only recognised where there is reasonable certainty as to their existence and value. Indeed, contingent assets are only disclosed in the notes where recovery is 'probable'. Thus, a contingent asset associated with a claim lodged by the company will only be mentioned in the notes if the company believes that it is likely to win its case.

Provisions and contingent liabilities might have associated assets. For example, the company might have to pay compensation and then reclaim those costs because of its insurance cover. In such cases the liability and the associated asset should be treated as two quite separate issues and should never be offset against one another. That could mean that the likely cost could be recognised as a provision and the associated reimbursement could be disclosed in the notes to the accounts if there is any doubt as to whether the amount will be forthcoming.

Summary

The word 'liability' is in common everyday usage and is clearly understood in normal conversation. In spite of that, it has created enormous difficulties for the accountancy profession and accounting standard-setters over the years. Companies have found ways to exclude liabilities for the sake of off-balance-sheet financing. They have also discovered that recognising provisions can enable them to manage their reported profit so that they can manufacture the impression of steady growth for a business that is quite volatile.

The accountancy profession deals with the threat of off-balance-sheet financing by requiring that the economic substance of agreements and relationships be accounted for rather than their legal form. In general, off-balance-sheet financing is only possible when a contract is structured in such a way that accounting for the literal wording of the document will create a misleading impression.

The threat of manipulating impressions of profit created by recognising liabilities is dealt with by having stringent recognition criteria before provisions can appear in the financial statements. That boils down to requiring that any amount recognised is due to a third party and that the payment is more likely than not.

Contingent liabilities act as a backstop if liabilities cannot be recognised because there is too much uncertainty about the timing or the amount of any payment. Any such matter will have to be disclosed in the notes to the financial statements. That will alert the readers to the existence of the problem, and shareholders will be able to seek further information and clarification from management.

Tutorial Questions

Question 1

R publishes local newspapers for each of the major towns in its region. It has recently signed a two-year lease with Country Bank's leasing company on a printing press that is suitable for R's very specific requirements. The press has to be able to produce relatively small numbers of newspapers, but also has to cope with very high volumes of output because the company publishes several titles.

The press itself is a highly modified Megapress that was purchased by Country Bank at R's specific request. It is a major piece of equipment that required a wall to be partially demolished to enable the old press to be dismantled and removed and the new press to be installed, a process that required it to be cemented into place with special concrete foundations.

R is responsible for the maintenance of the press while it is on its premises.

The press has an estimated useful life of ten years. It cost £1.2 million to buy it in its modified form.

The net present value of the two-year lease is £290 000.

The lease agreement says nothing about the possibility of extending the lease for future terms after the two-year period has expired.

Discuss the correct accounting treatment of this lease in R's financial statements. Your answer should indicate any further information that you would require before reaching a final conclusion.

Question 2

P entered into lease agreements for the following three assets on 1 January 20X2:

	Period of lease	Annual payment £	NPV of lease payments £	Normal cash price £
Lathe	10 years	2000	14 290	14 000
Delivery van	2 years	1500	2 865	8 000
Photocopier	4 years	3000	10 460	12 300

In each case, the first annual leasing payment was due on 1 January 20X2 (*Hint: take care when calculating the interest*). The interest rate implicit in each lease was 10%.

P is responsible for the maintenance and insurance of each of these assets throughout the period of the lease. The assets will almost certainly be returned to the lessor at the end of the agreed period. P is not required to guarantee the residual values of the assets at the conclusion of this period.

The normal cash price of the assets represents the amount that P would have paid if it had purchased the assets outright for cash on the open market.

P's depreciation policy is as follows:

> Lathes − 25% per annum (reducing balance)
> Delivery vehicles − 25% per annum (straight line)
> Office equipment − 10% per annum (straight line)

(a) Classify each of the three leases as either operating or finance, giving reasons for your decision in each case.
(b) Prepare any notes or other disclosures that would be required in respect of leases in P's financial statements for the year ended 31 December 20X2.

Question 3

J sells package holidays over the Internet to the public. J's directors are currently finalising their financial statements for the year ended 31 March 20X4. They are unsure about how to deal with the following items:

(i) A bus that was owned and operated by the company had not been properly maintained. The brakes failed while a group of 45 customers were being transferred from their destination airport to their holiday hotel. There were no fatalities, but many of the customers were injured, some very slightly and others quite seriously. The company has received a small number of claims from a few of these customers, but there are indications that many more claims will be received. J's lawyers have advised that the company will have to pay a substantial amount in order to settle these claims, but it will be impossible to estimate an accurate figure for the settlement until well after the financial statements have been published.

(ii) Twenty customers have claimed a total of £20 000 for lost luggage using the company's 'no loss guarantee'. The financial statements will be finalised before the claims can be processed and checked.

(iii) A claim has been received for £100 000 from a customer who claims that the weather was unpleasant throughout his holiday and that he suffered severe emotional distress because of this disappointment. The company's lawyers have indicated that this case can be ignored.

(iv) The company received claims totalling £300 000 during the year from the members of a large choir who were not permitted to practise in the grounds of their hotel because their singing was disturbing other guests. The choir claimed that their holiday had been ruined because of this. J's directors have decided to pay these customers 50% of the amount claimed as a goodwill gesture even though their lawyers say that they are under no obligation to do so. They have not, however, informed the members of the choir as yet.

(a) Identify the appropriate accounting treatment of each of the claims against J plc in respect of (i) to (iv) above. Your answer should have due regard to the requirements of IAS 37.

(b) It has been suggested that readers of financial statements do not always pay sufficient attention to contingent liabilities even though they may have serious implications for the future of the company.

    (i) Explain why insufficient attention might be paid to contingent liabilities.

(ii) Explain how IAS 37 prevents companies from treating liabilities that should be recognised in the statement of financial position as contingent liabilities.

Question 4

Partan is a manufacturing company. The company's trial balance as at 30 June 20X8 was as follows:

	£000	£000
Administration expenses	2 700	
Bank	600	
Corporation tax	200	
Cost of sales	18 000	
Deferred tax		1 100
Distribution costs	2 160	
Dividends	850	
Interest paid	560	
Inventory	1 500	
Long-term loans		4 000
Payments to Global Finance	2 500	
Plant and equipment	9 000	
Property	5 000	
Retained profit		7 770
Revenue		25 000
Share capital		5 000
Trade payables		2 300
Trade receivables	2 100	
	45 170	45 170

(i) Partan entered into a leasing agreement with Global Finance on 1 July 20X7. This involves a specialised piece of manufacturing machinery that was purchased by Global Finance to Partan's specifications. The contract involves an annual payment of £2.5 million per annum for five years, with the first payment made on 1 July 20X7. The fair value of the machinery as at the commencement of the contract was £10.6 million. The interest rate implicit in this lease is 9%. Partan is responsible for the maintenance of the machinery and is required to insure it against accidental damage. The machinery would normally be expected to have a useful life of approximately seven years. Partan depreciates its tangible fixed assets on the straight-line basis. No entries have been made in Partan's accounting records, apart from the recording of the first payment to Global Finance.

(ii) The balance on the corporation tax account is the amount remaining after settlement of the corporation tax on the profits for the year ended 30 June 2007.

(iii) The estimated corporation tax charge on the profits for the year ended 30 June 20X8 is £1.8 million. The provision for deferred taxation is to be reduced by £0.9 million.

(iv) The company's closing stocks were valued by means of a stock count at the year end. On 14 July 20X8 there was a fire at the Glasgow branch that destroyed stock valued at £0.4 million at the year end. The company's insurers have since found that the fire arose because of staff negligence and have refused the claim. On 20 July 20X8 the company discovered that stocks at the Edinburgh branch that had been valued at £0.7 million at the year end would have to be sold as scrap for only £5000 because of previously undetected manufacturing faults. The directors consider both of these matters to be material.

Prepare Partan's statement of comprehensive income and statement of changes in equity for the year ended 30 June 20X8 and its statement of financial position as at that date. These should be in a form suitable for publication and should be accompanied with notes as far as you are able to prepare these from the information provided.

Question 5

Lampe is a manufacturing company. The company's trial balance as at 30 June 20X9 was as follows:

	£000	£000
Administration expenses	4 800	
Bank	1 300	
Corporation tax		480
Cost of sales	27 000	
Distribution costs	4 400	
Dividends	2 000	
Interest paid	970	
Inventory at 30 June 20X9	3 900	
Long-term loans		10 000

Plant and equipment – cost	11 000	
Plant and equipment – depreciation		4 600
Property – valuation	48 000	
Property – depreciation		4 800
Retained profit		7 770
Revaluation reserve		2 000
Revenue		54 000
Share capital		19 720
Trade payables		4 700
Trade receivables	4 700	
	108 070	108 070

(i)   The directors have estimated the tax charge for the year at £2.6 million. The balance on the corporation tax account is the amount remaining after the settlement of the liability for the year ended 30 June 20X8.

(ii)   Depreciation has still to be charged for the year. Property is depreciated at 2% of valuation every year, and plant and equipment at 25% on the reducing balance basis.

(iii)   The directors had the property revalued at 30 June 20X9. The valuation of £50 million should be shown in the financial statements.

(iv)   During the year, the company purchased additional plant and equipment costing £3 million. These additions are included in the trial balance figures. A full year's depreciation is to be charged in the year of acquisition. There were no disposals.

(v)   Lampe is being sued for damages in respect of an injury sustained by a customer. The company's lawyers have indicated that it is uncertain whether the case will succeed in the event that it comes to court. The claimant is waiting for medical complications arising from the injury to stabilise before entering into detailed negotiations. Depending on the severity of the long-term effects of the injury, the company could be forced to pay damages of anywhere between £50 000 and £2 million.

(vi)   The company has unwittingly breached a patent in the manufacture of a new product. The patent holder has requested compensation, which has yet to be determined. Lampe's lawyers do not feel that there is any point in disputing the claim. It is likely that the company will have to pay £3 million, but there is a slim possibility that it will have to pay as much as £7 million. Lampe plc's directors are considering providing the full £7 million because the company has had a disappointing year and there is nothing to be lost from setting aside an excessive provision that can always be reversed if found to be unnecessary.

(a) Prepare a statement of comprehensive income, a statement of changes in equity, and a statement of financial position for Lampe. These should be in a form suitable for publication and should be accompanied with notes (in so far as is possible given the information provided).
(b) Explain your treatment of the matters described in notes (v) and (vi) above.

Further Work

The answers to these end-of-chapter questions can be found at the back of the book.

Question 1

Q is a publishing company. The following trial balance has been extracted from the enterprise's financial records:

Q
Trial balance at 31 December 20X5

	£m	£m
Administrative expenses	128	
Cash and cash equivalents	196	
Corporation tax		34
Cost of sales	2 284	
Deferred tax		642
Distribution costs	281	
Dividend paid	600	
Interest	144	
Interest-bearing borrowings (repayable 20Y8)		2 900
Inventories as at 31 December 20X5	112	
Lease payments	15	
Plant and equipment – cost	1 588	
Plant and equipment – depreciation to date		648
Property – cost or valuation	8 912	
Property – depreciation to date		2 222
Retained profit brought forward		2 600
Sales		5 940

Share capital		1 200
Trade payables		54
Trade receivables	1 980	
	16 240	16 240

(i) The balance on the corporation tax account is the amount remaining after settling the tax provision for the year ended 31 December 20X4.
(ii) The directors have estimated the tax charge for the year at £230 million.
(iii) The provision for deferred tax should be decreased by £17 million.
(iv) Depreciation for the year has still to be charged as follows:

Property	2% of cost
Plant and equipment	25% reducing balance

A whole year's depreciation is charged in the year of acquisition and none in the year of disposal.
(v) The balance on the lease payments account has arisen from the payments made on two new leases that were entered into during the financial year. The terms of those leases are as follows:
  • *Office building.* The directors took out a two-year lease on 1 January 20X5 on an office building at an annual lease payment of £2 million, paid annually in advance. The net present value of the lease payments at the start of the lease at an interest rate of 10% was £3.8 million. The estimated market valuation of the building on 1 January 20X5 was £18 million.
  • *Print works.* The directors took out a twenty-year lease on a purpose-built print factory at an annual lease payment of £13 million, paid annually in advance. The net present value of the lease payments at the start of the lease at an interest rate of 10% was £123 million. The estimated market valuation of the building on 1 January 20X5 was £130 million.
    The only entries made in respect of these leases are the recording of the lease payments.
(vi) Apart from the transactions involving leases, there were no acquisitions or disposals of fixed assets during the year.

Prepare Q's statement of comprehensive income and statement of changes in equity for the year ended 31 December 20X5 and its statement of financial position as at that date. These should be in a form suitable for publication and should be accompanied with notes as far as you are able to prepare these from the information provided.

Question 2

L is a company that manufactures protective clothing and overalls for sale to specialist retailers. The following trial balance has been extracted from the company's financial records:

L
Trial balance at 30 June 20X5

	£m	£m
Accumulated profits		38
Administration salaries	22	
Bank	45	
Cost of sales	208	
Distribution costs	51	
Dividend	96	
Equipment – cost	46	
Equipment – depreciation		14
Interest paid	5	
Inventory as at 30 June 20X5	16	
Loans (repayable 20Y5)		76
Plant – cost	290	
Plant – depreciation		99
Property – cost	534	
Property – depreciation		178
Revenue		755
Share capital		100
Share premium		60
Taxation		10
Trade payables		13
Trade receivables	57	
Warranties		27
	1 370	1 370

(i) The company gives a three-year warranty on all of its products. The balance on the warranties account represents the provision for future warranty costs as estimated at 30 June 20X4. The balance as at 30 June 20X5 should be modified to £35 million.

(ii) There was a fire at the company's premises during the year ended 30 June 20X5. The directors have been notified of the following claims arising from this:

- A group of employees was seriously injured. Their lawyers have lodged claims totalling £2 million. The company's lawyers have advised the directors to settle for this amount as soon as possible. It is unclear whether such a settlement will be reached within the next year.
- Close relatives of an injured employee have lodged a claim for £1 million in respect of post-traumatic stress associated with the incident. The company's lawyers have advised the company to contest this claim, in spite of the fact that the courts have been known to make awards in respect of such claims.

(iii) Plant that had cost £42 million was sold at its book value of £23 million during the year. New plant was purchased for £55 million. These transactions have been included in the above figures. There were no other transactions involving fixed assets.

(iv) Depreciation for the year has still to be charged as follows:

Property	2% of cost
Equipment	25% reducing balance
Plant	25% reducing balance

A whole year's depreciation is charged in the year of acquisition and none in the year of disposal.

(v) The directors have estimated the tax charge for the year at £30 million. The balance on the taxation account is the amount remaining after settling the liability for the year ended 30 June 20X4.

Prepare L's statement of comprehensive income and statement of changes in equity for the year ended 30 June 20X5 and its statement of financial position as at that date.

Question 3

The chief accountant of a construction company is finalising the work on the financial statements for the year ended 31 December 20X4. She has prepared a list of all the matters that might require some adjustment or disclosure under the requirements of IAS 37:

(i) A customer has lodged a claim for repairs to an office block built by the company. A large crack has appeared in a load-bearing wall, and it appears that this is due to negligence in construction. The company is negotiating with the customer and will probably have to pay for repairs that will cost approximately £300 000.

(ii) The wall in (i) above was installed by a subcontractor employed by the company. The company's lawyers are confident that the company has a strong claim to recover the whole of any costs from the subcontractor. The chief accountant has obtained the subcontractor's latest financial statements. The subcontractor appears to be almost insolvent with few assets.

(iii) Whenever the company finishes a project it gives customers a period of three months to notify any construction defects. These are repaired immediately. The statement of financial position as at 31 December 20X3 carried a provision of £180 000 for future repairs. The estimated cost of repairs to completed contracts as at 31 December 20X4 is £120 000.

(iv) During the year ended 31 December 20X4 the company lodged a claim against a large firm of electrical engineers who had delayed the completion of a contract. The engineering company's directors have agreed in principle to pay £230 000 compensation. The company's chief accountant is confident that this amount will be received before the end of March 20X5.

(v) An architect has lodged a claim against the company for the loss of a notebook computer during a site visit. He alleges that the company did not take sufficient care to secure the site office and that this led to the computer being stolen while he inspected the project. He is claiming for consequential losses of £100 000 for the value of the vital files that were on the computer. The company's lawyers have indicated that the company might have to pay a trivial sum in compensation for the computer hardware. There is almost no likelihood that the courts would award damages for the lost files because the architect should have backed them up if they were important.

Explain how each of the matters (i) to (v) should be accounted for. Assume that all amounts stated are material.

References

Lennox, C. (2003), Opinion shopping and the role of audit committees when audit firms are dismissed: the US experience. Research report published by The Institute of Chartered Accountants of Scotland.

Lu, T. (2006), Does opinion shopping impair auditor independence and audit quality? *Journal of Accounting Research*, **44**(3), 561–583.

INTRODUCTION TO GROUP ACCOUNTS

12

Contents

Learning Objectives

After studying this chapter you should be able to:

- explain why businesses are organised as groups;
- explain why consolidated financial statements are necessary;
- explain the basic approach to preparing consolidated financial statements;
- outline the legal background to the publication of consolidated financial statements.

Introduction

The process of preparing consolidated financial statements ('group accounts') lies at the very heart of financial reporting. This is partly because most large businesses are organised as groups and partly because many of the controversies that have arisen in the past with financial reporting have related to the problems associated with accounting for groups of companies.

There are a number of very practical skills associated with preparing group accounts, and we will be discussing these in Chapter 13. This chapter will set the scene by describing some of the issues associated with consolidation.

Groups of Companies

In practice, companies rarely operate independently. It is very common for companies to operate in a group structure. This usually involves a *parent company*, which normally owns a controlling interest in each of the other companies in the group, and various *subsidiaries*, which are united by virtue of the fact that they are all under the common control of the parent company.

There are several reasons why it is better to operate in this way, rather than having one large company:

- Sometimes the easiest way to expand is by buying other companies. It would be possible to transfer all of the purchased companies' assets and staff after it has been taken over, but that would be expensive (because of the need to transfer titles to assets and employment contracts). It would also lead to the loss of business names that could have some value on the market. Therefore, it is usually simpler and cheaper to let the existing companies continue as before, albeit under new ownership.
- In future years it might be desirable to sell off part of the business that is a distraction from the core activities or that is not generating sufficient profit. It will be much easier to sell a company because it will be possible to show purchasers audited financial statements for the business that they are buying. It will also be much easier to identify the assets and liabilities belonging to a company that is being sold off than it would be to identify the boundaries of a division that was part of a larger company.
- In desperate situations, a company that runs into difficulty can be allowed to fail. The parent company need not have any legal responsibility for the debts of a failing subsidiary. It might create bad publicity to leave a subsidiary to collapse while it has unpaid bills, but that is a matter for the parent company's senior management to decide. If all of the companies had been merged into one large company, then one failing segment could pull the whole business down.

If you obtain the published accounts of almost any business, even a relatively small one, you will almost certainly find that it is either the parent company of a group or a subsidiary. If it is listed on a stock exchange, then it is more or less bound to be a parent company.

Imagine . . .

Imagine a world with no group accounts. Picture the following situation. Mega plc is a major quoted company that prospects, extracts, and refines oil all over the world. Surprisingly, it has a very simple statement of financial position:

Mega plc	
Statement of Financial Position as at ????	
	£m
Non-current asset investments	
Mega Drilling Ltd	2 000
Mega Shipping Ltd	2 300
Mega Refining Ltd	1 900
Mega Retail Ltd	1 300
Mega Management Ltd	120
	7 620
Current assets	
Bank	90
	7 710
Share capital	5 000
Retained profits	2 710
	7 710

Mega plc owns all of the shares of each of the five companies listed under the heading of non-current asset investments. The first four companies listed operate in many different parts of the world, finding, extracting, and processing oil and natural gas and selling the resulting products. Mega Management Ltd employs the board of directors who manage Mega plc and owns and operates the head office and employs all of the staff who work there (see figure on next page).

Mega plc has a bank account, but rarely has much cash in it. From time to time the companies that it owns pay dividends. Sometimes the cash is used to invest in other companies and sometimes it is used to pay dividends to Mega plc's shareholders.

You might have noticed that the statement of financial position is undated. That is because the figures themselves will never change much, unless Mega plc decides to buy another company or sell one of its existing holdings. There might be

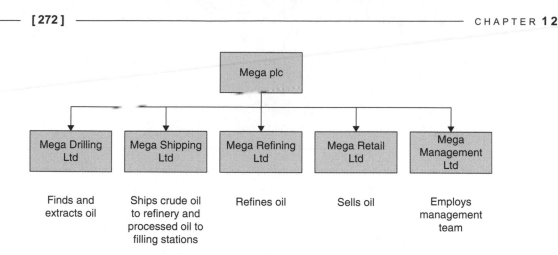

some fluctuation in the bank balance while it receives dividends and passes those on to its own shareholders, but the statement of financial position will otherwise remain as it is.

We could have shown Mega plc's income statement, but that would have been just as unrevealing as its statement of financial position. Its only income would be dividends received. It would have no expenses.

You would not find these financial statements terribly helpful if you were a shareholder in Mega plc. It would be impossible to tell whether the companies that it owns are doing well or badly. Provided the companies continue to pay their dividends (which they might do even if they make losses), everything will appear to be in order regardless of the true position.

Economic Reality

The solution to this problem sounds simple, although it has proved to be one of the biggest sources of problems for accounting regulators over the years. Rather than telling the shareholders about their *legal* rights with respect to the company, we could tell them about their *economic* rights. In terms of strict, legalistic theory, the shareholders of Mega plc own shares in a 'parent company' that enters into very few transactions and merely acts as a vehicle for owning all the shares of a series of other companies known as 'subsidiaries'. There is, however, an economic reality, which is that the shareholders in Mega Ltd see themselves as owning shares in an enterprise that extracts, refines, and sells oil (see figure on next page).

Consolidated financial statements are intended to bridge the gap between the *legal form* and the *economic substance* of the relationship between the group companies.

Suppose our statement of financial position actually relates to 31 December 20X8. The following schedule relates to Mega plc and its subsidiary companies:

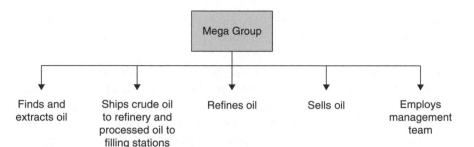

Statements of Financial Position as at 31 December 20X8							
	Mega plc £m	Mega Drilling Ltd £m	Mega Shipping Ltd £m	Mega Refining Ltd £m	Mega Retail Ltd £m	Mega Management Ltd £m	Total £m
Property, plant, and equipment							
Land and buildings		200	100	300	700	100	1 400
Plant and equipment		1 600	1 900	1 500	400	10	5 410
	-	1 800	2 000	1 800	1 100	110	6 810
Fixed asset investments							
Mega Drilling Ltd	2 000						2 000
Mega Shipping Ltd	2 300						2 300
Mega Refining Ltd	1 900						1 900
Mega Retail Ltd	1 300						1 300
Mega Management Ltd	120						120
	7 620	-	-	-	-	-	7 620
Current assets							
Inventory		8	5	25	50		88
Trade receivables		6	13	10	30		59
Due from group members		10	14	38	-	6	68
Bank	90	7	9	7	8	5	126
	90	31	41	80	88	11	341
	7 710	1 831	2 041	1 880	1 188	121	14 771
Share capital	5 000	1600	1800	1500	1 000	60	10 960
Retained profits	2 710	215	212	347	128	58	3 670
	7 710	1 815	2 012	1 847	1 128	118	14 630
Current liabilities							
Trade payables		14	21	15	20	3	73
Due to group members		2	8	18	40		68
	-	16	29	33	60	3	141
	7 710	1 831	2 041	1 880	1 188	121	14 771

This is a complicated table, but take a few minutes to study it closely.

Firstly, we can see that the directors of Mega plc can control 'real', tangible assets worth a total of £6.810 billion. They can manage current assets worth approximately £341 million. They can make these assets work together in an efficient manner. If, for example, Mega Retail Ltd requires a short-term loan, they could tell the directors of Mega Refining Ltd to transfer cash or to wait for payment for supplies.

While this table is a massive improvement on the statement of financial position of Mega plc on its own, it is still complicated because it still retains the artificial distinctions between each of the companies in this 'group'. As far as the shareholders in Mega plc are concerned, this is just one large business that produces and sells oil. The assets and liabilities of the separate companies are of little importance to them.

One way around this would be to publish just the total column from the extreme right-hand edge of the table. That would simplify the document, but it would not be entirely satisfactory in presenting the economic reality. The reason for that is that the individual statements of financial position contain a host of *internal* relationships *between* companies. The most obvious of these are the current assets of balances due from group members and the liabilities of balances due to group members. These are valid entries in the financial statements of the group members themselves, but they are quite misleading when we try to present the companies collectively, as a single economic entity. The solution to this is to cancel these offsetting amounts against one another.

There are some less obvious internal relationships between the group members. Mega plc's statement of financial position shows a variety of investments in other companies. Those companies have corresponding equity balances that reflect the share capital and reserves purchased at the time of Mega plc's investment. Again, the secret is to cancel these. That process is slightly more complex than the process used on the intercompany balances, and so we will return to it in Chapter 13.

Once all of the cancellations have been made and the statement tidied up, we are left with the following statement of financial position:

Mega Group
Consolidated statement of financial position as at
31 December 20X8

	£m
Property, plant, and equipment	
Land and buildings	1 400
Plant and equipment	5 410
	6 810
Current assets	
Inventory	74
Trade receivables	59
Bank	126
	259
	7 069
Share capital	5 000
Retained profits	1 996
	6 996
Current liabilities	
Trade payables	73
	7,069

Many of the figures are simply the totals of the separate statements. Inventory is slightly more complicated because much of the stock would have been bought and sold between group members at a slightly artificial price. The inventory figure stated in the consolidated statement of financial position represents the cost to the group, ignoring any internal transfers. We will return to the calculation of inventory in Chapter 13. There is insufficient information in the case for you to derive the amount shown above.

The most complex figure to derive of all is that for retained profits. Again, there is insufficient information to derive this figure in the case, and, again, we will have to return to the topic in Chapter 13. Calculating the figure for retained profits is complicated because some of the balances on the subsidiaries' retained earnings will have to be cancelled against the parent company's investment in them.

The Mega Group statement of financial position illustrates the point of preparing consolidated financial statements. We can tell at a glance what resources were available to the directors of Mega plc. This makes them far more accountable to their shareholders. We can also see what the overall liquidity of the group is, what liabilities it owes, and how it has changed since last year. We can prepare a consolidated income statement that will enable us to see exactly how profitable the group has been. Even though this is a very simple example, it illustrates why we need group financial statements.

A Few Words of Warning

The title of the statement of financial position sheet makes it very clear that this is a *consolidated* statement relating to a *group* of companies. This is important because the statement is intended to show an *economic* entity in a realistic manner. It is not, however, a *legal* entity. There are, therefore, a number of areas in which you have to take care when reading consolidated financial statements:

• A group of companies has no legal identity of its own. You can enter into a contract with any of the companies in the group, but not with the group itself. In an extreme case, the group might not choose to support a company that has got into difficulties. The group statement of financial position might leave you with a false sense of security. It is, however, possible to benefit from the fact that a subsidiary is part of a larger group. The secret is to ask for a formal, written guarantee from the parent company or from other group companies. That means that you could make a loan to, say, Mega Management Ltd that was guaranteed by Mega plc. If Mega Management Ltd defaulted on the loan, you could use the guarantee to demand settlement from the parent company.

- The directors of the parent company can normally control all of the activities of the subsidiaries, but there can be extreme situations where that is not so. For example, if one of the subsidiaries was based overseas in a country that had 'exchange controls' in force, it would be necessary to seek government approval before sending cash home. There is no guarantee, therefore, that Mega Group can call on all of the £126 million in cash in its statement of financial position. Everything depends on the location of those subsidiaries.
- Some subsidiaries may be only part owned. That can sometimes constrain the actions of the parent company because the 'minority' shareholders of the subsidiary might have rights if they feel that their welfare has been compromised. For example, the parent company might ask the subsidiary to make an interest-free loan to a fellow group member. In certain circumstances, minority shareholders in the lending company might be able to bar such an action.

The difficulties outlined above are unlikely to arise in practice, but they are sufficiently important for us to ensure that we make the nature of the statements clear by always including the words 'group' and 'consolidated' in their titles.

What is a Subsidiary?

The parent company/subsidiary company relationship is not expressed in terms of ownership because our interest is in the exercise of economic control. It is possible to control another company without owning all of the shares or even more than half of the voting shares. For example, a parent company could have total control if it owned, say, 40% of the shares and a third (otherwise independent) party owns another 40% and has agreed to support any decision made by the parent.

IAS 27 *Consolidated and Separate Financial Statements* defines a subsidiary as 'an entity . . . that is controlled by another entity (known as the parent)'. The IAS goes on to define control as 'the power to govern the financial and operating policies of an entity so as to obtain benefits from its activities'.

The most obvious way to acquire a subsidiary is to buy more than half of the voting rights, but it is possible to have a subsidiary without owning any shares in the company. IAS 27 identifies the following situations:

- power over more than half of the voting rights by virtue of an agreement with other investors;
- power to govern the financial and operating policies of the entity under a statute or an agreement;

- power to appoint or remove the majority of the members of the board of directors or equivalent governing body and control of the entity is by that board or body; or
- power to cast the majority of votes at meetings of the board of directors or equivalent governing body and control of the entity is by that board or body.

If a subsidiary company has a subsidiary of its own, then the 'sub-subsidiary' will be subject to the dominant influence of the subsidiary's parent company and so all three companies will be part of the group.

IAS 27 deals with the issue of potential voting rights. The ownership of options or other financial instruments that can be converted into voting shares should be taken into account when deciding whether or not the owner has control. That is provided the potential voting rights are currently exercisable or convertible. Management's intentions are specifically excluded from this aspect of deciding whether control exists. That might seem like a very rigid and potentially misleading rule, but it reduces the scope for avoiding the rules.

For example, suppose that Alpha owns 40% of the voting shares issued by Beta. Alpha also has the right to acquire a further 20% of the voting shares at any time by exercising the right to buy a block of shares that is presently held by a third party. IAS 27 requires that Beta be treated as Alpha's subsidiary because Alpha has the potential to obtain a controlling interest through exercising its rights, even though it does not intend to do so in the foreseeable future. If Alpha's directors were permitted to argue that they did not intend to exercise their right to buy, then they would be free to exclude Beta from the consolidated financial statements. The fact that they could take control at any time would grant them a great deal of power over Beta's directors, and so they could have effective control even though none exists on paper.

If You've Got It, Why not Flaunt It?

The definition of a subsidiary might appear to be unnecessarily complicated, but there are good historical reasons for that. There have been problems in the past with parent companies deliberately creating 'controlled non-subsidiaries' or quasi-subsidiaries that were excluded from the formal definitions that existed at the time. There were various reasons for doing this:

- A 'non-subsidiary' could be used to borrow money from third parties and then make it available to group companies. For example, it might use the money raised to purchase assets and then make a series of very short-term operating leases to subsidiaries. The fact that the liabilities were excluded from the consolidated statement of financial position means that the group's gearing ratio would be very much lower because of this.

- If the group owned assets that made little or no return, then they could be sold to a non-subsidiary and, again, made available to the group using short-term operating leases. This would have the effect of increasing the group's return on capital employed. This was one of the techniques used by Enron to bolster its profitability in the late 1990s and early 2000s.
- If the group had business interests that might appear to be socially or morally unacceptable, then they could be transferred to a 'non-subsidiary' so that it might continue without the associated bad publicity.

These motives have led to a number of scandals involving misleading consolidated statements of financial position that excluded 'actual' subsidiaries that were effectively part of the group but that were excluded from the formal definitions of subsidiaries. This has led to the development of wider definitions of the parent company/subsidiary company relationship, so that it is far more difficult to exclude anything from it. Previously, the definition was based largely on ownership. In general, owning more than 50% of the voting rights was sufficient to create a subsidiary. This was where the abuse tended to come in, because it was relatively common for parent companies to structure their relationships with certain sensitive subsidiaries so that the formal definitions did not come into effect. For example, merchant banks might be given sufficient cash to acquire a controlling interest. They would be paid a fee and given guarantees against any losses from holding the shares. In return, they would use their control to manage the company exactly as the parent company wished.

IAS 27's definition is based on control because that reflects the economic reality that the standard-setters are trying to capture. If one company controls another, then the other company is a subsidiary, even if no shares are owned. Thus, control through a contractual agreement with a bank, as described in the previous paragraph, would create a subsidiary.

Reporting Requirements

IAS 27 requires all parent companies to publish consolidated financial statements. There are some exceptions to this. The main ones arise when the parent/subsidiary relationship arises within a group:

- If the parent is itself a wholly owned subsidiary, then it is exempt.
- If the parent is a partially owned subsidiary of another entity, then it can be exempt provided its other owners have been informed that it will not prepare group accounts and they agree to this.

For example, consider the companies in the A Group:

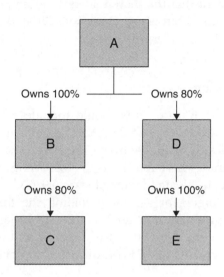

A is required to publish consolidated financial statements that will include subsidiaries B, C, D, and E (unless A fulfils one of the other conditions for exemptions that are discussed below).

B is C's parent, but it is exempt from the requirement to prepare group accounts because it is a 100% subsidiary of A.

D is E's parent, but may be exempt provided the shareholders who hold the other 20% of D's share capital have been informed that the company does not wish to publish group financial statements and they agree to this.

IAS 27 also grants exemptions to parents whose debt or equity are not traded in any public markets or who have not filed financial statements with a view to issuing debt or equity securities in a public market. Thus, A might be exempt if none of its securities is publicly traded.

Finally, a parent is exempt if its ultimate or any intermediate parent publishes consolidated financial statements that comply with IFRS. Thus, D could be exempt on the basis that A will publish group financial statements that comply with IFRS.

Thus, if a parent company is quoted on any stock exchange, then it must publish consolidated financial statements unless it is itself the subsidiary of another company. Providing an exemption for parents that are subsidiaries is quite logical because subgroups such as the D Group in our diagram above are not independent economic entities. The directors of D are subject to A's control, and so there is no real point in preparing financial statements that consolidate the financial statements of D and E.

The exemption for parents that are unquoted is less easy to justify, although there may be an argument that the shareholders of an unquoted parent company could simply require their directors to prepare consolidated financial statements if they so wished.

Excluding Subsidiaries

The consolidated financial statements should include all subsidiaries that fall within the definition laid down by IAS 27. IAS 27 specifically includes subsidiaries whose business activities are dissimilar from those of the rest of the group and even requires parent companies whose interest is that of a venture capital organisation or similar to prepare consolidated financial statements.

There could be an argument against including the financial statements of companies whose activities are unrelated to those of other group members, but these are outweighed by the threat that the directors will use such arguments to distort the impression created by the consolidated financial statements.

Summary

Most businesses of any great size are organised as groups of companies. There are several practical and legal reasons why it is convenient to do so.

Unfortunately, the financial statements of a company that owns shares in other businesses would tell its shareholders very little in the way of useful information. Group financial statements overcome this problem by portraying the group as an economic entity, even though it is actually organised as a series of independent legal entities.

The key to preparing group financial statements is to identify offsetting balances and totals between the individual companies' accounts, cancel these, and then add the remainder together. While that sounds simple, it can require several adjustments, and these will be discussed in detail in later modules.

Parent companies are required to publish a consolidated profit and loss account and a consolidated statement of financial position. These statements must include each and every subsidiary, defined in terms of the parent company's ability to exercise control. There are very few exceptions to the requirement to prepare group accounts or to include every subsidiary. Parent companies that are wholly owned subsidiaries are, however, exempt.

Tutorial Questions

Question 1

A owns 52% of B.

B Ltd owns 51% of C.

A plc owns 10% of the shares in D, but also has the right to appoint a majority of the voting members of D's board.

Identify the members of the A Group, explaining why each should be included.

Question 2

The following statements of financial position have been prepared for G and its two wholly owned subsidiaries, H and K, as at 31 March 20X4:

	G £000	H £000	K £000
Property, plant, and equipment	26	9	8
Investment in H Ltd	15		
Investment in K Ltd	10		
Current assets	2	4	3
	53	13	11
Share capital	34	7	7
Retained earnings	19	6	4
	53	13	11

None of the companies owned any inventory.

Prepare a consolidated statement of financial position and explain what each figure in the statement means.

Hint:
• Assets equals capital + liabilities.

Question 3

M plc owns 60% of the share capital of N plc. Explain whether the M Group consolidated statement of financial position should include 60% or 100% of the balances in N plc's financial statements.

Hint:
- Think about the purpose of consolidated financial statements.

Question 4

You have been asked to make a loan to Aitch, a wholly owned subsidiary of the Aitch Worldwide Group. The directors of Aitch have shown you their company's statement of financial position, which is not impressive, and a copy of their parent company's group statement of financial position, which is. Explain why you should be careful in relying on the group financial statements before making a loan to a member of the Aitch Worldwide Group.

Question 5

The directors of Y have asked for your advice. Their group of companies manufactures clothing and sells much of this through its own shops. One group company brews vinegar and sells this to supermarkets that are not part of the Y Group. The directors are concerned that it is misleading to include the figures from the vinegar company in the group accounts and have asked for your advice.

Explain whether it is logical to include the vinegar company in the group accounts. Explain whether it is likely that the directors would be permitted to exclude the company.

Further Work

The answers to these end-of-chapter questions can be found at the back of the book.

Question 1

One of your friends owns shares in Parent plc and has asked you a number of questions about the company's annual report. She has access to the financial statements of the individual group members and is concerned about the following points:

- She cannot reconcile the total sales of the individual group members to the figure according to the consolidated income statement in Parent plc's annual report. She is concerned that there has been some fraudulent understatement.

• The total figure for the retained profits of all of the group members is far short of the retained profits according to the consolidated statement of financial position. Again, this appears to suggest fraud or error in the preparation of the group accounts.

Advise your friend.

Question 2

Explain why the identification of subsidiary companies has been such a difficult area in accounting regulation.

Question 3

Discuss the potential conflict between the objectives of IAS 27 and IFRS 8 *Operating Segments*.

Question 4

Discuss the difficulties of reading and understanding a set of consolidated financial statements.

THE MECHANICS OF CONSOLIDATION

13

Contents

Learning Objectives

After studying this chapter you should be able to:

- prepare simple group balance sheets, dealing with adjustments for pre-acquisition retained earnings, goodwill on acquisition, and non-controlling interests;
- reconcile and cancel intercompany balances;
- prepare a consolidated income statement.

Introduction

The mechanics of preparing consolidated financial statements is relatively straightforward and involves thinking about the logic underlying consolidation. The starting point will always be the financial statements of the individual group members. The next step is to identify and deal with any internal relationships between group members. Finally, the group accounts themselves are prepared by totalling the individual figures and adjustments.

This chapter will introduce some of the basics of preparing group accounts. It would be possible to devote a sizeable textbook to consolidations alone if all of the complexities and adjustments were taken into account.

The Basic Problem

Consolidation is essentially a two-stage process:

• cancel any and all balances or transactions that exist between group members;
• combine the remaining figures to show the group as a single economic entity.

This chapter will introduce some of the basic mechanics of combining the financial statements. The focus will be on the logic behind the preparation of group accounts.

A Brief Word About Methods

Any consolidation question starts with two or more sets of financial statements. These have to be adjusted by cancelling any items that exist within the group. The most straightforward approach is to use double-entry bookkeeping to present any adjustments as journal entries.[1] This has the advantage of providing a systematic approach to presenting workings that reduces the risk of ending up with a consolidated statement of financial position that does not square. It is also the approach that is used in the real world. In practice, accountants who are responsible for preparing consolidated financial statements use journal entries.

This chapter recommends that you use the double-entry approach, but will briefly explain the alternative approach in passing. You should decide which suits you best.

---

[1] A journal entry is simply an adjustment comprising equal debit and credit entries to show which balances should be amended.

Consolidated Statement of Financial Position

The starting point is the preparation of a set of financial statements for each group member, accompanied with some additional information. The following example deals with the simplest possible case.

H Ltd acquired 100% of the shares in S on 31 December 20X8. The statements of financial position of the two companies at that date were as follows:

	H £000	S £000
Property, plant, and equipment	8	6
Investment in S	10	
Current assets	12	10
	30	16
Share capital	20	10
Current liabilities	10	6
	30	16

Think!

What figures might the consolidated statement contain?

The following points are all relevant:

• The group controls property, plant, and equipment worth a total of £14 000 (£8000 + 6000), has current assets worth £22 000, and owes current liabilities of £16 000.
• H's statement of financial position includes an asset of £10 000 for its investment in S, which matches exactly the £10 000 of equity that S shows as the amount due to its 100% shareholder.

We can cancel the offsetting balances with the following journal:

Debit	Share capital	10 000
Credit	Investment in S	10 000

Once these figures have been adjusted, the consolidated statement of financial position is as follows:

H Group
Consolidated statement of financial position
as at 31 December 20X8

	£000
Property, plant, and equipment	14
Current assets	22
	36
Share capital	20
Current liabilities	16
	36

This is the simplest possible case. Now we need to deal with some additional complexities.

Pre-Acquisition Retained Earnings

The amount paid by the holding company is deemed to represent a payment for the relevant proportion of the equity purchased as at that date. This includes *all* equity balances, including share premium, revaluation reserves, and retained earnings.

For example, P Ltd acquired 100% of the shares issued by Q Ltd on 31 December 20X3. The companies' statements of financial position as at that date were as follows:

	P	Q
	£000	£000
Property, plant, and equipment	25	10

Investment in Q	13	
Current assets	8	7
	46	17
Share capital	20	10
Retained earnings	20	3
Total equity	40	13
Current liabilities	6	4
	46	17

In this case, the holding company has paid £13 000 for equity worth £13 000 according to the subsidiary's books. The journal that we need to cancel this relationship is:

Debit	Share capital	10 000
Debit	Retained earnings	3 000
Credit	Investment in Q	13 000

This gives us the following consolidated statement of financial position:

P Group
Consolidated statement of financial position
as at 31 December 20X3

	£000
Property, plant, and equipment	35
Current assets	15
	50
Share capital	20
Retained earnings	20
Total equity	40
Current liabilities	10
	50

Post-Acquisition Retained Earnings

The amount paid for the investment in the subsidiary is deemed to represent the parent company's payment for its stake in the equity of the subsidiary *as at the time of acquisition*. In other words, the subsidiary's retained earnings up to the date it became part of the group are cancelled against the parent's investment.

Think!

What figures will appear in the consolidated statement of financial position in respect of retained earnings?

The consolidated statement of financial position will show retained earnings comprising the parent company's figures plus the earnings that the subsidiaries have retained since they joined the group. (As this chapter unfolds, we will see that there are some further adjustments that have to be made.)

Returning to the P Group example, but four years later, the statements of financial position of the same two group members were as follows:

Statement of financial position as at 31 December 20X7

	P £000	Q £000
Property, plant, and equipment	34	19
Investment in Q	13	
Current assets	15	10
	62	29
Share capital	20	10
Retained earnings	30	13
Total equity	50	23
Current liabilities	12	6
	62	29

The same adjustment is required to cancel the parent company's investment against the obligation according to the subsidiary company's equity. The holding company's £13 000 is still offset against equity valued at £13 000. The journal that we need to cancel this relationship remains:[2]

Debit	Share capital	10 000
Debit	Retained earnings	3 000
Credit	Investment in Q	13 000

Making this adjustment gives the following consolidated statement:

P Group
Consolidated statement of financial position
as at 31 December 20X7

	£000
Property, plant, and equipment	53
Current assets	25
	78
Share capital	20
Retained earnings	40
Total equity	60
Current liabilities	18
	78

---

[2] A true story. The author worked for a large accounting firm that took on a client that had been audited by another firm for many years. The audit of group financial statements proved difficult because there was no independent evidence to prove that the pre-acquisition profits had been correctly stated in this journal. The only copies of the relevant audited figures were in the previous auditor's files, and that firm refused to assist a competitor.

Another Way of Thinking About Retained Earnings

The double-entry approach used above is arguably the most efficient way to present workings. It is not, however, the only way. It is possible to calculate group retained earnings as:

• parent company retained earnings, plus
• the group share of all *post-acquisition* earnings made by subsidiaries.

In our example, the holding company's retained earnings are £30 000 and the group is entitled to 100% of the post-acquisition earnings of the subsidiary, which are £13 000 − 3000 = £10 000. Thus, group retained earnings are £30 000 + 10 000 = £40 000.

Goodwill on Acquisition

In the real world it is highly unlikely that the amount paid by the holding company will equal the book value of the equity acquired according to the subsidiary's financial statements.

If the two figures are different, then they cannot be cancelled against one another as they are. A balancing figure is required, otherwise the consolidated statement of financial position will not balance. This is accomplished by inserting 'goodwill on acquisition' into the consolidated statement of financial position.

For example, T acquired all of the share capital in V on 31 December 20X3. At that date the two companies' statements of financial position were as follows:

	T £000	V £000
Property, plant, and equipment	8	6
Investment in V	15	
Current assets	2	4
	25	10
Share capital	22	8
Retained earnings	3	2
Total equity	25	10

We have already seen that T's asset of £15 000 must be offset against V's equity of £8000 + 2000 = £10 000. The problem is that these figures differ by £5000.

First things first. It is now time to start laying out workings in a more organised manner. The T accounts that we revised in the appendix to Chapter 1 provide an excellent system for doing so:

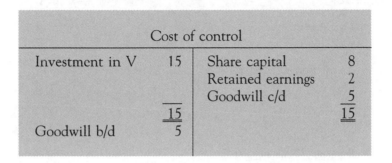

Cost of control				
Investment in V	15	Share capital	8
		Retained earnings	2
		Goodwill c/d	5
	15		15
Goodwill b/d	5		

We use the 'cost of control' account to organise the workings for cancelling the parent's investment against the subsidiary's equity. In this case there is a debit balance on the cost of control account, which means that T has paid a premium of £5000 over the nominal value of the share capital and reserves acquired. We describe this as 'goodwill' in the consolidated statement of financial position.

This system can also be used to provide workings for the total retained earnings figure:

Retained earnings			
Cost of control	2	Balance b/d	3
Balance c/d	3	Balance b/d	2
	5		5
		Balance b/d	3

The consolidated statement of financial position will show the goodwill as a non-current asset:

T Group
Consolidated statement of financial position
as at 31 December 20X3

	£000
Property, plant, and equipment	14
Goodwill	5
Total non-current assets	19
Current assets	6
	25
Share capital	22
Retained earnings	3
Total equity	25

Think!

What does this goodwill figure represent?

A great deal of care has to be taken in interpreting the goodwill figure. It reflects the difference between the book value of the subsidiary's equity and the amount that the parent paid, but it does not necessarily mean much more than that. The purchase price may have been agreed on the open market between the parent and the previous owners of the shares, but even that price may not mean a great deal. For example, the parent company may have paid more than the 'real' economic value of the company, either because the directors were mistaken or badly advised or because they were desperate to make a successful bid and acquire a subsidiary.

We discussed the accounting treatment of intangibles in Chapter 9. The goodwill is normally carried in the consolidated statement of financial position without adjustment unless an adjustment for impairment is required.

Non-Controlling Interests

In Chapter 12 we saw that there is no need to own 100% of the equity in order to have control. Interests in the subsidiary's equity that are not attributable to the parent are called 'non-controlling interests', although their former title of 'minority interests' might be slightly easier to understand.

The calculation of non-controlling interests is normally very straightforward. The percentage or proportion of the equity that was not purchased by the parent company is attributable to the non-controlling interests. There is no need to distinguish pre- or post-acquisition earnings. The minority shareholders are entitled to a full share of all of the equity according to the subsidiary statement of financial position.

Accounting for non-controlling interests is also fairly straightforward. The balance is treated as an element of equity in the consolidated statement but is shown separately from the equity attributable to the parent's shareholders.

For example, Q acquired 75% of R's equity on 31 December 20X4. R's retained earnings at that date were £8000:

Statements of financial position as at 31 December 20X7	Q £000	R £000
Property, plant, and equipment	33	28
Investment in R	25	
Total non-current assets	58	28
Current assets	11	9
	69	37
Equity		
Share capital	40	20
Retained earnings	22	12
Total equity	62	32
Current liabilities	7	5
	69	37

As these questions get more complicated, it makes sense to work through the figures in a systematic way. It is helpful to start with the cost of control account because that requires a clear understanding of what has been purchased. In this case, the parent paid £25 000 for 75% of the equity, which comprised share capital of £20 000 and retained earnings of £8000; 75% of those figures comes to £15 000 and £6000 respectively:

Cost of control				
Investment in R	25	Share capital	15	
		Retained earnings	6	
		Goodwill c/d	4	
	25		25	
Goodwill b/d	4			

The investment is offset against the equity that was acquired *at the time of acquisition, as valued at that date.* That leaves a goodwill balance of £4000.

The minority shareholders are entitled to 25% of the equity in the subsidiary's statement of financial position:

Non-controlling interest			
		Share capital	5
Balance c/d	8	Retained earnings	3
	8		8
		Balance b/d	8

Thus, the minority shareholders are entitled to £8000 of equity. Finally, the account for retained earnings is as follows:

Retained earnings			
Cost of control	6	Balance b/d	22
Non-controlling interest	3	Balance b/d	12
Balance c/d	25		
	34		34
		Balance b/d	25

The advantage of leaving the retained earnings account until last is that we can fill in many of the figures simply by completing double entry for the adjustments that have already been made. The cost of control account shows a credit of £6000, with the corresponding debit going to retained earnings, and the non-controlling interest account has a credit of £3000, for which a corresponding debit is required.

Now that we have completed the workings, we can prepare the statement:

Q Group
Consolidated statement of financial position
as at 31 December 20X7

	£000
Property, plant, and equipment	61
Goodwill	4
Total non-current assets	65
Current assets	20
	85
Share capital	40
Retained earnings	25
	65
Non-controlling interests	8
Total equity	73
Current liabilities	12
	85

It would have been possible to calculate these figures without resorting to T accounts.

Retained earnings should equal the group share of all post-acquisition earnings. That amounts to the parent's balance of £22 000 plus 75% of the amount generated by R since it joined the group. That is, $75\% \times (12\,000 - 8000) = £3000$, £22 000 + 3000 = £25 000.

The non-controlling interest is 25% of the subsidiary's equity of £32 000 = £8000.[3]

---

[3] The risk of thinking through the balances without detailed workings is that there is more scope to make a careless error.

Intercompany Balances

All balances between group members must be cancelled. This means a thorough check through all receivables and payables to ensure that all amounts are cancelled.

The cancellation process can be complicated by the fact that different companies can record the same transaction at different times, so that the figures disagree.

For example, E's trade payables show a balance of £3000 due to F, a fellow group member. F's trade receivables include a balance of £10 000 due from E.

Think!

How could this difference have arisen?

An investigation of the difference revealed that, three days before the year end, F despatched inventory worth £5000 to E. This inventory did not arrive until after the year end. Four days before the year end, E sent a cheque for £2000 to F. This cheque was still in the post at the year end.

Correcting these timing differences involves either pretending that the transactions were completed by both parties or pretending that the transactions had not taken place in either company. The end result will be the same.

If we assume that E had received its inventory, then the value of its inventory will increase by £5000 and trade payables will increase by the same amount.

If we assume that F had received the cheque, then bank will increase by £2000 and receivables will decrease by that amount.

Both E and F will show the same balance of £8000 due/from the other, and this can now be cancelled.

This sequence of adjustments can be shown as the following series of journal entries:

Debit	Inventory	5000
Credit	Trade payables	5000
Debit	Bank	2000
Credit	Trade receivables	2000
Debit	Trade payables	8000
Credit	Trade receivables	8000

Consolidated Income Statement

Creampie plc is a bakery company. It owns 100% of the share capital of Dairyfarm Ltd, a company that operates a dairy farm and manufactures fresh cream. Dairyfarm Ltd sells all of its output to Creampie plc and makes no sales to third parties.

The income statements for the two companies are as follows:

Income Statements for the year ended 30 June 20X4	Creampie plc £000	Dairyfarm Ltd £000
Revenue	5 000	2 000
Cost of sales	(2 400)	(700)
Gross profit	2 600	1 300
Other charges	(900)	(300)
Net profit	1 700	1 000

Both companies sell highly perishable products, and so neither had any closing inventory as at the year end.

Preparing the consolidated income statement involves the following thought process:

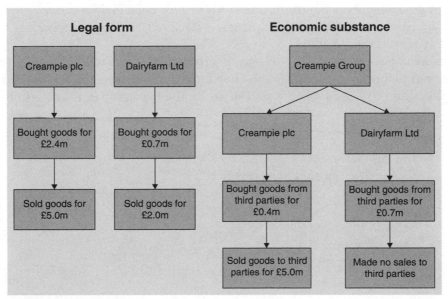

Legally, both companies have separate legal identities. All of the sales made by each company are 'real' sales in the eyes of the law. That does not alter the fact that the Creampie Group's shareholders, and any others who are interested in these companies, will disregard any sales made between group members. In this case, we have to cancel £2.0m of sales shown in Dairyfarm Ltd's income statement against the corresponding £2.0m of purchases shown in Creampie plc's. Making these adjustments gives us the following consolidated income statement:

Creampie Group
Consolidated income statement for the year ended
30 June 20X4

	£000
Revenues	5 000
Cost of sales	(1 100)
Gross profit	3 900
Other charges	(1 200)
Net profit	2 700

This statement portrays the group as a single economic entity. All of the transactions included in these figures are with third parties.

It is only slightly more complicated if both companies make a mixture of sales to fellow group members and third parties. All that we need to do is cancel any sales that appear in one group member's income statement from the corresponding sales that appear in the other's.

For example, Newsday plc publishes a daily newspaper. It sells 90% of its daily print run to third parties and 10% to Shop Ltd. Newsday owns 100% of the shares in Shop Ltd. The latest income statements for the two companies are as follows:

Income statements
for the year ended 31 December 20X3

	Newsday plc	Shop Ltd
	£000	£000
Sales to third parties	9 000	3 000
Sales to Shop Ltd	1 000	
	10 000	3 000

Cost of sales, excluding purchases from Newsday	(5 200)	(800)
Purchases from Newsday		(1 000)
Gross profit	4 800	1 200
Other charges	(2 200)	(400)
Net profit	2 600	800

Combining the sales and expenses, but ignoring the transactions between group members, gives:

Newsday Group
Consolidated income statement for the year
ended 31 December 20X3

	£000
Revenues	12 000
Cost of sales	(6 000)
Gross profit	6 000
Other charges	(2 600)
Net profit	3 400

Closing Inventory

So far, all of our consolidated profit figures have been equal to the total of the profit figures for the individual group members. This will not always be the case. Our examples have been of companies that sell cream or newspapers that are too perishable to be kept in inventory. This is unlikely to be very realistic for most groups.

Typically, groups of companies are created for some commercial logic. Group members might have very similar businesses, and that will give them greater influence over their markets. There could, however, be a 'vertical integration', which means that there is scope for group members to trade with one another for their mutual benefit. For example, a holding company might buy a company that builds cars and another company that makes car radios. The car maker might buy its radios from the radio maker and so both might benefit – the car maker has a reliable source of radios and the radio maker has a steady customer. The problem arises at the year end, when the car maker has an inventory of radios that it purchased from the radio manufacturer. Normal commercial practices will often mean that this inventory is overvalued for the purposes of the group financial statements.

You Want *How* Much?

Sales between group members are normally priced at the same selling prices that would be charged to any third party. There are several reasons for this:

- Sales priced in any other way might attract the attention of the tax authorities. Sometimes a group of companies can save tax by either under- or overpricing sales between group members. This is most likely to work where one is in a country with a low tax rate and the other is in a country where business tax is high. A seller in a low-rate country might overprice sales so that most of the profit is 'earned' in a country with lighter taxes. Most countries have laws to prevent this and usually demand that sales between group members are on normal, commercial terms.
- Any minority shareholders in the radio company will be unhappy if the company is selling products for anything less than the normal unit price.

The simplest and easiest way to prevent any difficulties is for group members to sell to each other at their normal selling prices. This means that the profit from each item sold is earned in instalments as it moves through the group. For example, suppose it costs the radio maker £10 to build a car radio that it sells for £18, and suppose the car maker pays £18 for a radio and sells it for £25. The group's profit on each radio is recognised as follows:

	Radio maker	Car maker
Selling price	£18	£25
Cost	£10	£18
Profit	£8	£7

The cost of a radio to the group is £10 and its ultimate selling price to a third party customer is £25. The total profit of £15 (£25 − 10) is split between the group members, £8 and £7 respectively. Goods that are purchased from another group member and then resold to a third party customer before the year end do not create any problems. But what if the radio is still in the car maker's closing inventory at the year end?

	Radio maker	Car maker
Selling price	£18	
Cost	£10	£18
Profit	£8	

This piece of stock cost the group £10, but it is shown in the car maker's statement of financial position at a purchase price of £18. The radio maker is currently showing a profit of £8, even though the group has not yet sold the unit to a customer. This means that we need to make two adjustments:

- *Reduce* closing stock in the statement of financial position by £8 to bring stock down to the actual cost to the group.
- *Reduce* gross profit (or increase cost of sales) by £8 to cancel the unearned profit that has been recognised by one of the group members.

These adjustments must be made in addition to any cancellation of inter-company sales and purchases.

Always Read the Question

The biggest source of errors in these calculations has nothing to do with the complexities of group accounts. There are many ways in which the question might describe the basis on which the selling prices charged to fellow group members have been set. It is important to read the question closely just to be sure of the arithmetical adjustments that are required to determine the unrealised profit in closing inventory.

For example, Long plc owns 100% of the share capital of Short Ltd. The latest income statements for the two companies are as follows:

Income statements for the year ended 30 June 20X4	Long plc £000	Short Ltd £000
Revenues	12 000	4 000
Cost of sales	(5 000)	(2 500)
Gross profit	7 000	1 500
Other expenses	(4 800)	(600)
Net profit	2 200	900

1. Long plc made sales of £1 100 000 to Short Ltd during the year.
2. Short Ltd's closing inventory includes £60 000 of stock that had been purchased from Long plc. Long plc's selling prices are set at cost plus 50%.

In order to prepare a consolidated income statement, we need to do two things. Firstly, sales and cost of sales both need to be reduced by £1 100 000 in order to cancel the internal transactions. Secondly, we need to calculate the unearned profit included in group closing inventory and adjust for that.

Long plc's selling prices are cost plus 50%. That means that the £60 000 of closing inventory is valued at 150% of its original cost to the group. Dividing by 150 and multiplying by 100 gives us £40 000. We can check this easily because £40 000 + 50% = £60 000.

Reducing closing inventory by £20 000 (£60 000 − 40 000) will have the effect of increasing cost of sales by £20 000. Thus, the group cost of sales figure is £5 000 000 + 2 500 000 − 1 100 000 + 20 000 = £6 420 000. Group sales = £12 000 000 + 4 000 000 − 1 100 000 = £14 900 000. This gives us:

Long Group Consolidated income statement for the year ended 30 June 20X4	£000
Revenues	14 900

Cost of sales	(6 420)
Gross profit	8 480
Other expenses	(5 400)
Net profit	3 080

Non-Controlling Interests

The minority shareholders are entitled to a share of the subsidiary's profits in line with their holding in the company. That share is deducted from profit after tax.

An Example

Rail plc owns 75% of Pale Ltd. The latest income statements for the two companies are as follows:

**Income statements
for the year ended 30 June 20X4**

	Rail plc £000	Pale Ltd £000
Revenues	17 000	9 000
Cost of sales	(9 000)	(3 800)
Gross profit	8 000	5 200
Other expenses	(3 800)	(1 300)
Net profit	4 200	3 900
Tax	(1 100)	(600)
Profit after tax	3 100	3 300

1. During the year, Rail plc made sales of £2.6 million to Pale Ltd.
2. At the year end, Pale Ltd had £150 000 of inventory bought from Rail plc. Rail plc priced these items at cost plus 20%.

Workings

Reduce both sales and purchases by £2.6 million in order to cancel the inter-company trading.

The profit included in closing inventory equals £150 000 × 20/120 = £25 000.

The minority shareholders are entitled to 25% of the profit after tax (= £3.3 million × 25% = £825 000).

After making these adjustments, the consolidated income statement is as follows:

Rail Group
Consolidated income statement for the year
ended 30 June 20X4

	£000
Revenues	23 400
Cost of sales	(10 225)
Gross profit	13 175
Other operating expenses	(5 100)
Net profit before tax	8 075
Tax	(1 700)
	6 375
Non-controlling interests	(825)
	5 550

Summary

Preparing the consolidated financial statements is really quite a mechanical process. In the real world, the greatest problems are associated with identifying subsidiaries. The actual mechanics of drawing up the consolidated statements themselves is really just a bookkeeping process.

The secret to preparing group accounts is to draw up a clear set of workings and keep the objectives of group accounting in mind.

Tutorial Questions

Question 1

Prepare a consolidated statement of financial position from the following information.

C Ltd acquired all of the share capital of D Ltd on 31/12/X1 when the balance on D Ltd's retained earnings was £3000:

Statements of financial position as at 31/12/X4

	C Ltd £000	D Ltd £000
Non-current assets		
Property, plant, and equipment	18	15
Investment in D	19	—
Current assets	7	10
	44	25
Share capital	25	12
Retained earnings	17	8
	42	20
Current liabilities	2	5
	44	25

Question 2

Prepare a consolidated statement of financial position from the following information.

H plc acquired 80% of the share capital of I Ltd on 1 January 20X4.

The statements of financial position of H plc and I Ltd were as follows as at 31 December 20X6:

	£000	H plc £000	£000	I Ltd £000
Non-current assets				
Tangible property		54		77
Plant and equipment		70		26
		124		103
Investment in I Ltd		150		—
		274		103

Current assets

Inventory	40		35
Trade receivables	80		45
I Ltd current a/c	22		—
Bank	5		6
		147	86
		421	189

Share capital		200	75
Retained earnings		141	60
		341	135

Current liabilities

Trade payables	65		38
Tax	15		9
H plc current a/c	—		7
		80	54
		421	189

1. I Ltd had retained earnings of £40 000 on 1 January 20X4.

2. I Ltd sent H plc a cheque for £3000 during December 20X6. This did not arrive until January 20X7.

3. H plc despatched inventory with an invoiced value of £12 000 in December 20X6. This was not received until after the year end. H plc made a profit of £3000 on this sale.

4. I Ltd's closing inventory at 31 December 20X6 includes goods that had been purchased from H plc for £8000. The profit element included in this amount was £1000.

Question 3

Parent plc acquired 80% of the share capital of Controlled Ltd on 30 June 20X1. At that date, Controlled Ltd had retained earnings of £1 050 000. Controlled has not issued any additional share capital since then.

The statements of financial position of the two companies as at 30 June 20X9 were as follows:

	Parent plc £000	Controlled Ltd £000
Non-current assets		
Investment in Controlled Ltd	6 000	
Property, plant, and equipment	2 800	1 200
	8 800	1 200
Current assets		
Inventory	450	300
Trade receivables	360	220
Bank	200	100
	1 010	620
Total assets	9 810	1 820
Equity		
Share capital	3 000	200
Share premium	1 000	100
Retained earnings	5 000	1 370
	9 000	1 670
Current liabilities		
Creditors	810	150
Total equity and liabilities	9 810	1 820

(i) £1 000 000 of the goodwill on acquisition is to be written off as a result of an impairment review.

(ii) At 30 June 20X9, Controlled Ltd showed a balance of £50 000 due to Parent plc. This did not match Parent plc's records, which showed a sum of £70 000 due from Controlled Ltd. An investigation revealed that Controlled Ltd had sent a cheque for £5000 just before the end of June 20X9 that was not received by Parent plc until July. Furthermore, Parent plc despatched goods valued at £15 000 to Controlled Ltd in June 2009, but they did not arrive until July 20X9.

(iii) The goods referred to in (ii) above had cost Parent plc £10 000.

(iv) Controlled Ltd held inventory at 30 June 20X9 that had cost the group £50 000 but was valued at £75 000 in Controlled Ltd's books.

Prepare a consolidated statement of financial position for the Parent group as at 30 June 20X9.

Question 4

V plc purchased 90% of the share capital of Y plc when the balance on Y plc's retained profit was £400 000. The most recent statements of financial position for the two companies were as follows:

Statements of financial position as at 31 July 20X8

	V plc £000	V plc £000	Y plc £000	Y plc £000
Property, plant, and equipment		1 240		2 010
Investment in Y plc		1 800		—
Inventory	400		300	
Trade receivables	500		380	
Bank current account	70		—	
		970		680
		4 010		2 690
Share capital		2 000		900
Share premium		500		400
Retained profit		560		570
		3 060		1 870
Long-term loans		500		400
Trade payables	450		360	
Bank overdraft	—		60	
		450		420
		4 010		2 690

(i) During the year, V plc made sales of £700 000 to Y plc. These goods cost V plc £500 000. Y plc still held 20% of these goods at the year end.

(ii) V plc's trade receivables include £30 000 due from Y plc. Y plc's trade payables include £22 000 due to V plc. Y plc paid £8000 to V plc before the year end, but this payment was not received by V plc until after.

(iii) An impairment review of goodwill on consolidation as at 31 July 20X7 led to a write-down of £50 000. That was the only occasion on which an impairment write-down was required.

Required:

(a) Prepare a consolidated statement of financial position for the V Group as at 31 July 20X8.
(b) Explain the purpose of an impairment review of goodwill on consolidation and explain how the directors might have arrived at the figure for the write-down.
(c) Explain why it would not be appropriate to offset the positive balance in V plc's bank account against the overdraft in Y plc's.

Question 5

M plc paid £5.4 million for 60% of the share capital of N plc on 31 December 20X0. At that date, N plc had share capital of £2.5 million and retained profits of £3.6 million. M plc writes off goodwill on acquisition over five years.

During the year ended 31 December 20X4, M plc made sales to N plc of £3.0 million. N plc's closing stock includes £500 000 purchased from M plc. M plc's profit margin is 10% of selling price.

The two companies' income statements for the year ended 31 December 20X4 are as follows:

Income statements
for the year ended 31 December 20X4

	M plc £000	N plc £000
Revenues	19 000	11 000
Cost of sales	(11 000)	(4 600)
Gross profit	8 000	6 400
Other expenses	(2 600)	(800)
Profit before tax	5 400	5 600
Tax	(1 300)	(800)
Profit after tax	4 100	4 800

Prepare a consolidated income statement for the M Group for the year ended 31 December 20X4.

Question 6

Discuss the logic of treating goodwill on consolidation differently from internally generated goodwill.

Further Work

The answers to these end-of-chapter questions can be found at the back of the book

Question 1

Big plc acquired 100% of the share capital of Small Ltd on 31/12/X5, when the balance on Small's retained earnings was £3000:

Statements of financial position as at 31/12/X9

	Big plc £000	Small Ltd £000
Property, plant, and equipment	16	9
Investment in Small Ltd	15	—
Current assets	2	4
	33	13
Share capital	14	7
Retained earnings	19	6
	33	13

Prepare a consolidated statement of financial position for the Big Group.

Question 2

Hold plc acquired 80% of Sub plc's £1 ordinary shares three years ago. The balance on Sub plc's retained profits at that date was £1 500 000. Sub has not issued any shares since that date. The statements of financial position for the two companies were as follows as at 31 December 20X6:

	Hold plc £000	£000	Sub plc £000	£000
Non-current assets				
Tangible		15 460		9 000
Investments		8 500		–
		23 960		9 000
Current assets				
Inventories	1 800		770	
Trade receivables	1 000		650	

Bank	450		–	
		3 250		1 420
		27 210		10 420

Equity and liabilities
Equity

Ordinary shares		10 000		2 500
Retained profits		15 000		4 500
		25 000		7 000

Non-current liabilities

Loans		1 000		500

Current liabilities

Trade payables	800		2 000	
Tax	410		520	
Overdraft	–		400	
		1 210		2 920
		27 210		10 420

1. Hold plc's investments comprise the cost of its investment in Sub plc.

2. Hold plc sold goods to Sub plc for £140 000 during the year. These were transferred at a mark-up of 40% on cost. Three-quarters of these goods remained in Sub plc's closing stock at 31 December 20X6.

3. The group insists that all intercompany creditor balances are settled prior to the year end in order to facilitate the consolidation procedures. However, a cheque for £10 000 from Sub plc to Hold plc was not received until after the year end. Intercompany balances are included in trade payables and receivables as appropriate.

Prepare the consolidated statement of financial position of the Hold Group as at 31 December 20X6.

Question 3

S plc acquired 75% of the share capital of T plc for £6.0 million on 31 March 20X0.

During the year ended 31 March 20X4, S plc made sales of £1.9 million to T plc. This included £400 000 of stock that was still unsold by T plc at the year end. This stock had originally cost T plc £250 000.

During the year ended 31 March 20X4, T plc made a dividend payment of £1.0 million.

The income statements of the two companies for the year ended 31 March 20X4 were as follows:

Income statements
for the year ended 31 March 20X4

	S plc £000	T plc £000
Revenue	25 000	19 000
Cost of sales	(15 300)	(11 000)
Gross profit	9 700	8 000
Other expenses	(4 800)	(2 200)
Operating profit	4 900	5 800
Dividend income	750	–
	5 650	5 800
Tax	(900)	(600)
Profit after tax	4 750	5 200

Prepare a consolidated income statement for the S Group for the year ended 31 March 20X4.

REVIEW CHAPTER 14

Contents

Introduction

This chapter is intended to provide an overview of the others that have gone before. It is an opportunity both to think back and to reflect as well as to look forward.

Chapters 1 to 13

There is a grave risk that offering an overview of the body of the text will be viewed as an admission that there was no clear line of logic running from beginning to end and linking the various ideas that were discussed along the way. Having said that, it is often easier to look back and see how various thoughts and ideas worked with one another (or jarred in one another's company).

Experience suggests that the jump from the introductory stage to the intermediate stage of financial accounting is the most difficult for the vast majority of students. The material in a typical first-year course offers its own challenges, and there is quite a steep learning curve, but most of that material is fairly mechanical and procedural in nature. First-year questions usually have correct answers. The next step after learning the basics involves starting to think about how these simple questions have to be answered in the real world. There is no longer necessarily a correct answer to questions such as 'what profit did the company make?', 'what liabilities should appear in the financial statements?', or 'what information must be disclosed?'. In the real world, such questions are answered against a patchwork of aspirations and constraints. Many company directors wish to report honestly and accurately, but some are prepared to play fast and loose with the rules and regulations. The statements are prepared in accordance with the rules published by the accountancy profession, but those rules are often designed with anti-avoidance in mind rather than good accounting. Understanding the requirements of the rules often requires a history lesson in the malpractices that shaped the standards.

If it is any consolation, the jump to the next stage is not nearly as great. Some of the issues that have to be addressed are a little more complicated, but the effects of human nature are no worse, and that is the key to understanding accounting.

Returning to the matter at hand, the first thirteen chapters of this text covered a range of topics.

Chapter 1 was essentially a revision of the basics and an overview of the formats laid down by IAS 1 for the main financial statements.

Chapter 2 covered the regulations laid down by the IASB, their source, and some of the pressures that affect their development and enforcement.

Chapter 3 was designed to encourage readers to refer to real annual reports. There are many reasons for this. Certainly, it is a challenge to read an annual report and make sense of it. It might seem a daunting task at an early stage in one's studies, but a very senior professor of accounting, who had been a member of the UK's Accounting Standards Board, was quoted once as claiming that he never read the annual reports of the companies that he had invested in because he did not understand them.[1] It is worth persevering with annual reports if only because it is much easier to understand much of the material covered in this book if it can be seen working in practice.

Chapter 4 took a slight detour into the sources of news, information, and analysis that can be drawn upon out of interest in researching an essay or in planning a career in academia. Much of the focus of that chapter was on the academic literature. There is relatively little interaction between accounting academics and practitioners. The route into a teaching career is increasingly a

---

[1] Hopefully, this remark was made in jest, although there may well be a sense in which it is impossible to make a complex group of companies understandable to even the most expert of readers.

PhD in an accounting topic rather than a professional accountancy qualification, and, if anything, the gap between research and practice is widening. The material in Chapter 4 might help spark some curiosity to redress this movement. It can only be desirable for academics and practitioners to invest a little more time and effort in understanding one another.

Chapter 5 dealt with the attempt to devise a conceptual framework for accounting. One of the reasons that accountancy can be difficult to understand is that the various practices that have arisen over the years have developed in an ad hoc way in response to specific problems. Without a conceptual framework there is no formal agreement on the purpose of accounting. For example, it is possible to list potential users of financial statements without any controversy and to suggest what information is required by each. The problems start to arise when a choice has to be made that will put one user before another and it must be decided whose need will take priority.

Chapters 6 to 11 dealt with the accounting standards associated with specific figures or areas. Each chapter examined the application of one or more standards to a particular figure or set of figures. The topics chosen covered much of the income statement and statement of financial position, but did not go into any great depth on equity. The topics chosen were selected in the hope that they feature most prominently on a typical intermediate class. Taken as a whole, these chapters should underline the fact that accountancy is a mix of clear definitions and vague ideas (with lots of concepts falling somewhere between these extremes). Some of the accounting rules are clear and unambiguous and others require considerable judgement. Along the way, we have caught fleeting glimpses of the external auditor, whose report enables readers of financial statements to judge the credibility of the figures in the financial statements. In many respects the auditor is the primary beneficiary of clear and comprehensive rules because it is the auditor's responsibility to express a clear and unambiguous statement of opinion on whether the financial statements present fairly the performance and financial position of the business. One of the other lessons of history is that the auditor is often the first one to be blamed if there is any subsequent debate about whether the financial statements were misleading.

Chapters 12 and 13 introduced the concept of accounting for groups. That is an important area for accounting regulation because it has been one of the main ways in which creative accounting practices have led to shareholders and other readers being presented with financial statements that were factually correct and in accordance with the detailed requirements of the rules, but nevertheless misleading. One of the greatest problems associated with group financial statements arises with respect to identifying the various members of the group. Chapter 12 gave an overview of the rules, and Chapter 13 introduced the mechanics of applying those rules. Both chapters were very much introductory in scope, and consolidations will figure heavily in future studies.

Why Do Accountants Need Rules?

Accountancy can be viewed as both a mechanical process and as an ethical practice. Accountants are required to prepare financial statements in the knowledge that they will inform, and thereby affect, decisions made by readers. Those decisions could have implications for the accountants and directors who prepare the financial statements and also for the organisations who employ them.

Doing the Wrong Thing for the Right Reasons

Ethical arguments can crop up in the preparation of financial statements. For example, if an accountant knows that an honest report will deter a lender from helping the business, then the company could fail because of accounting choices. That could prove costly to the shareholders, employees, pensioners, suppliers, and others who depend on that company. Perhaps accountants should take the behaviour of the readers into account when preparing financial statements.

> **Think!**
>
> Is it acceptable for accountants to distort financial statements in order to protect jobs or shareholder wealth?

While it might be tempting for accountants to use their powers of presentation and communication for the good of society, it would be very dangerous for them to do so. This can be explained in several different ways.

Most countries give accountants professional status. The point about being a professional is that society grants certain privileges, such as the right to self-regulate or the ability to exclude non-members of the profession from some or all of the market for the profession's services. The status of accountants varies between countries, but accountancy is a well-paid and well-respected occupation in many countries, certainly throughout most of Europe and Asia. Arguably, those privileges are granted because accountants can be trusted to tell the truth. If accountants were caught distorting financial statements in order to protect the interests of other stakeholders, then they would quickly lose their status.

The moral arguments for manipulating the financial statements are also remarkably weak, even if the ultimate motive for doing so is to protect the company and its stakeholders. It is not the accountant's duty to protect jobs or enhance share prices when preparing or auditing financial statements, but it is the accountant's duty to report honestly. Dishonest reporting is not the only means by which lenders and other stakeholders can be persuaded to provide support, so it is possible to achieve the desired outcome honestly by other means. Manipulating the financial statements will always involve deception. Even ignoring the penalties and the damage that might be done to the profession, accountants should always tell the truth.

The manipulation of financial statements has been referred to repeatedly throughout this text, but the fact that accountants have misbehaved in a few high-profile scandals does not mean that their behaviour should be regarded as acceptable.[2]

Can Accountants Make Moral Judgements?

The process of making moral decisions has been studied by psychologists. This essentially ignores the morality of decisions and focuses instead on the underlying thought processes.

The process of resolving ethical decisions has been broken down into a four-stage model. The decision-maker must:

1. Recognise that there is a moral issue involved.
2. Be capable of selecting an appropriate action.
3. Attach priority to moral values, rather than, say, self-interest.
4. Have sufficient moral courage to put the choice made into practice.[3]

The second stage is the one that has attracted the greatest attention. That is because it is possible to design research instruments that can investigate this process in a robust way. It is not possible to study the other stages particularly easily because there is not always agreement as to whether a particular decision does involve an ethical dilemma, or, if there is, whether one resolution is any more correct than another.

Much of the research in this area draws on work done by Kohlberg. Kohlberg's work is summarised in many research studies and books on ethics.[4] In essence, Kohlberg argues that all individuals work through a series of stages in their ethical decision-making. At the earliest stages of childhood, decisions are based on a desire to avoid punishment. Later, decisions draw heavily on a desire to conform to

---

[2] The critics of the accountancy bodies argue that the small number of scandals represents the tip of the iceberg and use the fact that only small numbers of cases come to light as evidence that the regulation and supervision of accountants is inadequate.

[3] This model was proposed by Rest, the psychologist who designed the defining issues test described later in this section.

[4] An overview can be found in an ACCA research paper available from the ACCA's website (Dunn, McKernan, and O'Donnell (2003)).

the rules laid down by society in laws, standards, and other norms. Finally, decisions draw on principles and may set rules aside in cases where they conflict with 'what is right'. Kohlberg called this learning process moral development.

Rest developed a research instrument called the defining issues test (DIT). This returns a 'P score' which measures the tendency of the person completing the test to draw on principles rather than rules when deciding on moral dilemmas. A high P score indicates that the subject draws more heavily on principles. A low P score indicates that the subject is a rule-follower. That does not mean, in itself, that the subject with the higher P score is the better person.

The DIT has been used in thousands of studies on various occupation groups, age groups, and backgrounds. In general, the results indicate that the P score increases with both life experience and education, and that most individuals have an innate potential. Generally, graduates tend to have high P scores, while those who are less well educated tend to be rule-followers. The exception is accountants.

Accountants have been studied in many ways using this instrument. In general, the results indicate that accountants tend to be rule-followers, in spite of having high educational achievements. Accounting undergraduates at the start of their degrees have lower P scores than other students their age. Accounting graduates often have P scores that are lower than the average for those who have been to university. This raises some interesting questions as to whether accountants enter accountancy because it is an occupation that encourages rule-following and rule-followers or whether the emphasis attached to applying rules and standards constrains accountants' moral development.

One consolation of this body of research is that a healthy respect for the rules might help accountants produce financial statements that are consistent and therefore trustworthy.

Rules and Financial Reporting

Much of this text has presented financial reporting as being about designing clearer and more comprehensive rules that do not leave a great deal of room for professional judgement. While that might appear to undermine the accountant's professionalism, it also has the effect of protecting the accountant from any pressures that could be imposed by colleagues or superiors. An accountancy qualification is too valuable a commodity to risk by agreeing to sign off on a set of financial statements that are clearly incorrect in terms of the rules defining acceptable accounting practice.

The rules are also a source of support to accountants, whose preferred starting point in resolving ethical judgements is the body of rules that exists, although that may be a misleading argument because accounting standards address technical accounting issues rather than moral judgements. Furthermore, the rules implicit in

Kohlberg's stages of moral development include social norms as well as codified rules and regulations. The argument that 'everybody does it' might be enough to sway a rule-follower.

What Happens Next?

The completion of this text marks the end of the intermediate stage of study for financial accounting. The advanced stage is not that much more difficult, but there is usually a change in emphasis. The main difference is that the focus is generally on complex areas that are studied more in isolation. Typically, adjustments for costs and balances associated with pensions, complex financial instruments, and the like are studied, and their impacts on the financial statements are discussed.

The stage after that is study for professional exams. The focus there is different again because examiners for professional bodies tend to take the rules as given and are less inclined to ask for a candid discussion of any weaknesses or shortcomings in the regulations or for an analysis of the role that scandals might have had in the development of the rules. That leaves room in the curriculum for a more detailed examination of the technical aspects of the rules and regulations. Academic courses tend to teach and examine the rules in fairly broad terms, asking what they do to the financial statements. Professional courses tend to focus far more on the detail of what the rules actually say. In the (biased) opinion of the author, that means that a degree or diploma in accounting followed by a professional qualification is a far better grounding in accountancy than either one taken without the other.

Summary

This short chapter has provided a brief summary of the earlier chapters to indicate how the various academic and technical strands come together and (hopefully) complement one another.

The role that ethics might have to play in making accounting choices was discussed and, effectively, dismissed. Accountants should always tell the truth and report honestly and should leave the morality or otherwise of decisions based on accounting figures to the decision-makers. This led on to a brief overview of the psychology literature examining the extent to which accountants rely on rules in making moral judgements. Accountants tend to be far more dependent on rules than their peers in other professions and occupations, even though they have the same level of education and training.

Tutorial Questions

Question 1

Do the various accounting scandals that have been referred to in the course of this text indicate that accounting regulators are effective?

Question 2

Why do accountants need such significant education and training if the accounting standards lay down the correct approach?

Question 3

Does portraying accountants as rule-followers help or hinder recruitment to the profession?

Further Work

There are no questions with answers in this chapter. If you wish to explore further, then you could download some past exam papers from the website of the professional accountancy body that you are interested in joining after graduation. Compare the nature of the questions with the ones that you are used to. How do they differ?

Reference

Dunn, J., McKernan, J., and O'Donnell, P. (2003), Moral reasoning and the accountant. ACCA Occasional Research Paper No. 36, 2003.

ANSWERS TO END-OF-CHAPTER QUESTIONS

Chapter 1

Question 1

GHI Ltd
Statement of comprehensive income
for the year ended 31 December 20X1

	£000
Revenue	20 467
Cost of sales	(9 870)
Gross profit	10 597
Other operating income	160
Investment income	220
Administrative expenses	(2 742)
Distribution costs	(3 200)
Interest payable	(70)
Net profit	4 965

There was no other comprehensive income for the year.

GHI Ltd
Statement of changes in equity
for the year ended 31 December 20X1

	£000
Net profit	4 965
Dividend paid	(160)
Retained profits for year	4 805
Retained profits brought forward	2 900
Retained profits carried forward	7 705

GHI Ltd
Statement of financial position
as at 31 December 20X1

	Notes	£000
ASSETS		
Non-current assets		
Property, plant, and equipment	1	6 910
Investments		2 100
		9 010
Current assets		
Inventory		3 100
Trade receivables		1 400
Bank		600
		5 100
Total assets		14 110
EQUITY AND LIABILITIES		
Equity		
Issued capital		5 000
Retained profit		7 705
		12 705
Non-current liabilities		
Debentures		500
Current liabilities		
Payables	2	905
Total liabilities		1 405
Total equity and liabilities		14 110

Notes

1. Property, plant, and equipment

	Cost £000	Depreciation £000	Net book value £000
Land and buildings	4 500	−190	4 310
Plant and machinery	2 800	−1 300	1 500

Fixtures and fittings	1 500	−400	1 100
at 31 December 20X1	8 800	1 890	6 910

2. Payables

	£000
Trade payables	870
Accrued debenture interest	35
	905

Workings

Cost of sales

	£000
Manufacturing costs	10 880
Opening stock	2 090
Closing stock	(3 100)
	9 870

Administrative expenses

	£000
Trial balance	2 700
Audit fees	42
	2 742

Question 2

NOP plc
**Statement of comprehensive income
for the year ended 31 December 20X4**

	£000	£000
Revenue		700
Cost of sales (note 1)		300
Gross profit		400
Administrative expenses (note 2)	100	
Distribution costs (note 3)	150	
		250
Net profit		150

There was no other comprehensive income for the year.

NOP plc
Statement of changes in equity for the year ended 31 December 20X4

	£000
Net profit	150
Dividends	50
Retained profit for the year	100
Retained profit brought forward	350
Retained profit carried forward	450

NOP plc
Statement of financial position as at 31 December 20X4

	£000	£000
ASSETS		
Non-current assets (note 1)		900
Current assets		
Inventory	20	
Trade receivables	60	
Bank	10	
		90
Total assets		990
EQUITY AND LIABILITIES		
Share capital		200
Share premium		215
General reserve		100
Retained profit		450
		965
Current liabilities		
Trade payables		25
		990

Notes

1. Property, plant, and equipment

	Cost	Aggregate depreciation	Net book value
	£000	£000	£000
Factory	400	30	370

Machinery	400	120	280
Office equipment	150	70	80
Delivery vehicles	360	190	170
	1 310	410	900

Workings

Cost of sales

	£000
Opening stock	15
Purchases	200
Closing stock	(20)
Wages	50
Depreciation of factory	8
Depreciation of machinery	40
Loss on disposal of machinery	7
	300

Administrative expenses

	£000
Salaries	70
Depreciation of office equipment	30
	100

Distribution costs

	£000
Salesmen's wages	93
Depreciation of delivery vehicles	57
	150

Depreciation of factory

$$£400\,000 \times 2\% = £8000$$

This is added to the balance brought forward of £22 000 to give a closing balance on the depreciation account of £30 000.

Machinery

The adjustments required in respect of the disposal mean that it would be wise to produce T accounts to support this figure:

Disposal

Machinery cost	30	Bank	13
		Machinery depn	10
		Loss on disposal	7
	30		30

Machinery – cost

Bal b/d	430	Disposal	30
		Bal c/d	400
	430		430
Bal b/d	400		

Machinery – depreciation

Disposal	10	Bal b/d	90
Bal c/d	120	Charge for year	40*
	130		130
		Bal b/d	120

Office equipment

$$\text{Depreciation} = £150\,000 \times 20\% + £30\,000$$

This gives a balance carried forward on the depreciation account of £40 000 + £30 000 = £70 000.

Vehicles

Depreciation is to be calculated on the reducing balance basis. This means that the charge = $(360\,000 - 133\,000) \times 25\% = £57\,000$ (rounded off to the nearest thousand).

The balance carried forward on the depreciation account (£133 000 + 57 000) = £190 000.

———————————

*The depreciation charge is based on the cost of £400 000 × 10% = £40 000.

Note that the figures in the question were expressed in thousands, and so the calculation of the depreciation charge was also rounded off to the nearest thousand. It is always wise to work in the same units as are used in the question. There should be no penalty for sensible rounding.

Chapter 6

Question 1

Tax charge

	£000
Current tax	
Charge for year	80
Underprovision brought forward	6
	86

Income statement extract

	£000
Profit before tax	300
Tax	86
Profit after tax	214

Statement of financial position
Current liabilities

Tax	80

Question 2

WV plc
Statement of comprehensive income
for the year ended 31 December 20X1

	Notes	£000
Revenue		3 500
Cost of sales		(1 595)
Gross profit		1 905
Other income		493
Distribution costs		(434)
Administrative expenses		(410)

Finance costs		(17)
Profit before tax		1 537
Income tax expense	1	(484)
Profit for the year		1 053
Other comprehensive income		
Gain on revaluation		432
Total comprehensive income		1 485

WV plc
Statement of changes in equity
for the year ended 31 December 20X1

	Retained earnings £000	Revaluation reserve £000	Total £000
Opening balance	208	—	208
Net profit	1 053		1 053
Dividends	(18)		(18)
Gain on revaluation		432	432
Closing balance	1 243	432	1 675

WV plc
Statement of financial position
as at 31 December 20X1

	Notes	£000
ASSETS		
Non-current assets		
Property, plant, and equipment	2	1 775
Current assets		
Inventory	3	840
Trade receivables		278
Investments		14
		1 132
Total assets		2 907
EQUITY AND LIABILITIES		
Equity		
Called-up share capital		300
Share premium account		100

Revaluation reserve		432
Retained earnings		1 243
Total equity		2 075
Non-current liabilities		
Deferred tax	4	72
Current liabilities	5	760
Total of equity and liabilities		2 907

Notes

1. Tax

	£000
Current tax	
Charge for year	460
Underprovision brought forward	7
	467
Future tax	
Increase in provision for deferred tax	17
	484

2. Property, plant, and equipment

	Property £000	Plant and machinery £000	Total £000
Cost or valuation			
At 1 January 20X1	600	1 575	2 175
Disposal		(30)	(30)
Adjustment on revaluation	200		200
At 31 December 20X1	800	1 545	2 345
Depreciation			
At 1 January 20X1	220	285	505
Disposal		(24)	(24)
Charge for year	12	309	321
Adjustment on revaluation	(232)		(232)
At 31 December 20X1	—	570	570

Net book value

At 31 December 20X1	800	975	1 775
At 1 January 20X1	580	1 290	1 670

3. Inventory

Closing inventories comprise:

	£000
Raw materials	260
Work in progress	170
Finished goods	410
	840

4. Deferred tax

	£000
Balance as at 1 January 20X1	55
Increase	17
Balance as at 31 December 20X1	72

5. Current liabilities

	£000
Bank overdraft	140
Trade payables	160
Tax	460
	760

Workings

Cost of sales

Manufacturing overheads	370
Opening stocks – finished goods	320
Opening stocks – raw materials	185
Opening stocks – work in progress	205
Purchases of raw materials	640
Wages – manufacturing	400
Closing stocks – raw materials	(260)
Closing stocks – work in progress	(170)

Closing stocks – finished goods	(410)
Gain on disposal	(6)
Depreciation – plant and machinery	309
Depreciation – property	12
	1 595

Disposal

Cost	30	Depreciation	24
Gain	6	Proceeds	12
	36		36

Plant – cost

Bal b/d	1 575	Disposal	30
		Bal c/d	1 545
	1 575		1 575
Bal b/d	1 545		

Plant – depreciation

Disposal	24	Bal b/d	285
Bal c/d	570	Charge	309
	594		594
		Bal b/d	570

Distribution

Bad debts	22
Increase in provision for bad debt	2
Selling and advertising	240
Wages	170
	434

Admin

Trial balance	200
Wages	210
	410

Question 3

Halflife
Statement of comprehensive income
for the year ended 30 September 20X9

	Notes	£000
Revenue		15 000
Cost of sales		(8 270)
Gross profit		6 730
Distribution costs	(434)	
Administrative expenses	(280)	
		(714)
Operating profit		6 016
Finance costs		(180)
Profit before tax		5 836
Income tax expense	1	(107)
Profit for the year		5 729
Other comprehensive income		
Gain on revaluation		4 260
Total comprehensive income		9 989

Halflife
Statement of changes in equity
for the year ended 30 September 20X9

	Retained earnings £000	Revaluation reserve £000	Total £000
Opening balance	974	—	974
Net profit	5 729		5 729
Dividends	(200)		(200)
Gain on revaluation		4 260	4 260
Closing balance	6 503	4 260	10 763

Halflife
Statement of financial position
as at 30 September 20X9

	Notes	£000
ASSETS		
Non-current assets		
Property, plant, and equipment	2	12 862

Current assets

Inventory		730
Trade receivables		1 552
Bank		19
		2 301
Total assets		15 163

EQUITY AND LIABILITIES

Equity

Called-up share capital		1 500
Revaluation reserve		4 260
Retained earnings		6 503
Total equity		12 263

Non-current liabilities

Loan		1,200
Deferred tax	3	750
		1,950

Current liabilities	4	950
Total of equity and liabilities		15,163

Notes

1. Tax

	£000
Current tax	
Charge for year	150
Underprovision brought forward	7
	157
Future tax	
Decrease in provision for deferred tax	(50)
	107

2. Property, plant, and equipment

	Property £000	Equipment £000	Vehicles £000	Total £000
Cost or valuation				
At 1 October 20X8	8 000	1 800	120	9 920

Disposal			(30)	(30)
Adjustment on revaluation	4 000			4 000
At 30 September 20X9	12 000	1 800	90	13 890

Depreciation

At 1 October 20X8	260	540	78	878
Disposal			(18)	(18)
Charge for year	240	180	8	428
Adjustment on revaluation	(260)			(260)
At 30 September 20X9	240	720	68	1 028

Net book value

At 30 September 20X9	11 760	1 080	22	12 862
At 1 October 20X8	7 740	1 260	42	9 042

3. Deferred tax

	£000
Balance as at 1 October 20X8	800
Decrease	(50)
Balance as at 30 September 20X9	750

4. Current liabilities

	£000
Trade payables	720
Tax	150
Accrual	80
	950

Workings

Cost of sales

Opening inventory	610
Purchases	6 800
Manufacturing	190

Wages	980
Factory depreciation	240
Equipment depreciation	180
Closing inventory	(730)
	8 270

Depreciation on factory = 2% × £12 million = £240 000
Depreciation on equipment = 10% × £1.8 million = £180 000

Disposal

Cost	30	Depreciation	18
		Proceeds	10
		Loss	2
	30		30

Vehicles – cost

Bal b/d	120	Disposal	30
		Bal c/d	90
	120		120
Bal b/d	90		

Vehicles – depreciation

Disposal	18	Bal b/d	78
Bal c/d	68	Charge for year	8
	86		86
		Bal b/d	68

Book value before depreciation = cost (90) − depreciation to date (78 − 18) = 30, charge = 30 × 25% = 8 (rounded)

Distribution costs

Sundry	72
Trade receivables written off	114
Increase in trade receivables	28

Wages	210
Loss on disposal	2
Depreciation charge	8
	434

Depreciation on disposal

Cost	30
Depreciation for y/e 30/9/X6	8
Book value at 1/10/06	22
Depreciation for y/e 30/9/X7	6
Book value at 1/10/07	16
Depreciation for y/e 30/9/X8	4
	12

Total depreciation = £18 000

Administrative expenses

Sundry	40
Wages	160
Audit fee	80
	280

Trade receivables

Trial balance	1 700
Write-off	(100)
Provision	(48)
	1 552

Chapter 7

Question 1

Remake plc
Statement of comprehensive income
for the year ended 31 December 20X7

	Notes	£000
Continuing activities		
Revenue		14 300
Cost of sales		(7 500)

Gross profit			6 800
Distribution costs			(2 200)
Administrative expenses			(2 000)
Operating profit			2 600
Reorganisation costs	1		(700)
Profit before tax and discontinued activities			1 900
Taxation	2		(1 500)
Profit after tax before discontinued activities			400

Discontinued operations

Profit after tax	3		3 700
Disposal costs after tax	3		(1 400)
			2 300
Profit after tax			2 700

Other comprehensive income

Gain on revaluation		2 450
Total comprehensive income		5 150

Note: the reorganisation costs did not need to be shown separately on the face of the statement. They could have been included in, say, cost of sales, and disclosed by a note.

Remake plc
Statement of changes in equity for the year ended 31 December 20X7

	Retained earnings £000	Revaluation reserve £000	Total £000
Opening balance	1 132	3 000	4 132
Profit for year	2 700		2 700
Dividend	(3 000)		(3 000)
Gain on revaluation		2 450	2 450
Closing balance	832	5 450	6 282

Remake plc
Statement of Financial Position as at 31 December 20X7

	Notes	£000	£000
Property, plant, and equipment			13 250
Current assets			
Inventory		800	
Trade receivables		900	
Bank		42	
			1742
			14 992
Share capital and reserves			
Share capital			5 000
Revaluation reserve			5 450
Retained earnings			832
			11 282
Non-current liabilities			
Deferred tax	4		1 600
Current liabilities			
Trade payables		310	
Tax		1 800	
			2 110
			14 992

Notes

1. Reorganisation costs

Reorganisation costs comprise the costs of redundancies and other expenses associated with the restructuring of the company's continuing activities.

2. Tax expense

	£000
Corporation tax charge for the year	1 600
Overprovision from previous year	(300)
Increase in provision for deferred tax	200
	1 500

3. Discontinued activity

Discontinued operations comprise the service centre operation that was closed during the year.

	£000
Revenue	9 000
Cost of sales	(3 000)
Gross profit	6 000
Distribution costs	(600)
Administrative expenses	(900)
Operating profit	4 500
Tax	(800)
Profit after tax	3 700

Gross closure costs	2 000
Tax relief on closure costs	(600)
Closure costs after tax	1 400

4. Deferred tax

	£000
Opening balance	1 400
Increase for the year	200
	1 600

Workings

Property, plant, and equipment

Cost per TB	15 000
Depreciation per TB	(4 200)
Revaluation adjustment	2 450
	13 250

Tax liability

Charge for year	2 400
Tax relief on closure costs	(600)
	1 800

Question 2

C plc
Statement of comprehensive income
for the year ended 31 December 20X3

	Notes	£m
Revenues		434
Cost of sales		(120)
Gross profit		314
Distribution costs		(20)
Administration expenses		(20)
Operating profit	1	274
Interest		(25)
		249
Tax expense	2	(41)
Profit after tax		208

There was no other comprehensive income for the year.

C plc
Statement of comprehensive income
for the year ended 31 December 20X3

	Retained earnings
Opening balance	26
Profit for year	208
Dividends	(50)
	184

C plc
Statement of financial position
as at 31 December 20X3

	Notes	£m
Property, plant and equipment		822
Current assets		
Inventory		15
Trade receivables		36
Bank		6
		57
Total assets		879

Equity

Share capital		217
Share premium		162
Retained earnings		184
		563

Non-current liabilities

Loans		255
Deferred tax	3	18
		273

Current liabilities

Trade payables	11
Tax	32
	43

Total equity + liabilities	879

Notes

1. Segmental information

	Turnover £m	Profit before interest and tax £m
Home	195	123
Republic of Arteria	152	96
Southland	52	33
Rest of the world	35	22
	434	274

2. Tax

	£m
Charge for year	32
Underprovision brought forward	3
	35
Increase in deferred tax	6
	41

3. Deferred tax

	£m
Balance as at 31 March 20X2	12
Increase for year	6
Balance as at 31 March 20X3	18

Workings

Deferred tax

Net book value	822
Tax written down value	762
Timing difference	60
Provision, at 30%	18
Increase (18 − 12)	6

Chapter 8

Question 1

Building costs	Definitely capital
Professional fees	Definitely capital *Even though this cost is in the form of professional fees, it is part of the cost of acquiring the use of the platform.*
Legal fees	Definitely capital *See professional fees.*
Transportation	Definitely capital *This is a cost that is directly attributable to bringing the asset to the location and condition necessary for it to be capable of operating in the manner intended.*
Annual repainting	Definitely revenue *This is really just a normal running cost.*

Major refits	Discretionary The refits could be viewed as part of the normal running costs. The fact that they do not occur annually, as with the repainting, is not particularly significant in itself. If management wish, they could argue that the refits meet the recognition criteria for non-current assets. Thus, there is scope for treating the refits as either capital or revenue expenditure.
Removal cost	Definitely capital This assumes that management can predict these costs with reasonable reliability. If not, then it would not be appropriate to make a provision. There is no discretion from the point of view of good accounting practice, but management could avoid making a provision by claiming that there was no reliable way to predict the anticipated costs.
Borrowing costs	During construction – definitely capital Since completion of construction – definitely revenue

Question 2

Historical cost

Ship	Original cost	Cumulative depreciation as at 1 January 20X7	Depreciation charge for year	Book value
A	$20m	$7.0m	$1.0m	$12.0m
B	$30m	$3.0m	$1.5m	$25.5m
C	$18m	$9.9m	$1.4m	$6.7m
D	$25m	$5.0m	$1.2m	$18.8m
			$5.1m	$63.0m

There is insufficient information in the question for us to tell whether ships C and D are impaired. That depends on whether the net present value of the cash flows from the ships over their remaining lives would exceed the book value. The fact that the market values are much smaller does not mean a great deal because these ships could be valuable to KL even if nobody else would wish to buy them.

Revaluation

Ship	Book value at 1 January 20X7	Valuation at 1 January 20X7	Gain/ (loss)	Depreciation	Book value at 31 December 20X7
A	$13m	$15.0m	$2m	$1.5m	$13.5m
B	$27m	$29.0m	$2m	$1.4m	$27.6m
C	$8.1m	$6.0m	($2.1m)	$1.5m	$4.5m
D	$20m	$19.0m	($1m)	$1.0m	$18.0m
				$5.4m	$63.6m

In this case, there is very little difference between the figures calculated under the two bases because two of the ships are revalued at a gain and the other two at a loss.

The depreciation charge under revaluation is a little higher, at $5.4 million rather than $5.1 million. There would also be a loss on revaluation of $3.1 million in the income statement because of the losses on ships C and D. The gains totalling $4.0 million on ships A and B would go to the revaluation reserve.

The fact that the ships are of a specialist nature means that it will be difficult to relate market prices for second-hand ships in general to these particular ships. The fact that they are specialised could make them more valuable if their type is in heavy demand, or they could be regarded as obsolete or redundant if there is little or no demand for these ships.

Even experts will find it difficult to evaluate the physical condition of a complicated asset such as a ship. Even if it is berthed in a dry dock, there will be large parts of the structure that are difficult to check and inspect.

Economic conditions can change very quickly, and that could easily have an impact on the market value of the ships, depending on their role. If, for example, they are used in support of oil exploration, then changes in the price of oil can make a huge difference to the economics of exploration.

Question 3

Host plc
Statement of comprehensive income
for the year ended 31 December 20X8

	Notes	£000
Revenue		92 000
Cost of sales		(58 000)
Gross profit		34 000
Distribution costs		(15 400)

Administrative expenses		(13 200)
Finance costs		(1 200)
Profit before tax		4 200
Income tax expense	1	(5 600)
Loss for the year		(1 400)
Other comprehensive income		
Gain on revaluation		2 500
Total comprehensive income		1 100

Host plc
Statement of changes in equity
for the year ended 31 December 20X8

	Share capital £000	Retained earnings £000	Revaluation reserve £000	Total £000
Opening balance	10 000	23 450	6 000	39 450
Net profit		(1 400)		(1 400)
Dividends		(7 000)		(7 000)
Gain on revaluation			2 500	2 500
Loss on revaluation			(500)	(500)
Closing balance	10 000	15 050	8 000	33 050

Host plc
Statement of financial position
as at 31 December 20X8

	Notes	£000
ASSETS		
Non-current assets		
Property, plant, and equipment		55 700
Current assets		
Inventory		3 200
Trade receivables		4 000
Bank		450
		7 650
Total assets		63 350

EQUITY AND LIABILITIES

Equity

Called-up share capital		10 000
Revaluation reserve		8 000
Retained earnings		15 050
Total equity		33 050

Non-current liabilities

Loans		15 000
Deferred tax	2	8 800
		23 800

Current liabilities	3	6 500
Total of equity and liabilities		63 350

Notes

1. Tax expense

	£000
Charge for year	4 200
Underprovision	600
Current tax	4 800
Increase in deferred tax	800
	5 600

2. Deferred tax

	£000
Opening balance	8 000
Increase for year	800
Closing balance	8 800

3. Current liabilities

	£000
Trade payables	2 300
Tax	4 200
	6 500

Workings

Impairment loss

Impairment value of coating line = £5.0 million
Book value of coating line = £7.8 million
Loss on impairment = £7.8 million − £5.0 million = £2.8 million

Revaluation

Perth factory = gain of £17.0 million − £14.5 = £2.5 million
Glenrothes factory = loss of £16.8 million − 16.5 million = £300 000 to revaluation reserve
Drymen factory = loss of £12.7 million − 8.0 million = £4.7 million = £200 000 to revaluation reserve and £4.5 million to income statement

Cost of sales

Opening inventory	2 500
Manufacturing costs	9 400
Purchases	26 000
Wages	16 000
Closing inventory	(3 200)
Impairment loss	2 800
Loss on revaluation	4 500
	58 000

Distribution

Per TB	6 400
Wages	9 000
	15 400

Admin

Per TB	7 200
Wages	6 000
	13 200

Property, plant, and equipment

Per TB – cost/valuation	75 000
Per TB – depreciation	(14 000)
Impairment	(2 800)

Gain on revaluation – Perth	2 500
Loss on revaluation – Glenrothes	(300)
Loss on revaluation – Drymen	(4 700)
	55 700

The flux line has an impairment value of £1.3 million, which is the present value of the cash flows that it will generate to the company if it is retained. That exceeds the net book value, so the asset is not impaired.

The coating line is worth a maximum of £5.0 million, which is less than the book value of £7.8 million. That means that this asset is impaired to the tune of £2.8 million.

Chapter 9

Question 1

(a) It is unlikely that H would continue to spend money on research if it did not expect to generate a profit from doing so. Arguably, the company's experience is that it can predict a reasonable correlation between research activity and future revenues and that this makes it possible to capitalise research costs. One argument might be that the research activities should be viewed as a whole rather than on a project-by-project basis. On that basis, research generates valuable knowledge that H can control through patents. A further argument might be that even 'failed' research will have ongoing value. Knowing that some particular approaches to problems do not work can be useful in itself. Also, a set of results that has no immediate use could prove valuable later when allied to some other findings.

(b) Companies that engage in research and development often spend very large amounts of money. The accounting treatment of these expenditures can have immense implications for the underlying financial statements. IAS 38 attempts to create a uniform treatment of these costs for all companies. The fact that there is very little discretion in the treatment of most research and development expenses means that it becomes easier to compare different companies in the same industry. This rigidity is important because otherwise it would be very easy to argue that almost any costs incurred could have future benefits (suggesting that they should be capitalised) and, possibly, that these benefits will continue almost indefinitely (suggesting that the costs should not be amortised). IAS 38 reduces the scope for such subjectivity by offering very little opportunity to capitalise costs, regardless of the company's confidence in its results.

(c) The accounting treatment of a transaction should have no effect on its underlying worth to the company. If a research project is likely to benefit the company (either on its own or as part of a portfolio of activities), then it should be pursued regardless of the accounting treatment. If necessary, readers can be reminded that the information in the financial statements must be read in the context of the regulations that affected their preparation. The fact that an investment has been written off in accordance with a set of rules does not mean that the company believes that it has been exhausted. Companies might, however, be discouraged from investing if they are concerned that share-holders will misinterpret the information – particularly if the readers are likely to read only the 'bottom line' and act on that, regardless of how that figure has been arrived at. Finally, if the accounting treatment has some tax conse-quences, then that might affect the company's willingness to invest – particularly if the accounting standards impose a treatment that is not tax effective.

(d) The freedom to depart from a standard is potentially useful because it can prevent companies from being forced to use misleading accounting policies. In such cases, the fact that they can use an alternative will be beneficial to the companies themselves and will also reduce the risk of damaging the IASB's reputation. There is a danger that the right to disregard a standard could be misinterpreted as a lack of confidence on the part of the IASB, because it implies that there will be situations in which the standards themselves could be unhelpful. The biggest danger associated with the right is that it might be used to justify an unacceptable treatment. For example, it is clear that H is precisely the type of company that the IASB wishes to have write off its research expenditure as it is incurred. It would undermine the intention behind the standard if the true and fair override could be applied in this case.

(e) The *music player* seems to meet all of the criteria laid down by the IAS for development. The project has a clear end in sight and appears to be commercially viable. Its costs should be capitalised. The *mobile phone* is research. This is because there is some doubt about whether the company has sufficient funding to complete the project. If it does not, then the project will lapse and the cash invested may be lost. Thus, the cost should be written off. The *microprocessor* is research. The company appears to have generated some useful knowledge that will probably lead to economic benefits in the future, but this is still a rather diffuse and long-term prospect. In the meantime, the company should write off the costs as they are incurred.

Question 2

(a)

Wave
Statement of comprehensive income
for the year ended 31 December 20X8

	Notes	£000	£000
Revenues			10 000
Cost of sales			(8 524)
Gross profit			1 476
Distribution costs	1	(1 600)	
Administration expenses		(800)	
			(2 400)
Operating loss			(924)
Interest			(1 680)
Loss for the year			(2 604)

There was no other comprehensive income for the year.

Wave
Statement of changes in equity
for the year ended 31 December 20X8

	Retained profit £000
Balance brought forward	380
Loss for year	(2 604)
	(2 224)

Wave
Statement of financial position
as at 31 December 20X8

	Notes	£000	£000
Non-current assets			
Property, plant, and equipment	2		19 256
Intangible	3		2 790
			22 046
Current assets			
Inventory		1 230	
Trade receivables		2 800	
			4 030
Total assets			26 076

Equity

Share capital	15,000
Retained earnings	(2 224)
	12 776

Non-current liabilities

Loan	12 000

Current liabilities

Bank overdraft	700	
Trade payables	600	
		1 300
Total equity + liabilities		26 076

Notes

1. **Distribution costs** The figure for distribution costs includes £1 million spent on attendance at a major trade fair.

2. **Property, plant, and equipment**

	Land and buildings £000	Machinery £000	Total £000
Cost at 1 January 20X8	17 200	13 000	30 200
Additions		600	600
Cost at 31 December 20X8	17 200	13 600	30 800
Depreciation at 1 January 20X8	1 800	8 000	9 800
Charge for year	344	1 400	1 744
Depreciation at 31 December 20X8	2 144	9 400	11 544
Net book value at 31 December 20X8	15 056	4 200	19 256
Net book value at 1 January 20X8	15 400	5 000	20 400

3. Intangible non-current assets

Development costs	Cost £000	Amortisation £000	Net book value £000
Balance brought forward	2 100	—	2 100
Additions	900	—	900
Charge for year	—	210	(210)
	3 000	(210)	2 790

These costs are being written off over ten years.

Workings

Cost of sales

Factory depreciation	344
Machinery depreciation	1 400
Factory running costs	1 200
Manufacturing wages	1 300
Opening inventory	1 300
Purchases	2 300
Applied research	1 700
Amortisation of development	210
Closing inventory	(1 230)
	8 524

Distribution

Sales salaries	600
Trade fair	1 000
	1 600

(b) (i). The calibrating equipment will be used for a range of projects, both research and development. It is, however, a piece of plant and should therefore be capitalised as a tangible non-current asset. The depreciation on this equipment should be written off as a normal operating expense unless the company keeps a detailed log of its usage and can allocate a proportion of that cost to specific development projects on the basis of actual time spent.

(ii). The long-range sonar project is technically feasible because it is an adaptation of an existing product. The project also appears to be commercially feasible because the company seems to be committed to bringing it to market in response to customer demand. Therefore, it is possible to capitalise these costs because they are within the definition of development expenditure as laid down by IAS 38. This is an application of the matching concept. The company will recognise the costs of developing this new product at the same time as the revenues that will accrue from it.

(iii). The diminishing echo project is applied research. The company is investigating a concept that may lead to a new product in the future, but the success of this cannot be guaranteed – either technically or commercially. Therefore, these costs cannot be capitalised within the rules laid down by IAS 38. Doing so would, in any case, breach the concept of prudence. Given that there is no particular reason to be confident that the company will earn any revenues from this project, it cannot realistically carry costs forward under that expectation.

(c) There are no rules about the correct accounting treatment of the trade fair. However, it is unlikely that the company could justify doing anything other than writing off the cost because there is no particular reason to believe that the costs will be recovered. It would be a different matter if the company had obtained number of orders from the fair. In that case, the cost could have been carried forward and offset against the turnover from those contracts. The amount involved is so substantial that the cost should be treated as an exceptional item. This is because it would be misleading to show the whole cost as a normal part of selling and distribution unless the company is in the habit of spending 10% of turnover on attending a trade fair.

Chapter 10

Question 1

Material

- Raw material = $10 000
- Work in progress = 5000 × $1.00 = $5000
- Finished goods = 40 000 × $1.00 = $40 000
- Total material = $55 000

Labour

- Work in progress = $\dfrac{\$400\,000}{400\,000} \times 5000 \times 50\% = \$2500$

- Finished goods = $\dfrac{\$400000}{400000} \times 40\,000 = \$40\,000$

- Total labour = $42 500

Overhead

- Work in progress $= \dfrac{\$40\,000}{400\,000} \times 5000 \times 50\% = \$250$

- Finished goods $= \dfrac{\$10\,000}{400\,000} \times 40\,000 = \$4000$

- Total labour $= \$4\,250$

$$\text{Total cost} = \$55\,000 + 42\,500 + \$4250 = \$101\,750$$

Note: labour and overhead costs were apportioned on the basis of normal production levels (400 000 units), using costs associated with manufacturing activities.

Net realisable values are based on forecasts about future demand and selling prices for products and materials. It is usually possible to obtain some assurance by looking at sales made after the year end. Unfortunately, the lines that are most likely to pose problems are those that are slow moving and for which there will be little or no post-balance-sheet information.

Joy is in a highly unusual situation because it has a single large customer that has placed a large order. Every item in Joy's inventory is either clearly acceptable to the customer or it is not. The customer will not buy any scarves or raw materials that are old patterns or colours and will probably forbid their sale to anybody else.

Current items that are planned to be sold to the customer in the immediate future have a readily determined net realisable value – Joy knows how much the customer has agreed to pay. The only problem is that the customer's problems could become worse, and that might affect its ability to take delivery of the stock and pay for it. Joy must form a view on whether the customer's restructuring is over and whether the company is sufficiently viable to pay the agreed price for the stock that it has ordered.

Question 2

It is too early to be certain that the contract can be renegotiated. The fact that the lawyers are only 'reasonably confident' indicates that there is a reasonable doubt that the increase will be received.

Motorway lights

Estimated total profit $= \$9.0$ million $- 1.4$ million $- 5.6$ million $= \$2.0$ million
Profit to date $= \$2.0$ million $\times 2.8/9.0 = \$0.62$ million

Turnover = $2.8 million
Cost of sales = $2.8 milion − 0.62 million = $2.18 million

These figures are cumulative, but it is the first year of the contract.
Gross amount due to customers:
• Costs incurred to date = $1.4 million
• Recognised profit to date = $0.62 million
• Invoiced to date = $2.8 million
• Gross amount due = $1.4 million + 0.62 million − 2.8 million = $0.78 million

Retention:

• Invoiced to date = $2.8 million
• Cash received to date = $2.6 million
• Retention = $0.2 million

Pedestrian footbridge

Estimated total loss = $8.0 million − 2.9 million − 5.2 million = ($0.1 million)
Loss to date = ($0.1 million)
Turnover = $3.0 million
Cost of sales = $3.0 million + 0.1 million = $3.1 million

These figures are cumulative, but it is the first year of the contract.
Gross amount due to customers:
• Costs incurred to date = $2.9 million
• Recognised loss to date = ($0.1 million)
• Invoiced to date = $3.0 million
• Gross amount due = $2.9 million − 0.1 million − 3.0 million = $0.2 million

Retention:

• Invoiced to date = $3.0 million
• Cash received to date = $3.4 million
• Retention = $0.4 million

The income statement will include:
• Revenues of $2.8 million + 3.0 million = $5.8 million
• Cost of sales of $2.18 million + 3.1 million = $5.28 million

The statement of financial position will show:

Current assets
    • Retentions $0.2 million

Current liabilities
- Advances $0.4 million
- Gross amount due to customers for contract work of $0.78 + 0.2 million = $0.98 million

Chapter 11

Question 1

Q
**Statement of comprehensive income
for the year ended 31 December 20X5**

	Notes	£m	£m
Revenues			5 940
Cost of sales			(2 709)
Gross profit			3 231
Distribution costs		(281)	
Administration expenses		(130)	
			(411)
Operating loss			2 820
Interest	1		(156)
Profit before tax			2 664
Tax	2		(179)
Profit after tax			2 485

There was no other comprehensive income for the year.

Q
**Statement of changes in equity
for the year ended 31 December 20X5**

	Retained profit £m
Balance brought forward	2 600
Profit for year	2 485
Dividend	(600)
	4 485

Q

**Statement of financial position
as at 31 December 20X5**

	Notes	£m	£m
Property, plant, and equipment	3		7 328
Current assets			
Inventory		112	
Trade receivables		1 980	
Bank		196	
			2 288
Total assets			9 616
Equity			
Share capital			1 200
Retained earnings			4 485
			5 685
Non-current liabilities			
Loan		2 900	
Lease	4	120	
Deferred tax	5	625	
			3 645
Current liabilities			
Trade payables		54	
Lease		2	
Tax		230	
			286
Total equity + liabilities			9 616

Notes

1. Finance charges

	£m
Interest on loan	144
Finance charge on lease	12
	156

2. Tax expense

	£m
Charge for year	230
Less: overprovision brought forward	(34)
	196
Decrease in provision for deferred tax	(17)
	179

3. Property, plant, and equipment

	Property £m	Plant and equipment £m	Total £m
Cost at 1 January 20X5	8 912	1 588	10 500
Additions	123		123
Cost at 31 December 20X8	9 035	1 588	10 623
Depreciation at 1 January 20X5	2 222	648	2 870
Charge for year	190	235	425
Depreciation at 31 December 20X5	2 412	883	3 295
Net book value at 31 December 20X5	6 623	705	7 328
Net book value at 1 January 20X5	6 690	940	7 630

Property includes a leased factory that has a net book value of £111 million

4. Leases

	Minimum lease payments £m	Present value of minimum lease payments £m
Within one year	13	2
Greater than one year but less than five years	52	10

Greater than five years		182	110
Total minimum lease payments		247	122

The company has an operating lease on an office building with a minimum lease payment of £2 million that will conclude within one year.

5. Deferred tax

	£m
Balance at 1 January 20X5	642
Decrease in provision	(17)
	625

Workings
Cost of sales

Cost of sales	2 284
Factory depreciation	12
Property depreciation	178
Plant and equipment depreciation	235
	2 709

Administration

Trial balance	128
Operating lease on offices	2
	130

Finance lease

Finance lease

1/1/X5	Bank	13	1/1/X5	Property	123
31/12/X5	Bal c/d	122	31/12/X5	Interest	12
		135			135
1/1/X6	Bank	13	1/1/X6	Bal b/d	122
31/12/X6	Bal c/d	120	31/12/X6	Interest	11
		133			133
1/1/X7	Bank	13	1/1/X7	Bal b/d	120
31/12/X7	Bal c/d	118	31/12/X7	Interest	11
		131			131

1/1/X8	Bank	13	1/1/X8	Bal b/d	118
31/12/X8	Bal c/d	116	31/12/X8	Interest	11
		129			129
1/1/X9	Bank	13	1/1/X9	Bal b/d	116
31/12/X9	Bal c/d	113	31/12/X9	Interest	10
		126			126
1/1/Y0	Bank	13	1/1/Y0	Bal b/d	113
31/12/Y0	Bal c/d	110	31/12/Y0	Interest	10
		123			123
			1/1/Y1	Bal b/d	110

Finance charge for year ended 31 December 20X5 = £12 million

Balance due at 31 December 20X5 = £122 million, analysed:

£13 million − 11 million = £2 million current liability
£122 million − 2 million = £120 million non-current liability
£13 million × 4 = £52 million, less interest of 11 + 11 + 10 + 10 = £10 million
  due between 2 and 5 years
£120 million − 11 million = £109 million due after 5 years

Question 2

L
Statement of comprehensive income
for the year ended 30 June 20X5

	Notes	£m	£m
Revenues			755
Cost of sales			(285)
Gross profit			470
Distribution costs		(51)	
Administration expenses		(22)	
			(73)
Operating profit			397
Interest			(5)
Profit before tax			392
Tax expense	1		(20)
Profit after tax			372

L
Statement of changes in equity
for the year ended 30 June 20X5

	Retained profit £m
Retained profit at 30 June 20X4	38
Profit for year	372
Dividends	(96)
Retained profit at 30 June 20X5	314

L
Statement of financial position
as at 30 June 20X5

	Notes	£m	£m
Property, plant, and equipment	2		512
Current assets			
Inventory		16	
Trade receivables		57	
Bank		45	
			118
Total assets			630
Equity			
Share capital			100
Share premium			60
Retained earnings			314
			474
Non-current liabilities			
Loans			76
Current liabilities			
Trade payables		13	
Tax		30	
Damages claim		2	
Warranty costs		35	
			80
Total equity + liabilities			630

Notes

1. Tax

	£m
Charge for year	30
Overprovision brought forward	(10)
	20

2. Property, plant, and equipment

	Land and buildings £m	Equipment £m	Plant £m	Total £m
Cost or valuation				
As at 30 June 20X4	534	46	277	857
Additions			55	55
Disposals			(42)	(42)
As at 30 June 20X5	534	46	290	870
Depreciation				
As at 30 June 20X4	178	14	118	310
Disposals			(19)	(19)
Charge for year	11	8	48	67
As at 30 June 20X5	189	22	147	358
Net book value				
As at 30 June 20X5	345	24	143	512
As at 30 June 20X4	356	32	159	547

3. **Contingent liability** A claim for £1 million has been lodged against the company. The directors are contesting this.

Workings

Cost of sales

Trial balance	208
Increase in provision for warranty costs	8

Provision for damages	2
Depreciation – equipment	8
Depreciation – plant	48
Depreciation – buildings	11
	285

Question 3

(i) This liability is virtually certain to arise, and the amount can be accurately predicted. The full cost should be accrued as an expense and as a current liability.

(ii) This is an asset, but its recovery is remote because the subcontractor has insufficient assets to meet the claim against it. No mention should be made of this counterclaim in the financial statements.

(iii) This liability will probably arise. The enterprise should recognise the closing balance of £120 000 as a current liability. The increase of £40 000 in the provision should be taken to the income statement and treated as part of the cost of repairs.

(iv) This asset will probably be recovered. Given that there is no written agreement, it would be safer to disclose this as a note to the financial statements.

(v) There is a remote possibility of a material payment. This matter should not be mentioned in the financial statements, not even in the notes. The prospects of making a payment are so unlikely that it would be misleading to say anything.

Chapter 12

Question 1

It is very unlikely that this discrepancy is due to fraudulent misstatement. The sales according to the consolidated financial statements will deliberately exclude the effects of any intercompany sales between group members. That means that the group accounts present the total for sales to third parties, which is a much more relevant performance measure than total sales without adjustment.

The figure for retained profit is also adjusted for the effect of intercompany balances. In this case, the cancellation will be between the cost of subsidiaries in the parent company's statement of financial position and the retained earnings that were acquired for that price.

Question 2

The main problem has been the attitude of preparers of financial statements. The directors of parent companies have often gone to great lengths to justify the exclusion of subsidiaries, mainly so that those companies can be used to indulge in off-balance-sheet financing for the group.

The ability to exclude subsidiary companies was enhanced in the past because there are always third parties who are willing to assist in putting together an artificial arrangement so that the figures can be factually correct but nevertheless misleading. When the parent/subsidiary relationship was defined in terms of ownership, it was possible for companies to find banks and other institutions that would hold the shares in return for a fee and a guarantee against loss of capital. That gave the parent control without the corresponding ownership.

IAS 27 has tightened the definition of subsidiaries to make it far more difficult to exclude them from the group financial statements.

Question 3

The potential conflict arises because IAS 27 attempts to build the group up into a single economic entity, while IFRS 8 tries to break the resulting totals down into separate operating segments.

Arguably, there is no real conflict between the two standards. The purpose of group accounts is to describe the group members as a single economic entity. They may not operate as a single unit in each and every respect, but there is a sense in which the group members will interact and support one another.

Segmental reporting enables readers to see how their single unified business is exposed to a variety of risks if it operates in a range of industries and geographical areas. The need to do this is not specifically restricted to groups. An independent company can have a variety of operating activities and can require a segmental analysis to make any sense of its results.

Question 4

The main problem is that the economic entity portrayed by the group accounts may be highly misleading in certain circumstances. The directors of the parent company can generally control the actions of group members in great detail, but there can be occasions when this integration does not occur. One example would be where a group member runs into difficulty and none of the other group companies makes any attempt to help. That is unlikely to happen, although there could be extreme cases where the group does not wish to support a failing subsidiary or where it cannot do so without suffering unduly because of the costs.

The group accounts may require further investigation to establish whether there are guarantees in place to enable third parties to make a claim against the group as a whole if a particular subsidiary runs into difficulty.

Chapter 13

Question 1

Workings

Cost of control

Investment	15	Share capital		7
		Retained earnings		3
		Goodwill c/d		5
	15			15
Goodwill b/d	5			

Retained earnings

Cost of control	3	Bal b/d	19
Bal c/d	22	Bal b/d	6
	25		25
		Bal b/d	22

Big Group
Consolidated statement of financial position
as at 31 December 20X9

	£000
Property, plant, and equipment	25
Goodwill on acquisition	5
Current assets	6
	36
Share capital	14
Retained earnings	22
	36

Question 2

Cost of control

Investment	8 500	Share capital	2 000
		Retained earnings	1 200
		Goodwill c/d	5 300
	8 500		8 500
Goodwill b/d	5 300		

Unrealised profit on inventory = $75\% \times (140\,000 \times 40/140) = 30$

Dr Retained profit		30
Cr Inventory		30

Hold's balance due from Sub = 10
Sub's balance due to Hold = 0 (cash in transit)

Dr Bank		10
Cr Receivables		10

Non-controlling interests

		Share capital	500
Bal c/d	1 400	Retained earnings	900
	1 400		1 400
		Bal b/d	1 400

Retained earnings

Cost of control	1 200	Bal b/d	15 000
Inventory	30	Bal b/d	4 500
Non-controlling interest	900		
Bal c/d	17 370		
	19 500		19 500
		Bal b/d	17 370

Hold Group
Consolidated statement of financial position
as at 31 December 20X6

	£000
Property, plant, and equipment	24 460

Goodwill on acquisition	5 300
	29 760
Current assets	
Inventories	2 540
Trade receivables	1 640
Bank	460
	4 640
	34 400
Share capital	10 000
Retained earnings	17 370
	27 370
Non-controlling interests	1 400
Total equity	28 770
Non-current liabilities	
Loans	1 500
Current liabilities	
Trade payables	2 800
Tax	930
Overdraft	400
	4 130
Total equity + liabilities	34 400

Question 3

Revenue = 25 000 + 19 000 − 1900 = 42 100
Unrealised profit in closing inventory = 400 − 250 = 150
Cost of sales = 15 300 + 11 000 − 1900 + 150 = 24 550
Non-controlling interest = 5200 × 25% = 1300

Dividend income from within group, so cancelled.

S Group
Consolidated income statements
for the year ended 31 March 20X4

	£000
Revenue	42 100

Cost of sales	(24 550)
Gross profit	17 550
Other expenses	(7 000)
Operating profit	10 550
Tax	(1 500)
Profit after tax before non-controlling interest	9 050
Non-controlling interest	(1 300)
Profit after non-controlling interest	7 750

INDEX

Note: Page numbers in *italics* refer to footnotes